Focused Group Analytic Psychotherapy

This practical text lays out a new form of focused, time-limited group analytic psychotherapy, built on new and existing research, and integrating clinical experience from across the field.

Presented in three parts, *Focused Group Analytic Psychotherapy* clearly introduces the therapeutic approach, fully explores all the elements involved, from considering suitable patients to composing the group and the role of the therapist, and provides an in-depth examination of clinical quality assurance, research and the integration of supervision. Peppered with examples and vignettes from carefully designed research by the author and others, the chapters demonstrate how this approach can be used in group therapy with patients facing specific psychological problems, symptomatic distress and/or a problematic relationship to self or others.

This book will be an essential guide for psychotherapists who have primarily focused on individual psychotherapy and who want to learn more about groups, and to those, including group analysts, who have experience with long-term groups and want to learn more about time-limited groups.

Steinar Lorentzen, PhD, is a professor emeritus in psychiatry at the University of Oslo, Norway. He has trained as a psychoanalyst and group analyst and is a founding member of the Institute of Group Analysis and Group Psychotherapy in Norway, where he was a training analyst for many years. He has published book chapters, two books and numerous papers on different clinical psychiatric issues, with a particular focus on psychotherapy, psychodynamic groups and group analysis.

"Ever since Freud, mental health professionals have been wrestling with the dilemma of how to reconcile the scientific rigours of classification with the imaginative concepts underpinning the analytic process. Professor Lorentzen's research takes us a significant step forward on this journey. In clear, down-to-earth language and with clinical group analysis as his focus, he provides us with a welcome bridge over the divide".

Dr Harold Behr, FRCPsych, Hon Member IGA London, former editor of the journal *Group Analysis*

"Dr. Lorentzen is an expert on group analysis. Focused Group Analytic Psychotherapy (FGAP) combines decades of clinical wisdom with rigorous research to inform beginning and advanced clinicians. I highly recommend FGAP as a significant contribution to the field".

Gary Burlingame, PhD, Professor and Chair of Psychology and President of the American Group Psychotherapy Association

Focused Group Analytic Psychotherapy

An Integration of Clinical Experience and Research

Steinar Lorentzen

LONDON AND NEW YORK

Cover image: Getty Images | diyun Zhu

First published 2022
by Routledge
4 Park Square, Milton Park, Abingdon, Oxon OX14 4RN

and by Routledge
605 Third Avenue, New York, NY 10158

Routledge is an imprint of the Taylor & Francis Group, an informa business

© 2022 Steinar Lorentzen

The right of Steinar Lorentzen to be identified as author of this work has been asserted in accordance with sections 77 and 78 of the Copyright, Designs and Patents Act 1988.

All rights reserved. No part of this book may be reprinted or reproduced or utilised in any form or by any electronic, mechanical, or other means, now known or hereafter invented, including photocopying and recording, or in any information storage or retrieval system, without permission in writing from the publishers.

Trademark notice: Product or corporate names may be trademarks or registered trademarks, and are used only for identification and explanation without intent to infringe.

British Library Cataloguing-in-Publication Data
A catalogue record for this book is available from the British Library

Library of Congress Cataloging-in-Publication Data
Names: Lorentzen, Steinar, author.
Title: Focused group analytic psychotherapy : an integration of clinical experience and research / Steinar Lorentzen.
Description: Milton Park, Abingdon, Oxon ; New York, NY : Routledge, 2022. | Includes bibliographical references and index. |
Identifiers: LCCN 2021046799 (print) | LCCN 2021046800 (ebook) | ISBN 9781032106465 (hardback) | ISBN 9781032106489 (paperback) | ISBN 9781003216377 (ebook)
Subjects: LCSH: Group psychoanalysis. | Group psychotherapy.
Classification: LCC RC510 .L668 2022 (print) | LCC RC510 (ebook) | DDC 616.89/14--dc23/eng/20211028
LC record available at https://lccn.loc.gov/2021046799
LC ebook record available at https://lccn.loc.gov/2021046800

ISBN: 978-1-032-10646-5 (hbk)
ISBN: 978-1-032-10648-9 (pbk)
ISBN: 978-1-003-21637-7 (ebk)

DOI: 10.4324/9781003216377

Typeset in Times New Roman
by Deanta Global Publishing Services, Chennai, India

Contents

Preface   xi
Abbreviations   xv

PART I
Introduction   1

1 Introduction   3
    A word about groups   3
    Definition   3
    Early systematic exploration of groups   3
    Book contents   4
    What is group psychotherapy?   5
    Classification of group therapies   5
    Short history of groups   7
    Psychodynamic groups   7
    Group analysis   8
        S.H. Foulkes   8
        Group analytic theories and concepts   9
        Views on the human being and on mental disorders   11
        Definition of group analysis   12
        Objectives of group analysis   12
    Are the similarities between psychodynamic groups greater than
       the differences?   12
    Group psychotherapy in Norway: a history   13
    Training in psychodynamic group therapy and group analysis   14
    Group therapy in Norway: a survey   14

PART II
Focused Group Analytic Psychotherapy 17

2 **Focused Group Analytic Psychotherapy (FGAP)** 19
 A brief description of the treatment 19
 Main features of FGAP 20
 The framework 22
  Time limitation 22
  Theoretical background 23
  The three dimensions of the group format 26
  Focus and objectives, individually and for the group 29
 Similarities and differences between FGAP and GA 30

3 **Who can benefit from Focused Group Analytic Psychotherapy?** 33
 Important conditions for benefiting from FGAP 34
  An interest in learning about oneself and others 34
  Help to explore ambivalence toward group psychotherapy 35
  An established treatment focus 36
  Personal resources 36
  Personality traits and ego functions 38

4 **Evaluation of patient suitability for Focused Group Analytic Psychotherapy** 45
 Overview 45
 Information from interviews and questionnaires 46
 Types of interviews 47
  The clinical interview 47
  The psychodynamic interview 48
  The diagnostic interview 51
 Clinical assessment of level of personality organization (STIPO) 52
 Questionnaires, patient self-report (psychometry) 57
  Measuring interpersonal problems (Inventory of Interpersonal Problems) 58
  What do the numbers mean? 59
  What do the different sub-scales represent? 59
  Use of IIP-C in the FGAP evaluation 61
 Clinical diagnosis 61
 Psychodynamic case formulation 64
  Areas to be covered in a psychodynamic case formulation 64
 Clinical ("surface") phenomena 65

Precipitating factors (stressors) 65
Predisposing factors (vulnerability) 66
  Personality 67
  Psychodynamic hypothesis 67
An overall evaluation 68
Treatment focus 69
  Clinical example 1 – *Mary, 39 years* 69
  Clinical example 2 – *Steve, 28 years* 70

5 Establishing and composing the group – introducing the demonstration group 72
  Some patients need extra preparation 72
  Contract between patient and therapist 78
  Overall group objectives 79
  Demonstration group 80
  Group composition guidelines 81
  Discussion of the composition of the demonstration group 83

6 The group process 85
  The process of Focused Group Analytic Psychotherapy 86
  Group analytic views on the therapy process 86
    Group-specific group factors 87
  The therapy process is formed by several elements 88
  What do patients and therapists bring to the therapy? 88
  Interaction and multidimensional response (feedback) 90
  Therapeutic factors 91
  Therapeutic alliance, group cohesion 93
  Groups developmental phases (stages) 94
    Opening (engagement, 2–4 sessions) 95
    Differentiation (2–4 sessions) 96
    Interpersonal work (8–12 sessions) 97
    Termination (2–3 sessions) 98

7 The therapist in Focused Group Analytic Psychotherapy (FGAP) 101
  Leadership role in FGAP: responsibilities and tasks 101
    The therapist as leader and authority 103
  Challenges for the FGAP therapist 104
    Higher level of activity 104
    Work in the here-and-now mode and within the treatment focus 104
    Less time to repair ruptures of the therapeutic alliance 105

Focus on group structure and boundaries 105
Greater attention to termination 106
The stance of the psychodynamic therapist. Objective perception or
transference? 106
The balance of support and interpretation (confrontation) 108
Guidelines for interventions in FGAP 109
Therapist observation 110
Therapist reflection 110
Is the time ripe for an intervention? 111
Therapist interventions: overview 112
Examples of specific types of interventions in FGAP 114
In the differentiation phase 117
When should one interpret on the individual level? 118
When should one not interpret individually? 119

PART III
Clinical quality assurance – Research – Supervision   123

8   Clinical quality assurance – evaluation of therapy outcomes
       and process   125
Why evaluate? 126
  *We do not know enough about whether and why patients
      change 126*
  Therapists have blind spots 126
  Evaluations can increase the impact of therapy 127
Are there any disadvantages of using measures? 128
Use of questionnaires in psychodynamic psychotherapy 128
Principles for selecting outcome measures in psychotherapy 129
What to evaluate? 129
  *Methods for planning and monitoring process and outcome of
      FGAP 129*
Choice of outcome measures 130
Choice of process measures 131
Procedures for data collection 131
  How to present a questionnaire to a patient? 131
  Time-points and procedures for data collection 131
Discussion of the results with patients 132
Interpretation and discussion of results 133
Note 134

Contents ix

9 Empirical research on group psychotherapy 135
  Research on group psychotherapy 135
  Why is research on groups so difficult? 136
    Group structure 138
    Patient variables 138
    Therapist variables 138
    Use of co-therapists 139
    Therapeutic factors 140
  Outcome research on group psychotherapy 141
  Psychodynamic short-term groups 143
  Our practice-based clinical research (background for FGAP) 144
    The effectiveness of long-term group analysis – a naturalistic study 144
    Short-term and long-term group analytic therapy – who needs what? 145
    The typical patient 145
    Patients with and without a personality disorder 146
    Change of interpersonal problems (IIP-C sub-scales) 146
    Change in self-concept 147
  Process research 147
    Group relationships, cohesion and alliance 147
    Cohesion and outcome in FGAP 148
    The development of group climate in short-term and long-term therapy 148
  Research challenges in the cohesion–outcome relationship 149
  Group Questionnaire (OQ-GQ Norwegian) 149

10 Supervision in Focused Group Analytic Psychotherapy (FGAP) 151
  What is supervision? 151
    Purpose/definition 151
    Differentiating supervision from other types of learning 152
  Why do candidates need supervision? 153
  Growing interest in psychodynamic time-limited group psychotherapy 154
    Training in psychodynamic group psychotherapy, including supervision 154
    Who needs supervision in FGAP? 155
    Establishing the supervisory situation 156
    Contract between supervisor and candidate 156
    How does the supervision take place? 157

*Advantages and disadvantages of individual and group
    supervision 159
What happens in the supervision session? 159
How and when does a supervisor intervene? 160
Frequency and duration of sessions 163
Examples of supervisory problems (FGAP) 163*
Countertransference reactions. Clinical example 164
Notes 165

Afterword	167
Appendix	168
Appendix 1 168	
Appendix 2 196	
Appendix 3 196	
References	200
Index	217

Preface

When, in the early 1970s, I started my training to become a specialist in psychiatry, mandatory supervision in psychotherapy had just been introduced as a part of the curriculum. There was great enthusiasm among older colleagues, who had fought for this for years. "Newcomers" easily, however, got the feeling that "the longer the psychotherapy lasted, the better". Today we know that most people with mental health problems can benefit from psychotherapy. Clinical experience and research, however, indicate that the *amount of time* different patients need to improve can vary greatly. Naturally, the *quality* of the treatment plays an important role, and so does the *specificity*, that is, the degree to which the therapy addresses the type of problems a patient is struggling with. Other important factors are the patient's *resources* and *opportunities* to develop, the *severity* of the disorder and the extent to which this is a chronic condition.

I have had a strong interest in psychotherapy from the very start of my career as a psychiatrist. My interests and type of work have also spurred me to complete training programs in psychoanalysis and psychodynamic therapy, both for individuals and groups. I have also, since the late 1980s, been involved in systematic research, especially in group psychotherapy.

Group therapy is a frequently used treatment approach within the Norwegian mental health care system. Early in my career I worked in a psychiatric clinic at Oslo University Hospital (Ullevål) on a ward that had, instead of putting patients into the traditional role of passive recipients of treatment, been organized as a group-based therapeutic community in which patients were co-workers in a joint project. They took part in the day-to-day operation of the ward, and were active in their own treatment as well as the treatment of their fellow patients.

I learned a lot about group processes during my service as a military psychiatrist in Brigade North (Norway), about the individual's relationship to their social context and, not least, about the importance of leadership to soldier well-being and even to their mental health. Later I worked at Gaustad hospital, the oldest psychiatric hospital in Norway, where a comprehensive change process was underway. This included leaving the old authoritarian structures behind, increasing the use of psychotherapy, including in groups and hiring more staff who had undergone training in psychotherapy. After becoming a specialist in psychiatry in 1977,

I went back to my old ward at Ullevål hospital and took part in its restructuring, which became necessary when the ward was given the primary responsibility for all crisis admissions from a borough of Oslo. The proportion of psychotic patients dramatically increased, the treatment program underwent a radical change and became based more on medication and supportive measures.

My first encounter with group analysis took place in the mid-1980s, at the end of my psychoanalytic training, when I had settled on being a practicing specialist. The high numbers of patients needing psychotherapy made initiating group therapy in my practice a good idea. I therefore, in 1984, signed up for a five-year training program in group analysis run by the Psychotherapy Committee of the Norwegian Psychiatric Association, teaching staff coming from the Institute of Group Analysis, London. Setting up a number of groups in my practice also allowed me to realize another prime interest – to carry out systematic research in psychotherapy. After completing the group training, I stayed on the program as a teacher and therapist for six years and I was also central in initiating and running a similar training program in Vilnius for another 12 years, for colleagues from the Baltic states.

My practice-based research led to a PhD in 2003 on treatment outcomes and processes for 69 patients who had been treated in three long-term psychodynamic groups. Shortly after this, I started in an academic position at the University of Oslo, this giving me both the time and opportunity to plan and organize a new research project: a randomized clinical trial with the primary aim of studying the significance of treatment length for outcome/change (see Chapter 9).

The main purpose of this book is, however, to describe a specific type of time-limited therapy, Focused Group Analytic Psychotherapy. This therapy is based on the integration of theory, clinical practice and research (my own and others), and is designed to treat patients with psychological problems and mental disorders.

The book begins with a general description of groups, their history, definition and classification, and the scope of groups used in mental health care in Norway and elsewhere. I then describe group analysis, a group therapy that developed in England in the late 1930s, which is probably the most commonly used psychodynamic group therapy used today at least in Europe (Chapter 1). I then describe the book's main theme, Focused Group Analytic Psychotherapy. The framework of this therapy is made up of the time-limitation, the theoretical background, the group dimensions, and the focus and goals of the therapy (Chapter 2). I describe in detail in Chapters 3 and 4 what kind of patients the treatment is suitable for, including problem areas, the personality resources and characteristics needed, and level of personality organization. I also describe how these properties can be evaluated using different types of interviews and psychometric methods. Rich clinical illustrations of both "the psychodynamic case formulation" and "treatment focus" are given. Chapter 5 is devoted to guidelines on how to assemble and compose a group. Eight patients who make up a demonstration group are described in some detail, to elucidate key theoretical issues presented in the previous chapters. Chapter 6 deals with aspects of the therapy process: what influences it, group relationships, therapeutic factors and its four phases (stages). Chapter 7 provides a comprehensive overview of the therapist's role, tasks, attitudes and interventions, illustrated with clinical examples. This is followed by a description of how patients and the group can be monitored and evaluated during therapy, the change in patients and the development of the therapy process (Chapter 8). In Chapter 9, I demonstrate why research into group psychotherapy is complex, and offer a broad review of key research in the field on outcomes, and in process and therapeutic factors. I also give my own research ample space, as this is one of the main reasons I wrote this book. The book concludes with a chapter on supervision in Focused Group Analytic Psychotherapy, both of individuals and groups (Chapter 10), with examples of some of the problems the group therapist will encounter.

This book is designed for professionals, both beginners and those with more experience. It can be useful to psychotherapists who have primarily focused on individual psychotherapy and who want to learn more about groups, and to those, including group analysts, who have experience with long-term groups and want to learn more about time-limited groups. I also believe that past and potential patients who want to know more about group therapy and how the therapist thinks and acts, and also those who are interested in our field, may find much of interest in this book.

Psychotherapy is a young science. It therefore lacks a solid core of knowledge on which the supporters of different theoretical directions can agree. The result is that similar clinical phenomena often are conceptualized in diverging ways, this limiting the possibilities for collection of knowledge. Another problem is what many professionals perceive as a "gap" that prevents the exchange of information between research and clinical practice. Clinicians often claim that researchers' findings have little relevance to day-to-day clinical work, while researchers claim that newer findings are often not read and applied to clinical work. A third problem may be that researchers put too much emphasis on "new discoveries" – old knowledge can easily be neglected or forgotten with the constant introduction of "new theoretical fads" in the clinical setting. I have sometimes seen that a thorough evaluation of individual patients is neglected in group therapy. This can result in some patients either remaining too long in therapy or failing to receive help with their most central problems. This problem may also be caused by many professionals, despite criticism from many quarters, putting too much emphasis on descriptive (phenomenological) diagnoses of behavioral traits as a starting point of psychotherapy.

The therapy described in this book is based on psychodynamic theory (object relations theory) and seeks to address some of the problems outlined above. Our research findings are largely based on clinical research that has been integrated with regular clinical work (see Chapter 9). I have therefore, in this book, placed great emphasis on an individual, dimensional evaluation (diagnosis) of personality organization in patients – partly to identify latent aspects of their problems as a starting point for choosing a treatment focus for the therapy, and partly to identify those who have the resources that can allow them to benefit from a time-limited therapy. Finally, FGAP is a psychodynamically oriented therapy that seeks to alleviate interpersonal problems and subjective suffering (symptoms) through the exploration and understanding of underlying, latent impulses, conflicts and defenses. We have found it fruitful to also include one or more behavioral tasks in the treatment focus of a number of patients. This method has been more widely used in behavioral therapies. We, however, consider it to be an effective method of challenging personal attitudes that maintain problematic behavior.

Many persons have directly and indirectly made it possible for me to write this book, and I can only name those who have been involved in my process of writing. I will primarily thank Søren Aagaard, Erik Larsen, Erik Stänicke and Ingrid Magnussen, all psychologists, and my colleague Theresa Wilberg, who all have read and commented on excerpts or chapters in the book. This has been important both as a corrective, but mostly as an encouragement. I especially want to thank Ingrid who in addition to going through parts of the manuscript, has lived with and related to my ups and downs during the writing process. I am also grateful to the psychologist Judy Ullevoldsæter Lystad for help with some of the graphics. Thanks also to my colleagues Svein Friis and Espen Bjerke, hospital chaplain Eileen Paus and head psychiatric nurse Helle Elvebredd for their contributions through important dialogues.

I am also grateful to psychiatrist and group analyst Harald Behr, London, who gave me first-hand experiences and knowledge by conducting a self-experience group where I participated for five years. He also supervised me for some years when I later conducted my own group and supervised in the same training program. Psychiatrist and researcher Roy MacKenzie, Vancouver, was someone who early inspired and encouraged me in my own group research. He unfortunately died too early, but has kept on inspiring me through his former papers and books. I am also grateful to the University, represented by administration coordinator Anette Sørensen, and the University Hospital of Oslo, represented by former head of section for treatment research, Erik Falkum, for providing good working conditions, helping with logistics, and for cooperation and good talks. Finally, I want to thank all who indirectly have contributed through conversations and encounters in my work as a psychiatrist: patients I have met in my long practice, participants in research groups and projects, co-authors, research fellows, therapists in the research project and other helpers. Thanks also to candidates and colleagues I have supervised or had in self-experience groups, or who have taken part in workshops in Norway or abroad.

Abbreviations

BPO	Borderline Personality Organization
CBT	Cognitive Behavioral Therapy
CGIS	The clinical global impression scale
CMHC	Community Mental Health Center
CORE-OM	Clinical Outcomes in Routine Evaluation-Outcome Measure
DSM-5	Diagnostic and Statistical Manual of Mental Disorders, 5th ed.
FGAP	Focused Group Analytic Psychotherapy
GA	Group Analysis
GAF	Global Assessment of Functioning
GCI	Global Change Index
GP	General practitioner
GCQ	Group Climate Questionnaire
GQ	Group Questionnaire
ICD-10 /ICD-11	International classification of diseases, 10th and 11th ed.
IIP-C	Inventory of Interpersonal Problems-Circumplex
MBT	Mentalization-based therapy
MINI-PLUS	Mini International Neuropsychiatric Interview
NPO	Neurotic Personality Organization
OQ-45	Outcome Questionnaire, 45 items
OQ-GQ	Outcome Questionnaire-Group Questionnaire
PD	Personality Disorder
PDM-2	Psychodynamic Diagnostic Manual, 2nd ed.
PO	Personality Organization
PPO	Psychotic Personality Organization
SASB	Structural Analysis of Social Behavior
SCID-5-PD	Structural Clinical Interview for DSM-5: Personality Disorders
SCL-90-R	Symptom Check List 90 – Revised
STIPO-R	Structured interview for personality organization – revised
STIPO	Structured interview for personality organization – clinical edition
WAI	Working Alliance Inventory

Part I

Introduction

Chapter 1

Introduction

A word about groups

Groups have been important throughout history for survival, for joining forces to find solutions to important problems and for the mutual satisfaction of less vital needs. Groups also provide the means for delegating tasks, for leadership and for developing ways of socializing, including communication. The use of the motivational powers of groups is probably as old as humanity itself.

Definition

Groups are made up of at least three individuals who are linked together for a shorter or longer period of time and for different reasons. They can be *natural groups* such as family, neighbors, people from one town or even nation, or can be formed for more *specific purposes* such as a choir or orchestra, a committee for organizing a party, a football team or a school class. Groups can, to different degrees, be organized. They can also have different characteristics or dimensions such as size, objectives, socializing norms, leadership, membership requirements, boundaries to the outside world and duration. Groups can be categorized as being small (4–15), medium (15–40) or large (50–500), and significantly higher numbers of individuals being referred to as a crowd. *Organizations* are groups of people who are linked together by complex tasks, are regulated by guidelines and laws and are governed by multi-level leadership.

The group has a central position in society, with awareness of the group's potent capacity for inducing change increasing in recent decades. The group has therefore assumed a central position in education, in politics, in industry, in business, in social situations and not least within the health system.

Early systematic exploration of groups

The sociologist Gustav Le Bon (1995) is known for his early, systematic explorations of group behavior, and for his study of the primitive behavior of crowds during the French Revolution (Behr, 2016). He, in his work, describes how a person in a large crowd acts in a "less human" way and becomes more regressive,

DOI: 10.4324/9781003216377-2

primitive and uncivilized. He believed that the "group soul" took control and that the individual was swallowed up by the crowd, being subjected to a hypnotic, collective control through this loss of their sense of personal responsibility. Man became a barbarian in a crowd, a creature ruled by instincts. The explanation for this was that group membership brought a feeling of great strength. This feeling was, however, also a contagion that spread and filled people with these feelings from the outside. The suggestibility of the individual also increased immensely when in a group.

The psychologist William McDougall (1920) also noted that man often behaved in a less civilized way when in a group. Groups could, he noted, also reinforce positive individual behavior where there was a certain level of organization in the group. This organization should include clear group goals, activity that was goal-directed and agreement on the preconditions for participation in the group.

Freud (1955) also contributed to the understanding of "groups" through his studies of the self (ego ideals). He described relationships within the army and the church, groups that we today consider to be organizations. Members need a sense of purpose, and activity goals are required for these "groups" to function. Clear leadership is also required, with members then developing libidinous ties both to their leader and to each other. Soldiers or a congregation can, furthermore, where there is clear leadership, take their superiors to be ego ideals and identify with their peers, so assuming the group's and the leader's goals, developing unity, community and solidarity. Freud maintained that a consequence of this is regression in the form of primitivization or uniformization, this pushing individual traits and needs into the background. This may explain some of the attraction and fear that joining a group can induce in a person. Group membership can, through association with a leader and a clear-set ideology, provide *security* by offering guidance, faith and meaning in one's life. Fear can also be generated through having to give up part of one's autonomy, freedom or uniqueness.

Book contents

The main objective of this book is to describe mental health enhancing groups. These are groups that are led by one or more therapists and which are established to help participants resolve or alleviate their psychological problems or suffering associated with mental disorders. In this book, I present one type of group therapy, Focused Group Analytic Psychotherapy (FGAP). This research-based, systematic approach seeks to help patients with their well-defined problems, within a limited time frame. This book therefore aims to provide a detailed, nuanced picture of this treatment, and to describe the treatment's framework, content, rationale, and how it is conducted, who can benefit from it and how participants can be evaluated and selected. I will begin with some general comments on treatment groups and an overview of treatment types, to provide the reader with a perspective.

Members of groups in mental health care services must have problems of a certain magnitude, must experience a certain degree of suffering and usually must have a clinical diagnosis. Group members must also have been evaluated by a professional for the social security reimbursement of treatment expenses.

The relationship between the therapist and patients has both personal and professional aspects. Interactions in groups are, however, guided by a different set of norms (rules) and expectations. These rules and expectations include that patients should make an effort to be open about their problems, seek to be faithful to the goals of the group and be constructive in transactions with other group members. This will be described in more detail in the discussion of FGAP evaluation and preparation (Chapter 3).

The therapist's role in the group is to apply their professional competence, personal faculties and life experience to assist the group and individual patients in their work with their problems and in the achievement of their treatment goals. Different group therapies and theoretical orientations, however, give different views of leadership and the leader's role in the group. The therapist in *psychodynamic groups* acts as an *administrator*, a *therapist* and a *group member*. The therapist administers the group and selects participants, but also represents professional expertise. The therapist is, however, also available in these groups as a relational object. Emphasis in group analytic groups is, however, placed on the therapeutic potential of the *group as a whole* and the other group members. The role of the therapist will be described in more detail in Chapter 7.

What is group psychotherapy?

Psychotherapy is a *systematic, psychological* and usually a *verbal* method that has been developed to treat mental health problems and disorders, traditionally in *individual* patients. The goal of a *therapy group*, which is normally the result of gathering five to ten patients and one or two therapists, is to ameliorate painful feelings, improve disturbed experiences of self and others and change dysfunctional external behavior. Patients often, however, have different needs for help. The group may therefore need to be adjusted to meet these needs. Some patients need to gain control of substance abuse or self-harm, others need to develop better self-esteem, a more stable mood or control anxiety. A number of conditions must, however, be met for a therapy to be effective, which is the essence of this book. One condition is that the therapist should be familiar with and be able to use the group's potential growth-promoting properties, including the supporting and learning-oriented factors that can promote positive change for the individual group member (see Chapter 6, "Therapeutic factors"). An updated and systematic overview of key research on the effects and use of group psychotherapy is given in Chapter 9. Numerous references are also made throughout the book to the key literature that underpins the text and provides additional information on specific issues.

Classification of group therapies

Professionals may hold different opinions on how groups should be classified. The most common way to classify group therapies is, however, by theoretical background. Most forms of group therapy have emerged in the wake of individual therapy, concepts therefore sometimes simplifying the more complex phenomena of groups. Some of the aspects used to categorize groups are outlined below. A specific group therapy may, however, be so composite that properties from two or more categories must be used to give a good, recognizable picture of the approach.

- *Theoretical background*. Psychodynamic groups, including Focused Group Analytic Psychotherapy (FGAP), are invariably based on a specific or a combination of psychoanalytic theories. Other types of groups can be based on cognitive, learning, behavior-oriented, systemic or existential theories. Some approaches combine elements from several theories to form more integrative models.
- *Patient characteristics* also define groups. Groups of patients with similar diagnoses such as substance abuse, schizophrenia or depression are often called "homogeneous groups". Groups of patients with clusters of symptoms such as anxiety disorders, eating disorders and personality disorders are also considered to be homogeneous groups. "Mixed" or "heterogeneous groups" are groups of patients with different diagnoses. The diagnostic systems currently in use, however, frequently assign several diagnoses to a patient (so-called comorbidity), making this classification sometimes arbitrary.
- *Treatment location and duration*. Groups can also be classified by where they take place. For example on a hospital ward, in a day care department, in an outpatient clinic or in private practice. Treatment duration – long-term, intermediate, short-term or ultra-short-term – can also be used to characterize therapies.
- *Patient flow*. *Open groups* start with a number of patients and enroll new patients as patients leave the group. *Closed groups* are groups in which all patients begin at the same time and are expected to remain together as a group until the group is dissolved at the end of the course.
- Some groups are *thematically oriented* and discuss topics such as beliefs, values, communication and social skills. Others are more *relationship-* and *process-oriented*, the relationships and interactions between participants *and* the group process being the central elements of the therapeutic work, and eventually the objects of analysis.

Group therapy has a broad background, and draws on theories from individually oriented therapy models, personality theory, field theory, social psychology and general systems theory. These theories do not stand still, but continuously develop through academic and clinical research, and clinical experience. Group therapy theory has also drawn on other fields such as psychiatry, psychology, social work, nursing, organization theory and pedagogics. This very broad theoretical background led Anthony (1971), one of Foulkes's co-authors, to characterize the history of group psychotherapy as being conglomerative, complex, confabulatory and conflictual.

Short history of groups

The Age of Enlightenment was a period in history from the early 1800s that focused on social welfare and the rights of the individual, this period leading to a humanization of the care of people who we today consider to be suffering from severe mental disorders. The use of punishment, chains and confinement upon those with mental disorders was abolished, and the person suffering from these was no longer considered to be evil but to have a disease. Greater emphasis was therefore placed on hygiene, living conditions, the value of activities and employment, and the significance of psychological dimensions in the patient's illness. Patients may have been assembled in therapy groups as early as in this period of reform, "the moral treatment" also being a part of this era (Borthwick et al., 2001). Joseph Pratt (1907), an internist from Boston, is often credited with being the pioneer of systematic group therapy. He brought tuberculosis patients together into groups in their homes and lectured them on aspects of the disease. The patients shared their experiences with each other, the symptoms, problems and challenges, and then discussed how these could be handled. Another group therapy pioneer was the Romanian Jacob L. Moreno (1889–1974), who was educated in philosophy, mathematics and medicine in Vienna. One of his primary ideas was that psychopathology was a consequence of a person executing too strict a control over their emotional life. He therefore started the "Theatre of spontaneity" in which participants, through dramatizing relationships and conflicts, were able to unleash their creative potential. He gradually became more engaged in therapeutic activity, this leading to his development of the psychodrama therapy method (Moreno, 1972).

The development of group therapy accelerated during and after World War II, in England and the United States in particular, as large numbers of military personnel returned from the war suffering from post-traumatic conditions. The most influential group therapy work in England at this time was the so-called Northfield experiments (Bion, 1946) at a military hospital in Birmingham. A number of prominent psychiatrists at the hospital (Bion, 1961; Foulkes, 1977; Ezriel, 1950; Main, 1946) abolished the traditional treatment ideology and engaged patients as active collaborators in their own treatment through introducing *the group* as a cornerstone of all hospital activities. All patients were a part of one or more groups, most activities being carried out in groups. This included psychotherapy, the planning of recreational activities and sharing and carrying out the everyday tasks needed for the hospital to function. These experiences were of great importance in the development of psychodynamic group therapy, administrative therapy and the concept of "the therapeutic community" (see next section).

Psychodynamic groups

This large "family" of group psychotherapies can, with some difficulty, be classified by the psychoanalytic theories they build on, such as object relations theory, interpersonal theory, self-psychology and intersubjective theories. Most therapies including FGAP, however, draw on many different theories, as demonstrated in the sections of this book. An important aspect of group theory is whether the focus is on the individual member or the "group as a whole". Theories that emphasize the individual are illustrated by the work of psychoanalysts Wolf and Schwarz (1962). They treated individual patients in groups using psychoanalysis, the other members being spectators. Other theories view the group as the patient, and address the group as a whole (Bion, 1961; Ezriel, 1950). Bion, in his approach, characterized patterns of group interactions based on what he believed to be basic assumptions about the participant's goals at the moment of observation. These include "dependency", "fight or flight", "pairing" and "a work group". Group analytic psychotherapy, which is the most commonly used psychodynamic group approach in Europe, focuses on *both* the group as a whole *and* on individual patients, assuming therefore a position between the two models described above. FGAP belongs to the "sub-family" of group analytic psychotherapy (or Group Analysis, GA). I will therefore describe some aspects of GA in more detail here. The next chapter will, however, be devoted to FGAP.

Group analysis

S.H. Foulkes

Group analysis was developed in the late 1930s by S.H. Foulkes (1898–1976), a German-Jewish psychiatrist and psychoanalyst who emigrated to England in 1933. He studied medicine and started, shortly after graduation, to specialize in neurology to achieve his goal of becoming a psychiatrist. He worked for a time in Frankfurt under Kurt Goldstein, a towering figure in neurology and gestalt psychology, and then spent two years in Vienna to undergo psychoanalytic training, including analysis with Helene Deutsch. He then returned to Frankfurt and became head of the clinic at the newly founded psychoanalytic institute, which was near the University's Sociological Institute led by Karl Mannheim and the Institute of Social Research led by Max Horkheimer. This later became the hearth of the so-called Frankfurt School of German sociology and philosophy. The Frankfurt School, psychoanalysis and his work within neurology and gestalt psychology were the three most important sources of inspiration for Foulkes in his development and formulation of group analytic theories. He, after seeing the dangers of the Nazi regime, moved in 1933 with his family to the United Kingdom, acquiring British citizenship in 1938. As a member of the British Psychoanalytic Association, he supported Anna Freud in the battle between M. Klein, A. Freud and "the Independents". Foulkes established a practice in Exeter in 1939 and made his debut as a group therapist at the outbreak of World War II, aged 42 (Foulkes & Lewis, 1944). In 1943 he was summoned by the army and stationed at the Northfield Military Neurotic Center, where soldiers and repatriated prisoners of war with post-traumatic disorders were treated. A number of the foremost

British psychiatrists worked at this hospital at that time. This became a crucial element in the development of new group-based therapies, psychotherapy in small groups, activity groups, large groups and network groups. Foulkes's experiences at Northfield therefore were an additional source of inspiration that contributed to the development of his group analytic method.

The transformation of Northfield from a traditional psychiatric hospital to a group-based, active therapeutic institution for traumatized soldiers was also of vital importance to the development of psychodynamic group psychotherapy. It was also of great importance to the development of administrative psychiatry (using all elements of the institution to advance its therapeutic potential) and the concept of the therapeutic community (Main, 1946). The experiences and ideas which later crystallized into the so-called "milieu therapy", radically changed the treatment of very many patients in and outside psychiatric institutions in many countries (Harrison & Clarke, 1992), including in Norway (Thomstad & Gydal, 1968).

Group analytic theories and concepts

Foulkes was primarily an ego-psychologically oriented psychoanalyst. This is evidenced by his support of Anna Freud in the conflicts that unfolded around her in the British Psychoanalytic Association. He was also greatly influenced by his early work with the neurologist and gestalt psychologist Kurt Goldstein, as shown by Foulkes's holistic approach to patients and the group, and by his view of the *figure* and *ground perspective*, the observer's view in his approach alternating between individual patients and the group as a whole, and therefore between the foreground and the background. His contact with the Frankfurt School and not least with his friend, sociologist Norbert Elias, had a significant influence on his understanding and theories of the individual's place and role within a sociological and social psychological framework.

Foulkes brought the understanding of the unconscious aspects of mental life and the phenomenon and concept of transference with him from psychoanalysis. Transference is evidenced by automatically adding (transferring) attitudes, feelings or wishes that originate in early, significant relationships, to successive encounters and transactions with new people, thus distorting the situation or the other person's unique presence. What is transferred can often be influenced by aspects of the sender's personality structure, for example a certain attachment style or an excessive use of certain (often immature) defense mechanisms. This can be observed where someone in a dialogue presents emotionally charged or verbal comments which seem irrelevant, exaggerated or in other ways "out of touch" with the situation or context. This occurs more or less automatically (unconsciously) and may lead to recurrent misunderstandings or friction or, even worse, to more serious conflicts in interpersonal situations.

Foulkes believed that a group's ability to devote itself to a "free-floating discussion" in line with the "free associations" in psychoanalysis, represented a difference between group analysis and other forms of group therapy. He believed that the therapist's laid back, pending attitude was of great importance in eliciting free associations, these having cues to latent themes which could be indicative of individual and more collective processes in the group as a whole (Foulkes, 1977; Pines, 1994). These could then become the subject of further exploration and scrutiny.

"The principle of interconnectedness" between human beings was a central issue in Foulkes's approach. I understand the principle of interconnectedness to be an axiom that states that we as persons and social beings are related, connected or tied up with each other as a consequence of common fate (Barwick & Weegmann, 2018). Foulkes argued that man is primarily a social being, meaning that the group is, *psychologically*, more basic than individuals, even though the individual is *biologically* the smallest entity. Foulkes was preoccupied with the interpersonal and the socially unconscious from the start of his theory building. However, he gradually toned down the interpersonal and placed more emphasis on the "social unconscious" (Foulkes & Anthony, 1984) as a central source of social and cultural influence upon the individual. I will now describe Foulkes's conceptualization of how the influence of society is brought into and developed further in the therapeutic group. Foulkes presented a "transpersonal perspective" and maintained that the individual constitutes "open systems", interactions and communication in a network of a group, not only being "between"' but also "through" people.

Matrix

Foulkes (1977, 1984, 1986) and Foulkes and Anthony (1984) have conceptualized a number of phenomena specific to the group, communication in a group being characterized (and driven) by what he referred to as the "foundation matrix" and "dynamic matrix". The *foundation matrix* is based on the fact that all human beings have a common biological and cultural background. We all have a body, we are all born into and socialized in a family, we depend on communication, we have a language and we need each other. He believed that these conditions were of vital importance to our understanding of each other. We take much of this background for granted "like the air we breathe", without really being aware of it. The *dynamic matrix* is a created and potentially intimate network developed by the members of the therapeutic group. It is defined as being "a hypothetical network of communication and relationships" or "the network of all individual mental processes, the psychological medium in which they meet, communicate and interact" (Foulkes, 1977). The Latin root of "matrix" is *mater*, which means mother (and also womb). What, however, is given birth to in the network? Individuals are at the intersection of communication and transactions as "open systems", and are both characterized by and help shape transactions in their own, unique way. The dynamic network (matrix) that gradually develops in a group and forms a central part of the group's history becomes the backdrop for understanding what the communication and interactions express for the group, and what it means personally to each patient. Foulkes considered the development of the matrix (through communication and interactions) and the repetitive correctives each group member receives on their interaction with others to be an important mechanism that contributed to learning and insight. He designated this "*ego-training-in-action*".

Foulkes was also concerned with the therapist's relationship to authority and leadership, which he emphasized as being central to group analysis. He recommended that the therapist should consciously tone down their authority, so mobilizing the treatment resources in individual members and the group as a whole. He also renamed the therapist "conductor", as in the conductor of an orchestra (Foulkes & Anthony, 1984).

Group-specific factors

Foulkes described a number of group-specific therapeutic factors.

  a. Socialization through the group. Opportunities for imitation and identification arise through the individual considering how others in the group, including the leader, behave in interpersonal situations. The group also provides the opportunity to try out new interpersonal strategies, and a tremendous opportunity for social training and learning.
  b. The mirror phenomenon. The group situation has been compared to a hall of mirrors in which an individual is confronted with different parts of his social, psychological and physical characteristics (body image) through the reactions of others.
  c. The condenser phenomenon. This term describes a sudden discharge of deep and primitive material or of a pooling of associated thoughts in the group.
  d. The chain phenomenon. Members of the group occasionally approach free association. This is characterized by their distinctive free-floating discussion. This often arises in a well-established group as a "chain reaction", each member forming an important and idiosyncratic link of the chain.
  e. Resonance indicates that communication strikes group members differently and leads to distinctive, individual responses.

Views on the human being and on mental disorders

Foulkes maintained that man is primarily a social being, and that individuality emerged late in social evolution. This also characterized his view of mental disorders. He referred to them as neuroses and character disorders, and saw them as being strongly related to human relationships. These manifest in the individual's relationships with the group, and often have their roots in the patient's relationship with his offspring family, or primary group. Mental disorders are defined by the person's relationship to the surroundings. He therefore believed that the best treatment would be participation in and analysis of the disorders of a group, this forming a starting point for a deeper understanding and correction of dysfunctional human relationships.

Definition of group analysis

Foulkes saw the individual as the target of treatment. The group was, however, the main element of treatment. The group's therapeutic potential was primarily mobilized by the therapist. Foulkes compared the therapist to the conductor of an orchestra, so diminishing the leader's authority and dominance, and gradually transferring parts of this to the group (Foulkes, 1977). One of the therapist's most important initial tasks is to involve team members in the treatment process. Communication in the group and the exploration and elaboration of this communication proceeds from manifest statements to understanding more latent aspects, and from symptom expressions to more interpersonal, relational meaning-bearing transactions. These verbal exchanges, according to Foulkes, constitute the group process itself. He introduced the concept of "translation" to describe this deepening of communication and felt the therapist should refrain from making traditional psychoanalytic interpretations if the group worked well. He operated with four levels of communication in the group: *current/immediate* such as "Pete is not coming" and "Lawrence felt hurt at last week's meeting", *transference* (whole object: "Holly responded to Hans as if he were her father"), *projection* (part-objects: group members project parts of themselves onto others) and the *primordial*, Foulkes referring here to Jung's archetypes and the collective unconscious. Refer to Thygesen and Aagaard (2002) and Hopper (2003) for more detailed information on this. GA is a long-term psychotherapy in which members participate over a number of years, Foulkes believing the optimal to be two to three years. The group is also characterized as being slow-open, which means that new patients are admitted when someone leaves.

Objectives of group analysis

Group analysis is an explorative therapy that aims to provide each patient with insight into their intrapsychic conflicts and irrational behaviors, including interactional patterns. This "translation" may allow earlier symptomatic behaviors, which Foulkes characterized as autistic, to be communicated in a way that is understandable to others. A clearer communication process can become an important medium for other therapeutic forces, and is therefore important in driving the therapeutic process forward and breaking the isolation from others that symptoms and deviant behavior may cause.

Are the similarities between psychodynamic groups greater than the differences?

Foulkes developed his own concepts for describing the many elements of the structure and process of the therapeutic group. GA, however, shares many of its basic elements with other psychoanalytically oriented therapies. These include a developmental perspective on personality, the existence of inner representations of early important interpersonal relationships, psychological causality, the effect of unconscious individual processes on behavior, the presence of psychic conflict and the existence of mental defense mechanisms. In the next chapter, I will take a closer look at areas where FGAP and GA differ.

Refer to Foulkes's articles and books (Foulkes and Anthony, 1984; Foulkes, 1977, 1984, 1986) and contributions of successors who have supplemented and expanded his theories within and outside his framework, for more in-depth information on group analysis (see, for example, Pines, 1983a, 1983b; Aagaard et al., 1994; Brown & Zinkin, 1994; Widlund, 1995; Nitsun, 1996, 2015; Dalal, 1998; Karterud, 1999; Thygesen, 2000; Behr & Hearst, 2005; Garland, 2010; Stokkebæk, 2011; Lorentzen, 2014, 2020; Nielsen & Sørensen, 2013; Sandahl et al., 2021; Schlapobersky, 2016; Barwick & Weegmann, 2018).

Group psychotherapy in Norway: a history

Systematic group psychotherapy was introduced in Norway in the early 1950s. It was inspired by English, German and later American psychiatry. The German influence adhered to the medical model of the psychiatric institution, group therapy being a supplement to the total psychiatric treatment program (Jørstad & Karterud, 1983). The British orientation was to mobilize the patients' resources by actively including them as collaborators in group therapy, and in groups that took part in the daily, practical activities of the ward. The group became both a fundamental organizing principle for therapy, and the primary unit for patients' belonging and identity in a type of ward named "the therapeutic community" (Main, 1946, 1977; Jones, 1971).

The new approach was received with enthusiasm in Norway, the numerous papers published on use of groups for different kinds of patients bearing witness to this (Astrup, 1958; Bratfos & Sagedal, 1961; Lange-Nielsen & Retterstøl, 1959; Askevold, 1958). Group psychotherapy continued in the 1960–1970s to be associated with the idea of the therapeutic community, a ward based on these principles being established at Ullevål Hospital in Oslo by the pioneer Herluf Thomstad (Thomstad & Gydal, 1968). A wave of interest in milieu therapy also spread to other parts of the country (Retterstøl, 1979). Attempts to change the traditional institutions were not, however, always successful. The lack of psychotherapeutic expertise among staff was a problem, and so were institutional leaders who were concerned by or shied away from change, partly due to this causing conflicts due to new demands on staff. Change, even where wanted, such as changing hospital routines to allow more time for therapeutic activities, also created this concern (Friis, 1977; Vaglum & Fossheim, 1980; Lorentzen, 1981). Outpatient group therapy was at that time almost non-existent, and was limited to the follow-up of previously hospitalized patients.

The national community mental health program of the early 1980s aimed to empty traditional psychiatric hospitals and establish treatment facilities closer to the homes of patients. This decentralization made it necessary to transfer resources from the old institutions to new psychiatric centers and outpatient clinics in the districts. More resourceful patients, who had previously carried and transferred the group therapy ideology to newly admitted patients, were no longer hospitalized. Group therapy, however, continued to play an important role in day care wards (Vaglum et al., 1984).

Milieu therapy and the therapeutic community are no longer prominent within our mental health care system. The hierarchical authority structure that this "democratization" was to change has been somewhat softened, group therapy today being mostly carried out at day care centers, outpatient clinics and private practice, where patient participation in day-to-day activities is no longer needed. Patients in emergency wards are often hospitalized for such a short period of time or function so poorly, that a therapeutic culture partly established and transferred by the patients is now difficult to implement.

Training in psychodynamic group therapy and group analysis

The history of group psychotherapy in Norway, particularly psychodynamic group therapy, includes the initiative in 1984 to start a training program for mental health professionals. A handful of Norwegian psychiatrists decided that a systematic training program in group psychotherapy was long overdue, and approached the Norwegian Psychiatric Association. The objectives of the program were to improve the standards of group work in psychiatry, and to make this training available to psychiatric health workers from all over Norway. This resulted in a year-long collaboration with the Institute of Group Analysis, London, administered initially by the Psychotherapy Committee of the Norwegian Psychiatric Association, and then from 1992 by the Institute for Group Analysis, Norway.

Expertise had to be imported. The course was therefore set up as a "block-training course", all participants coming to Oslo for five extended weekends a year, the teaching staff coming from London. This allowed participants from all of Norway to participate. The training was developed stepwise and eventually consisted of three levels (introductory, advanced, qualifying), the complete course taking five years. The training weekends provided self-experiences in small and large groups, theory seminars and lectures and supervision of the candidates' small group work (Lorentzen et al., 1995).

Group therapy in Norway: a survey

The setting up of decentralized, district-based mental health care units and a well-administered nationwide training program in systematic psychodynamic group psychotherapy, have together had an enormous impact on the quality of group therapy provided to patients within public mental care. Psychodynamic group therapy is, however, only one of several brands of group therapy available, as described below.

Group programs have primarily been developed in day care and outpatient clinics, rather than in acute wards (where group psychotherapy hardly exists). "The day care network", called since 2018 "The network for personality disorders", is a unit that is involved in research at Oslo University Hospital. The unit works with around 20 group units around the country. The network has a special interest in severe personality disorders and treatment, which is often mentalization-based (MBT; Bateman & Fonagy, 2016) and includes modules such as psychoeducation, individual and group psychotherapy. Some community mental health centers around the country have specialized group units that can provide a variety of group types – psychodynamic, cognitive behavioral therapy, psycho-educational, art/expression therapy groups, sometimes as combinations or successively.

There has been a lack of reliable information on the use of group psychotherapy in mental health services in Norway, including information such as theoretical background, objectives of therapy, type of interventions, structure and duration. There is also little data on the type of group therapy that patients with different diagnoses receive, and the characteristics of therapists including their professional background and training. Lorentzen and Ruud (2014) therefore sent a questionnaire to all national health enterprises that includes group (theory, objective, duration), patient (clinical data) and therapist (training, profession) related questions. Information from 426 groups representing all types of group therapy within all 25 health enterprises was received, the results therefore being considered to be representative of the field. "Types of group" were, based on the theoretical background, merged into nine categories. Psychodynamic groups were the most frequent, followed by cognitive behavioral therapy, psychoeducation, social skills/communication/coping, art/expression therapy, body awareness, physical activity, theme-oriented and mixed/eclectic groups. The most frequent primary diagnosis among the 2,391 patients was depression (22%), followed by personality disorder (17%), schizophrenia/psychosis (13%), social phobia (10%), substance abuse (7.5%) and bipolar disorder (6%). Most patients in *psychodynamic groups* had a primary diagnosis of depression or personality disorder. Patients with a psychosis/bipolar disorder were treated in *psychoeducative groups*, patients in *cognitive behavioral therapy* being spread across different diagnostic groups. About 60% of patients were in groups for less than six months, 40% attending for less than three months. The vast majority of therapists were nurses. Most had many years of experience in the field, but only around 50% had completed a systematic formal training of a moderate to long duration in group psychotherapy. This underscores the need for further training of more therapists, perhaps even a larger-scale program to train supervisors who can serve new group therapists throughout the country.

A number of research studies have shown that individual and group therapy are, on average, equally effective for patients with a range of mental disorders/problems (see Chapter 9). The question can, however, be asked of the extent to which these results reflect the use of group psychotherapy in public mental health care services in Norway? Bjerke (2018) reviewed information from the

Norwegian Patient Register (NPR) including *type of treatment* (individual or group), and compared this with whether the therapist characterized the session as a "group" or "individual" session. She found that 86% of two million consultations were registered as individual treatment, only 9% being registered as group treatment. The ratio was similar for different samples of adults. However, only 3% of consultations with children/youths were group treatment, 76% being individual treatment (Bjerke, 2018, pp. 70–97).

This book emphasizes a brand of group therapy that is based on psychodynamic and psychoanalytic theory. Those interested in reading more about the types of group therapy used and researched in Norway can refer to Lorentzen et al. (2015d).

Part II

Focused Group Analytic Psychotherapy

Chapter 2

Focused Group Analytic Psychotherapy (FGAP)

Focused Group Analytic Psychotherapy (FGAP) is based on a treatment manual I designed a few years ago (Lorentzen, 2005; Lorentzen, 2014) for use in a research project into the significance of duration of treatment. I have included many of the research results and important clinical experiences from the study in this book (for example, Chapter 9).

I will begin by providing a brief description of FGAP, and then give an overview of some important features of this new therapy. Then I will present the framework and key dimensions such as time perspective, choice of theory (psychoanalytic and group analytic), characteristics of the group, treatment focus and objectives for the patient and the group. The chapter ends with a discussion of the similarities and differences between FGAP and GA.

My hope is that the rationale of this treatment design will become clear through this description of FGAP. I will, however, also elucidate on this in all the remaining chapters of the book. There are repetitions in the text. However, I find this useful in the integration of the material.

A brief description of the treatment

Focused Group Analytic Psychotherapy (FGAP) is a time-limited, psychodynamic group treatment that aims to alleviate suffering in persons with psychological problems and/or mental disorders, by uncovering and resolving internal, psychic conflicts and/or by changing dysfunctional overt behavior (Lorentzen, 2018). A key feature of FGAP is that a treatment focus is developed for each patient. The treatment focus describes a set of problems that a patient is experiencing, which often encompasses dysfunctional relational patterns and which may be connected to symptoms or a negative sense of self. Central elements of the treatment are the process and structure that unfolds in a professionally conducted group. In this type of group, the therapist engages patients in the development of a treatment culture that emphasizes openness in communication and a high degree of interaction between participants, and in which dysfunctional patterns can be activated and then explored in the "here-and-now mode". This involves the manifest ongoing communication and interactions as they emerge in the group's current situation (context), the potential latent motives that underlie them and the consequences of each participant's input. A major challenge is the creation of a safe and open atmosphere by the therapist that all in the group can be a part of. This atmosphere can facilitate the emergence of more latent aspects of each patient's distorted patterns, which can then be explored jointly in the group. The objective of the treatment is to increase participants' awareness and understanding of their and others' relationship patterns (insight) through reflection, and through feedback from the therapist and other group members, these explorations representing a starting point for corrective emotional experiences (Alexander & French, 1946; Palvarini, 2010), new learning and a change in dysfunctional interpersonal strategies.

Groups are usually made up of seven to eight patients and one to two therapists. They are *closed*, which means that all participants begin and end at the same time and they remain together as a group throughout the process. There are normally 20 weekly sessions of 90 minutes in each course, treatment therefore running for around six months.

Main features of FGAP

The time limit and other key dimensions of the framework have the following consequences for therapy construction and execution.

a) FGAP is an *individual-oriented* treatment which is provided in and through the group – the therapist, the group and the other members play an important role in the treatment. Emphasis is therefore placed on psychoanalytic theories that permit a nuanced description of individuals in terms of symptoms, personality pathology and relational problems, and that capture individual characteristics such as personal resources. The most important group analytic theory in FGAP is, however, the *matrix* concept. This concept seeks to capture what we as people share with each other, and takes a number of forms. The *foundation matrix* is a concept that captures that we are all united by our origin being in a social context, the family, which is again a part of a larger social context, society. It also captures that we all have a body, and so share a large number of qualities and experiences, including that we have a need to communicate and to join forces to solve tasks and meet challenges in life. The *dynamic matrix* is a concept that seeks to capture the concept of the group as a whole, including that members of the therapeutic group are interconnected by what they create together through the network of participant communication and interaction. The psychoanalytic theories and group analytic theories pertinent to FGAP will be presented later in the chapter.

b) The treatment requires a *thorough clinical assessment* of each patient, including the mapping of key symptoms, relational and intrapsychic conflicts and personality-based resources.

The limited time available makes it necessary to choose a *focus for the therapy* that encompasses the patient's most central problems. The focus should be relatively circumscribed and coherent. Symptoms, interpersonal problems and one or more problematic relational pattern should also be dynamically linked. Dynamic means here that opposing internal forces are in conflict, and that the patients to a varying degree are aware of connections between their symptoms and internal conflicts. The same applies to *agency*, interpersonal friction being generated by the behavior of others or by something a person says or does. Symptoms may be due to rigid personality traits and internal conflicts that have roots in early relationships, which in turn are embodied in an inner world of more or less integrated representations of self and objects, leading to different degrees of functionality in patients. Giving the patient one or more *behavioral tasks* that challenge or break the patient's habitual, problematic relationship patterns, and that activate more latent aspects of the patients' overt behavior, can also prove to be an effective measure.

Designing a *psychodynamic case formulation* is a useful way to find and formulate a meaningful focus for the therapy. The formulation can provide a tentative hypothesis of the potential connections between current symptoms/ problems, personal vulnerable spots and acute or more persistent stressors in the patient's life situation (see Chapter 4).

Patients should have the personality resources required to be able to change and to benefit from a time-limited group. These resources are dependent on what is often referred to as "level of personality organization" (PO). A patient's PO is made up of a collection of specific domains of personality structure such as identity, quality of object relationships, affect tolerance and control, maturity of defense mechanisms and moral values. These qualities collectively represent an indication of the strength of a person's ability to withstand or master internal and external challenges, and should therefore be assessed carefully for each patient before therapy. Patients with normal, neurotic or high borderline PO usually benefit most from FGAP (see Chapter 4).

c) The treatment also requires the *preparation of patients* prior to treatment. This involves a review of the focus and the behavioral tasks the patient and therapist have agreed upon. The therapist can also inform the patient about the rules of participation, the need for the patient to contribute to the development of a treatment culture and possibly the challenges different phases of the therapy can involve. The preparation also gives patients the opportunity to express some final expectations for therapy that have not yet been ventilated. Preparation should help ensure that the therapy gets a "flying start", that effective use of the time available is made and that the patient quickly gets started on the therapeutic work.

d) FGAP's primary *objective* is to increase the patient's awareness of repetitive, dysfunctional ways of acting or feeling in relation to others and to self, of how these behaviors are triggered and maintained, and of how they can affect others and the experience of one-self. FGAP also involves an expectation of change and the replacement of problematic traits with more adaptive and/or constructive behaviors. The key words of this treatment are, however, *insight* and *change*. Expectations should not, however, be overwhelmingly high! Patients enter therapy with different degrees of insight into their inner world and dysfunctional interactional patterns, and may progress at different rates during therapy. The primary, *minimum* goal for all group participants should therefore be that they, through therapy, are able to initiate a process of reflection and change that can continue after the therapy has ended.

e) Treatment *in and by the group* is through the development of *a specific treatment culture*, which is characterized by a psychodynamic and group analytic understanding, the therapy treatment focus and objectives each patient shares with the group and the characteristic challenges that the different phases of the group process involve. The therapist is an important factor in this development as a role model through his attitude and how he intervenes, and through how he activates the other group members and keeps them accountable for their contributions.

f) The therapist in FGAP should exert *clear leadership* and is responsible for maintaining the group's boundaries, for keeping the group process in the here-and-now and for guiding the group members' attention *from* the group's *manifest content to* the exploration and analysis of more *latent connections* to individual patients and the group as a whole. This requires active observation and an empathic stance.

The therapists, in addition to being active observers and empathically registering the emotional waves in the group, must continuously reflect on what they see and experience, and intervene when the group is unproductive or stagnates. An FGAP therapist will therefore be more active, directing and didactic at times than a GA therapist. It is, however, important that they step back when group members become more active and work well.

The framework

Key FGAP framework factors are the time limit, theoretical background, dimensions of the group format and the objective and focus of the therapy. All these factors are important when shaping the requirements for the selection of patients and how each is prepared for participation in the group. They also have implications for group composition, treatment design, treatment techniques, understanding of change and, indirectly, also the treatment outcome.

Time limitation

Less time is available to work with each patient in FGAP. It is therefore important to use the time as effectively as possible. Two important ways of ensuring effective time use is to base the method on the dimensions that research and clinical experience have shown to be most effective, and to select patients that are of the type that have been shown to benefit from time-limited therapy (Poulsen, 2000/01a, 2000/01b, 2000/01c; Messer, 2001). Suitable therapists are those who have the skills and experience to quickly develop a treatment culture that is interactive, supportive and characterized by enthusiasm and communication.

The time-limited nature of this treatment may, for some patients, positively affect the therapy and change-process, the short time available suggesting that "time is important" so creating a sense of urgency. This could ignite a spark for patients with this quality and who believe that something important could be achieved within the time available, "opening up" and involving the therapist and other group members earlier than they would in longer term therapy. Patients do, however, have to have the *capacity to change*, this capacity depending both on the type of problems they want to work with, and on the resources needed to bring about change. All group members should share some common qualities (for example ability to reflect, interest in exploration of relationships, willingness to change), if the treatment culture is to develop well. The quality of the therapist's leadership is also an important factor. There has been relatively little research into the importance of the therapist's competence. Interest is, however, steadily increasing in this area (see, for example, Wampold & Imel, 2015; Hill & Knox, 2013; Knox & Hill, 2021).

Theoretical background

The theoretical background of FGAP arises from many sources. I would like in this book, however, to keep the presentation of FGAP relatively simple. I therefore emphasize here that FGAP has primarily relied on psychoanalytic/psychodynamic and group analytic theories and my and other professionals' clinical experiences and research in time-limited psychotherapy. (The concepts of psychoanalytic and psychodynamic are used interchangeably, if not otherwise stated.)

Psychoanalytic/psychodynamic theory

Psychodynamic therapies rely on psychoanalytic theories. These make important contributions to the understanding of personality development, and to the phenomenology and background of mental disorders and psychopathology as they appear as symptoms, internal conflicts and disturbed interpersonal relationships. Psychoanalysis has conceptual tools for capturing the interactions between the therapist and patients in the treatment situation, such as resistance, transference and countertransference. This provides important information that is useful in individual therapy and treatment in groups.

Foulkes was trained in classical ego psychology, a theory that describes well inter-systemic conflicts between the systems (id, ego, superego) and defense mechanisms (Freud, 1934). Ego psychology also highlights the development of the ego, the executive agency of the personality, as it seeks to regulate and mediate between tensions from within (drives, wishes, guilt, superego demands) and from the outside. Later authors have placed greater emphasis on interpersonal relationships (Sullivan, 1953a, 1953b; Leszcz & Malat, 2012) or have developed an object relations theory that primarily describes a child as object-seeking (Klein, 1952, 1975; Fairbairn, 1952; Winnicott, 1971). Interpersonal theory and object relations theory are also central to the advancement of self-psychology (Kernberg, 1975; Kohut, 1971; Stone, 1992; Brown, 1994), and to more intersubjective theories. These relationally oriented, post-classical theories (Messer, 2001) all originate from the two-person relationship (dyadic), but have also found their way into models of group psychotherapy. They all stress the importance of connectedness between persons and explain how the individual (the self) in concert with significant others, faces challenges from outside and from within, and gradually develops and builds an inner world which characterizes the perception of self and others, attachment style, cognition, emotionality and overt behavior. Aspects of this inner world affect personality development, contribute to psychopathology and dysfunctional behavior, and appear in the transference and countertransference reactions activated in the interview or group situation. These theories have increased our understanding of human motivation, and that the need for attachment, intimacy with others and affirmation of the self are separate motives that add to libidinous and aggressive drives. This opens more for that emotions and needs can become conflictual, even within one agency of the psyche. An example of an *intrasystemic conflict* is the coexistence of several contradictory self-images. This is a phenomenon that most are familiar with. Another example is a conflict between a desire for closeness and intimacy, this at the same time being a threat to the person's identity and wish for autonomy.

Psychoanalyst Otto Kernberg has modernized and developed psychoanalytic theory by integrating Freud's drive theory and ego psychology (structural model) into his version of object relations theory. He has also made valuable contributions to self-psychology (Kernberg, 1996) and has been extensively involved in the development of psychotherapeutic methods for patients with a more severe personality pathology (1975, 1980, 1984). His theories are also useful in understanding patients with neurotic and less severe personality problems. I will briefly outline a simplified version of this theory here as a background to understanding important aspects of FGAP. Two important themes are *suitability for the therapy* and *how patients are assessed*. These will be covered extensively in the next two chapters.

Object relations theory provides a model for how we, early in our development, begin to build an inner world that consists of memory traces and representations of relational episodes. *Part-self* and *part-object* representations that are affectively colored, merge gradually into more coherent, whole gestalts of the self and of external objects, external objects usually being caregivers and other significant family members. There is also, at the same time, a fusion of positive or negative affective qualities that make the emotional coloring of representations richer and more nuanced. A prerequisite is that experiences predominantly are positively colored. If experiences are predominantly negatively colored, then self and object representations will remain fragmentary (cf. splitting) and irrationally emotionally colored (cf. idealization, devaluation). Object relations theory maintains that this structuring and integration of an inner relational world is a key factor in personality development. It must, however, be emphasized that internal representations are not replicates of the outer world. They represent *how* the baby has perceived and "understood" transactions. One can say in general that a child, under favorable conditions and based on genetic equipment and temperament gradually, through interaction with significant caregivers, develops autonomy, a sense of identity and relational qualities, and gradually learns to distinguish between "inside" and "outside" and to see other people as separate from themselves. Good mental health means that the individual can face and resolve internal and external conflicts, and master challenges without developing symptoms, losing feelings of self-worth or the ability of psychosocial functioning.

Group analytic theory

The most central group analytic theories and concepts presented in the introductory chapter include a short biography of Foulkes, which describes the influence his psychoanalytic training, neurology/gestalt psychology, sociology and his work with traumatized soldiers had upon him. Some are particularly important to FGAP design, such as the *foundation matrix*, the *dynamic matrix*, the *transpersonal* perspective and the "ego-training-in-action" change mechanism.

One of Foulkes's most important contributions was to highlight the enormous importance that society and social relationships has upon the development of the individual. This is reflected in his *foundation matrix* concept. The term encapsulates the common experience background that all share, and which he believed was a prerequisite for understanding each other. Patients therefore bring their personal matrix that has been forged in relation to their group of origin to the therapy group, a new matrix forming from the interweaving of personal matrices as the group develops. This *dynamic matrix*, a term Foulkes uses to describe the group as a whole, becomes the background against which every communication can be understood. Each personal story and each interaction has a group meaning and a personal one. Foulkes defined the dynamic matrix as "the hypothetical web of communication and relationship in a given group" (Foulkes, 1986) or "the network of all individual mental processes, the psychological medium in which they meet, communicate and interact" (Foulkes & Anthony, 1984). He used an image (metaphor) of nerve tissue and intersecting fibers to represent communication and transactions, the individual being "a nodal point" at the intersection of fibers. He also presented the idea that members of the group act as an "open system" and that all communication "goes through" and affects all the participants in the group, depending on where they are developmentally and mentally at that point in time. He therefore moved from an interpersonal to a transpersonal level, and showed how group analytic psychotherapy was influenced by systems theory (Durkin, 1983; Agazarian, & Gantt, 2000; von Bertalanaffy, 1968).

Foulkes used the term "ego-training-in-action" for an important mechanism that only appears in groups and that contributes to insight and change. A patient, as a consequence of the interaction and communication between the participants in the group, receives constant correction as the group's matrix develops, leading to deeper levels of understanding. The new understanding and frequent corrections that each member receives, lead to modification of past behaviors and make the patient open to new learning. The "ego-training-in-action" group phenomenon has been compared to Freud's "working through" in individual psychoanalysis (Freud, 1958).

The three dimensions of the group format

Causes of mental disorders are complex and composite. Most symptoms and behavioral disorders are, however, related to human relationships. Disorders may have their origin in or show their first manifestations in a patient's early relationships with his primary group (the family). This makes *the group* an effective medium when activating, exploring, understanding and working through symptoms and interpersonal problems associated with such disorders. Extensive research of the outcome of group psychotherapy of patients suffering from a variety of mental disorders and problems has, furthermore, shown the efficacy and effectiveness of group psychotherapy (Burlingame et al., 2013; Blackmore et al., 2012; Burlingame & Strauss, 2021).

A key frame factor for group therapy is the group format itself. FGAP and other group analytic therapies all contain three important dimensions. These are structure, process and content (Foulkes & Anthony, 1984; de Maré, 1972).

Structure

Structure consists of the *physical aspects* that define the group, localization, time aspect, duration and frequency of sessions, financial terms and explicit rules that apply within and outside of the group. Physical conditions are, however, accompanied by aspects that define the *psychological structure* of the group. Walls, windows, doors and sound insulation delineate a room and separate it from other rooms. Psychological space is, however, determined by the group's boundaries defined by explicit and implicit rules. All participants have sought help for psychological problems. They have all been evaluated and been granted access to the group based on these. Participation, however, takes place within a given time frame and is based on the framework and rules, and how these are perceived and interpreted. Patients are expected to expose and work with their own problematic relationships. They should also share the time available and respond to the inputs of fellow patients. They should refrain from meeting outside the group between sessions, leave the group when the session is over and pay for services at the designated times. They can expect, in return, to receive assistance in teasing out the problems they are struggling with.

The psychological space is influenced by physical conditions such as the size of the room, furniture and colors. Is it spacious, welcoming, bright and friendly, or does it seem drab, dark and cramped? Does it feel safe, or does poor insulation or an open door set off fantasies that others are listening? Are there windows that let in daylight or is there only electric light? What is the temperature? Is it cold, warm or too hot? Time relates to the length of sessions and the therapy course. It also relates to the time of day sessions are held, and not least their frequency. These affect the intensity of therapy. Financial conditions such as fees and payment terms are also important structural factors. The structure is, furthermore, affected by the composition of the group (patient selection), that the group is closed, that sessions are held every week and that they are attended by the same persons. These all represent predictable aspects.

Each member's idiosyncratic behavior often becomes visible or is easier to spot against the "background" of the group's structure. A group can, however, also come under stress if a number of patients enact problematic behavior at the same time. Common examples are patients who are undisciplined and frequently arrive late, skip sessions and do not respect the financial terms. Group members can also make problematic suggestions such as that the group should move outside onto the lawn "because the weather is so nice". Another suggestion I have experienced is that a group member brought glasses and a bottle of champagne to the group, and wanted everyone to join him in celebrating his birthday. The therapist, who was responsible for maintaining the structure and for intervening in this type of "boundary issue" situation, acknowledged the importance of the occasion, but asked him to wait and asked the group to reflect on the initiative. The patient in response, however, swiftly handed out the glasses and was ready to pour! The therapist, after "corking the bottle" commented on the attempt to change the group's purpose. Only then was it possible for the group to start reflecting on what had happened. The two vignettes above describe incidents that can be characterized as "attacks" on the group's structure.

Process

The process consists of the way communications and other interactions develop during a session, and from session to session. The ideal is to develop a working group (Bion, 1961) which is characterized by it being task-oriented, and by being aimed at working on the problems that have caused the group members to seek help. All members participate in this type of group. Communication is therefore characterized by a free group discussion in which members constructively address the inputs of other members, the group over time developing an investigative, personal and open tone. Therapists play an important role in this, by contributing to the development of such a culture through their stance and interventions.

The group process is the same for all members in closed groups. Group members therefore follow each other through the process, from start to end. A number of researchers and clinicians have observed and described a sequence of phases in such groups (Brabrender & Fallon, 2009). Four phases are highlighted in FGAP, engagement, differentiation, interpersonal work and termination. Each phase has a distinctive character and presents specific challenges to the therapist, the patients and the group. These must be met and resolved for the group to progress and for the patients to change (MacKenzie, 1997, p. 143; Lorentzen, 2014). A brief description of the phases is given here, and will be further elaborated in Chapter 6. In the *engagement* phase, patients introduce themselves and start to become acquainted with each other. Each member can decide *how* they present themselves and how much of themselves they want to reveal. They should all, however, present the *therapy focus* and *behavioral tasks* they decided on with the therapist during the evaluation. The main concern of patients at this stage is whether they will be accepted by the others in the group. The therapist asks clarifying questions, invites comments to each presentation and makes connections between similar topics or problems, thus stimulating the members to participate in the development of a treatment culture in the group. In the *differentiation* phase, patients begin to position themselves in relation to the therapist and each other. Group members start to test out strategies for giving feedback to others and for disclosing themselves, endeavoring to keep interactions constructive. The therapist is an important moderator in these transactions, modeling how feedback is given through comments and interventions. The *interpersonal work* phase is the longest. Greater emphasis is now placed on the treatment focus of each patient, including aspects of dysfunctional relationship patterns that are tied up in the patient's problems or symptoms. The therapist tries to create a safe "work situation", in which problematic individual inputs are met with acceptance, interest and reflection. This can provide new learning and be the starting point for change. In the *termination* phase, anxiety about separation and having to manage without the support of the group is activated, participants evaluating the outcome of therapy and summing up what they have learned. Patients may be reminded that they should awaken old or potentially new relationships, and take up activities and use the skills they possess, to meaningfully nurture themselves when the treatment is over.

Content

The content of a group consists mainly of communication and interactions, and how the group members (including the therapist) work toward a deeper understanding of these. "Deeper" in this context means to explore and get in touch with more latent (pre-conscious or unconscious) meanings and determinants of what individual members, member subgroups and the group as a whole feels and does. Foulkes (1977) identified four levels of communication that need to be addressed. These are the immediate level, the transference level, the projective level and the primordial level. Examples are given under "Definition of GA", Chapter 1. Phenomena such as dysfunctional relational patterns in the group will usually be connected to more latent dynamic forces in individual patients and the group as a whole. These forces are often understood as expressions of psychological causality, the main role of the therapist being to assist individual patients and the group in exploring and clarifying these connections. The short-term group works in the here-and-now situation in particular, but will also be able to move toward the individual history of group members and the social (collective) unconscious. See Thygesen and Aagaard (2002) and Hopper (2003), for example, for a more detailed discussion of the relationships between the personal and the social unconscious.

Focus and objectives, individually and for the group

The *treatment focus* and the *aims of the therapy* are the last two key factors of the framework. FGAP's point of departure is a more limited, circumscribed problem area for each patient that is placed at the center of the therapeutic work. The foci usually encompass parts of dysfunctional relationship patterns that are recurrent and "anchored" in the patient. These can be seen as being problematic aspects of the patient's regular repertoire of interpersonal strategies, examples of this including a lack of self-assertion, a tendency to withdraw from other people (social avoidance) or different types of dismissive or aggressive behavior. A central objective in FGAP is that each individual should learn more about their "inappropriate" relationship patterns, which is a *prerequisite* for a patient to change. These patterns can sometimes underlie or at other times be a consequence of problematic relationships with others, with the person themselves (impaired self-esteem regulation) and can be an expression of persistent internal conflicts of another nature.

It is important to point out that each patient's therapy objective should be clear before the therapy starts. Revisions to this can, of course, be made as new understanding emerges during therapy. Therapy objectives should be attainable within the scheduled time, and patients should have fairly realistic expectations of what is achievable in 20 sessions. All goals are not always achieved in the course (six months). The main objective of FGAP is, however, not to "cure", but to initiate a constructive process of change that hopefully will continue after therapy has ended. Patients who have been trapped in a locked pattern or life situation might need to "get the ball rolling again", or learn enough through therapy to "move on in life".

The relationships between interpersonal problems, disturbed self-esteem, internal conflicts and symptoms are often complex. Assessments are therefore carried out and specific, central patterns of behavior are selected as a focus, to address aspects that can have ripple effects if change is achieved. Examples include a person who, by becoming less avoidant, receives more attention and confirmation from others, which may cause the person to feel less lonely and sad. The adaption of more adequate, controlled and better articulated ways of expressing aggression could lead to fewer broken relationships, improved self-esteem and less symptoms such as suspiciousness or phobic avoidance of social situations.

The psychogenetic perspective, which is "the root" of these patterns in early life, has traditionally been given much more attention in psychodynamic therapy and psychoanalysis than in modern psychotherapy (which is less concerned with a meticulous reconstruction of the past). Research and clinical experience shows that reactivation of dysfunctional, emotionally charged patterns followed by explorations in the here-and-now situation often provide a better basis for insight and change than a more intellectual and simplified explanation.

The group also has a supra-ordinate objective that lends itself to all patients working with dysfunctional relationship patterns. It can be argued that FGAP is, based on this, a "homogeneous" group in which all group members intend to work with interpersonal, relational problems.

Similarities and differences between FGAP and GA

I want to close this chapter by comparing some key features of FGAP and GA, and through this to provide the reader with more clarification. FGAP is a specific time-limited psychodynamic psychotherapy and also a group analytic psychotherapy that shares a number of features with GA (Table 2.1).

The individual, both patients and the therapist, plays a more central role in FGAP than in GA. The therapist works in a more individual and focused way with interpersonal transactions and intrapsychic conflicts in FGAP, addressing the group as a whole less and the individual member and interactions between patients more. Every patient in a group setting is an important collaborator in psychotherapy. The patient carries the energy, and is the one who can act, create, change and make choices, including in their own life (Krogh, 1998). FGAP's individual orientation is reflected in a more careful assessment of personality and personal characteristics. It is also reflected in a certain PO level and circumscribed treatment focus being considered as prerequisites for successful therapy. The therapist also acts more as a specialist and can direct and lead, for example, by encouraging patients to disclose their treatment focus and behavioral tasks in the first session. The therapist is often more active, and stimulates development of the treatment culture by trying to establish connections between patients early in the process, reminding them of their focus and keeping them, as much as possible, in a here-and-now mode. Patients in FGAP are assigned behavioral tasks that are to be carried out *in* and *between* sessions, which is unusual in traditional psychodynamic therapy. Examples of this may be that an avoidant and distancing person is, at least once every session, to disclose something personal and emotional to the group. Other group members may be requested to be more assertive, delimit themselves from others or be more expectant and reflecting. GA therapists will traditionally be more laid back and delegate more of the initiative and responsibility for progress to the group and its members.

Table 2.1 Comparisons between Focused Group Analytic Psychotherapy and Group Analysis

Characteristic	Focused Group Analytic Psychotherapy (FGAP)	Group Analysis (GA)
Time factor/intake.	Time-limited, closed group. Patients follow the course together from start to end.	Slow-open, long-term group. Patients end when they are finished, new patients therefore entering and changing the group.
Assessment/selection of patients. Orientation toward individual patient or group as a whole.	Mapping of personality and personal characteristics (pathology and resources) and level of personality organization (PO) must be relatively high for the patient to benefit from the therapy. Establish a focus for the therapy, consisting of symptoms, interpersonal problems and behavioral tasks.	Patients are assessed, but emphasis is not usually on specific focus. Individual-oriented, but also great emphasis on the group as a whole. Patients may have lower levels of PO and still benefit from the therapy. Transference is activated through free group discussion.
Objective.	Increased insight into the relationship between the elements in the therapy focus and their connections to internal conflicts. Achieve change in experiences of and behavior toward self and others.	More open treatment agreement. Wider and less concrete objectives. Increased insight into own conflicts and improved behavior in relation to self and others.
Therapist role/activity level.	The therapist plays a more specialist role, active and knowing, more directive and more of a leader. Keeps the process in the here-and-now modus and patients' attention on their therapy focus. Interpretation of transference in the here-and-now and related to therapy focus.	The therapist is more expectant and laid-back. Leaves more process initiative and responsibility to the group, what is disclosed and feedback. Less concerned with focus. Interprets transference, addressing both individuals and the group as a whole.
Therapy process – structure.	The process is structured and has four stages: engagement, differentiation, interpersonal work and termination. Each phase has its own distinctive character and challenges for patients and therapist. Patients stay together as a group throughout therapy.	The process is less structured. Patients are included at different times into an established treatment culture. It takes some time before new patients are socialized into the culture, the group's progression suffering. Interaction in both the here-and-now and there-and-then modes.
Theory Psychoanalytic.	Psychoanalytic object relations theory is central in assessing the level of personality organization and in working with transference-countertransference reactions.	Psychoanalytic theory is especially important for working with transference-countertransference reactions.
Group analytic.	Group analytic theory is especially important in describing the role of the group through the concept of matrix (the group as a whole).	Group analytic theory is important in describing both the role/stance of the therapist and the significance of the group as a whole (matrix).

FGAP is a more structured therapy, the process being more clearly divided into specific phases, and the therapist actively referring to these phases and the group's boundaries as a clarifying and structuring technique (Brabrender & Fallon, 2009). These conditions are more closely described in Chapter 5. Psychoanalytic theories are equally important in both therapies to the development of an understanding of patients, phenomena in the therapy and transactions between the participants in the group. Assessment and evaluation of *the person* includes assessment and evaluation of personality and personal qualities, diagnosis, resources and psychopathology. Personal qualities include attachment mode and defense mechanisms, and affect tolerance and control. The concepts of transference, countertransference and resistance are used similarly in the two therapies to understand many aspects of the group process. There are, however, differences in how the therapist relates to this understanding, for example to interventions in the group. The therapist and patient together choose a focus for treatment work that is more limited in FGAP than in GA, each patient having more time at their disposal in GA. The therapist may also handle transference differently, the therapist in FGAP primarily exploring and interpreting transference in the light of the group's current context (here-and-now) and primarily addressing aspects that can be tied to elements of the patient's treatment focus. In GA, transference is explored and understood in the context of the group, but the therapist/other group members can also use more time to explore similar episodes outside the group, in current or past relationships.

The *matrix* concept, represented in group analytic theory by the metaphor of an interconnected network, is also highly relevant in FGAP where interactions and communications are central to actualizing transference in the here-and-now situation. The limited time in FGAP does not provide the same opportunity to develop a strong common treatment culture as in GA. It is, however, still of vital importance. The FGAP therapist tries to compensate for this by allocating more time to a thorough assessment and preparation of patients *ahead of therapy*, the focus each patient discloses in the first session ideally giving FGAP patients "a flying start".

Chapter 3

Who can benefit from Focused Group Analytic Psychotherapy?

A thorough assessment is the basis for all good treatment. It is also a prerequisite for deciding *whether* a person needs treatment, and for forming a qualified opinion of the *kind of treatment* a person needs. In this chapter, I describe the problems patients seek help for. I also describe how a therapist plans a strategy for the alleviation of these problems, partly in concert with the patient, and I describe the patient characteristics that are instrumental to benefiting from FGAP. The resources a patient has and the type of problems they are struggling with are, in all forms of psychotherapy, important aspects. Choosing the best approach therefore depends on the type of mental disorders/problems a patient is experiencing, and their resources and preferences. All forms of psychodynamic group psychotherapy ideally require some patient qualities. The qualities required at the start of a time-limited therapy, however, differ from those required at the start of longer-term therapy. Two of these qualities are the ability to mentalize (psychological mindedness) and the ability to experience and control emotions (affect tolerance/ control). Both can be developed during therapy. A patient must, however, have a certain level of these two qualities at the start of short-term group therapy because of the limited time available. This will be demonstrated in this chapter, with special reference to FGAP.

Health authorities require professionals to give patients a clinical diagnosis. The diagnostic system used in Norway is ICD-10 (World Health Organization, 1992). This descriptive taxonomy can be sufficient for classifying mental disorders. It has, however, only limited value in predicting prognoses and developing psychotherapy strategy. The American Psychiatric Association has also developed a similar multiaxial system called the Diagnostic and Statistical Manual of Mental Disorders (DSM-5; American Psychiatric Association, 2013). The pros and cons of using descriptive, categorical diagnoses will be discussed in the next chapter.

The *type of problems* a patient has (treatment focus) and the *quality of the key features* of that person must be carefully assessed to determine whether a patient can benefit from FGAP. Key features can include a sense of identity, quality of object relations, maturity of defense mechanisms, affect tolerance/control, moral values and the quality of social conditions. A patient's level of personality organization (PO) can be determined collectively from these domains, this also providing an indication of the level of benefit a patient can draw from time-limited therapy. It is also useful to have a picture of the type and degree of the impairment of each personality domain for planning of therapy.

The psychodynamic diagnostics of personality is a somewhat neglected area of group psychotherapy. This neglect is partly due to this area being difficult, and requiring specific training and experience. It is also neglected because descriptive diagnoses are more easily obtained. Some therapists may also overestimate the curative potential of long-term groups, and enroll new patients into groups without developing plans and targets for the therapy, "trusting the group itself" to tease this out during the course of therapy. This could be a serious mistake in FGAP, but may be more acceptable in longer-term therapy. Clinical experience suggests, however, that long-term therapies in some cases could be shortened, if specific details about each patient's personality pathology had been teased out before therapy started.

I will go into more detail in this and the next chapter on the individual's distinctive character. In this chapter I will, however, describe the *qualities* that are considered to be important for FGAP patients; *how* these properties are assessed will be covered in the next chapter.

Important conditions for benefiting from FGAP

Psychotherapy is more of a collaborative project between therapist and patient than treatment within other areas of the health care system, patients often being a "passive recipient" in these areas. Most types of psychotherapy are therefore and because of this challenging, with patients having to meet a set of preconditions to profit from it. The challenges associated with FGAP mainly relate to aspects of the framework outlined in the previous chapter. These aspects include its time-limited nature, the group format itself and the psychodynamic orientation. It also requires a wish and will to acquire increased insight into and to change problematic behavior, such as dysfunctional relationship patterns.

An interest in learning about oneself and others

Psychodynamic therapy is exploratory. Symptoms, which are usually very troublesome, are in psychoanalytic theory often considered to be "surface phenomena" that express underlying, often repressed and unresolved intrapsychic conflicts. It is therefore important that patients are not too fixated on the symptoms, but also can see that these may be due to other aspects of their psychic life. Increasing insight into intrapsychic conflicts and learning, and applying new, more appropriate interpersonal strategies have been shown to relate to long-term improvement. Showing an active interest in understanding and learning more about themselves and others is also a prerequisite for patients taking part in a meaningful therapeutic exploration of personality traits and problematic relationships. Some people are more down to earth and fact-oriented. They want clear advice and help to get rid of troublesome symptoms and are less interested in exploring latent or underlying determinants. Others may be directly dismissive of the idea that there exists "an internal life" that influences how they feel or act, a stance that can alone contribute to the eruption of symptoms. Patients should also have some degree of "psychological mindedness" when consulting a therapist, if they are to take full advantage of time-limited therapy. This allows symptoms to be discussed, explored and reformulated in operationalized terms during the evaluation and assessment, which can then act as a focus/objective for therapy, and be shared with the group in the first session.

The ideal is that a patient expresses, after evaluation and preparation, a wish for treatment rather than having to be persuaded. This is, however, not a necessity for a patient to improve. Most clinicians have experienced patients who have benefited from time-limited therapy, despite an initial ambivalence or negative attitude to treatment. A negative attitude may, in fact, be a better prognostic sign than a patient "passively" accepting a therapist's advice about entering therapy. Strong resistance can sometimes be based on irrational notions about the group and other patients, these fading for many as soon as the group starts. Therapists should be more active in this exploration and in challenging the objections patients bring to the evaluation (see below).

Help to explore ambivalence toward group psychotherapy

Many patients, despite research showing that group therapy and individual therapy are equally effective (Burlingame et al., 2016a), prefer individual therapy. Patient choice of therapy is, however, something that therapists do not always adequately explore or question. This may be due to therapists not having the skills required to run groups or not being familiar with the research literature. My experience is, however, that most patient objections to joining a group are associated with the problems they seek help for, objections including the fear of "not being understood by the other members", that "the problems of the other patients could be contagious" (rub off on them) or that "they will not get enough therapist time and attention". A mental disorder usually implies having problems interacting with others. The concerns of patients around group therapy are therefore often fuelled by a discomfort activated *by the thought of the challenges* they think they will meet in the group. These connections can become evident to the patient through a detailed exploration and discussion of these ideas. The therapist may, through this, come to see the patients' fearful expectations to be variations of a behavioral pattern that could form part of the patient's treatment focus in FGAP. Therapists can also explain to patients that getting so quickly in touch with problematic interpersonal issues can mean that they can start working on these issues earlier in a group than in individual psychotherapy.

An established treatment focus

Time-limited groups are often used in the treatment of patients with similar (homogeneous) symptoms or diagnoses. Examples include groups for those struggling with substance abuse, eating disorders or pathological grief. The belief is that groups made up of patients facing similar struggles will more quickly develop into a cohesive group, group members being able to more easily understand and help each other in a short period of time. The "homogeneity" in FGAP is that all members have central dysfunctional interpersonal relationship patterns, which are often combined with negative experiences of themselves (self-esteem problems). These patterns create or maintain problems for the patients and the people they are surrounded by, and are usually repetitive and distinctive. They are considered to be tied to inner self and object representations, and often form an integrated part of personality traits. The patterns can be activated in relation to random people, but appear in particular in close relationships.

Another prerequisite for a patient to benefit from FGAP is that current problems and patterns should be limited and can be formulated in operationalized terms. A patient's problematic attitudes are ambiguously expressed, and may be more or less unconscious to them. Problematic attitudes will, however, be disclosed through the way in which they think and express themselves, in words or in behavior, toward others or themselves. This can be captured by the therapist and others. It is important to assist the patient in the translation of experienced problems or symptoms into relational terms, and therefore into a treatment focus that can be a natural starting point for participation in a group. The therapist must therefore use his or her total understanding of the patient as a person, and be active in suggesting and engaging him/her in a circumscribed problem area, which may require negotiations before consensus can be reached. A focus should cover the problematic areas and relational patterns that are central to the patient's persistent problems. Change process initiation during treatment must also be realistic, the degree to which this is realistic being determined by the type and scope of problems, and the patient's resources.

Personal resources

A patient's personal resources play a significant role in determining the effect of FGAP; these resources include the patient's personality characteristics and the features imbedded in them. The description below is partly general and partly in terms of professional concepts developed within the psychodynamic theories that are used to characterize defined resources. I describe resources under the headings of personality, personality traits, ego functions, degree of structural integration of personality and social conditions.

Personality

Personality is more about who you are than about the disturbances you have. The word comes from the Greek word "persona" and was used about the masks actors wore when they played a role. Personality descriptions are based on features that characterize a person over time and across contexts, the traits of a person being of greater interest than how they act in a particular situation. The personality encompasses relatively stable, habitual patterns of thinking, registers of emotional expression and patterns of behavior, including ways of relating to others. Thought patterns include what persons believe in and how they understand themselves and others, including their moral values and ideals. We have distinctive, often idiosyncratic ways of understanding and explaining experiences, and of interpreting and translating moral values into action. We also have distinctive ways of experiencing and expressing emotions, this often being within a repertoire such as lively, cheerful and poignant or consistently sad, gloomy and pessimistic. All patterns of behavior disclose something about how people try to adapt to life's demands, to keep anxiety, grief and threats to self-esteem to a minimum. We adapt and protect ourselves in different ways and have a varying ability to integrate this into the endeavors of everyday social life, so that they remain hidden from others. Some patterns become more adaptive than others, the adaptive extent depending on a person's cultural background, professional involvement, family responsibilities and other social obligations. Some processes are conscious, others are unconscious and automatic (McWilliams, 2011).

It is common, in psychodynamic theory, to characterize personality using two dimensions: personality style and type and level of personality organization (Lingiardi & McWilliams, 2017). Personality style implies that one can have only one personality. This is considered to be a prototype that the person falls into. Different types, styles or syndromes include a depressive, dependent, anxious, evasive, compulsive, hysterical (histrionic) or narcissistic style. There is, however, no clear distinction between personality style/type and personality disorder. A person can therefore be characterized as having a compulsive or narcissistic personality without having a *personality disorder* (PD). The term "personality disorder" is first used when there is a degree of rigidity or where there are other deviances that cause significant problems for the person or for others. For example, when there is a significant loss of function (in work, in close relationships or in social situations), and when the person has been this way since adolescence. An example might be a person with obsessive-compulsive PD. This person both controls others, is controlled as a person, and has extensive compulsions and obsessional thoughts which interfere with everyday life. The person cherishes intellect, reason and logic, emotions being rejected or devalued, and a lot of time is spent on rituals, the control of family members and checking own behaviors, activities that seriously affect the person's ability to engage in work. Another example is a person with a narcissistic PD. This person has, since late puberty, felt himself to be more important than or "above others", and has limited interest in the usual demands of social interaction. They are strongly focused on the importance of their own person, most of the input received from others being interpreted in the light of their wish to be confirmed and admired. If others disagree with them in discussions, then they take this to be a personal insult. If others succeed or are praised for an achievement, they feel envy and perceive this to be criticism of themselves. They are, at work, frequently involved in unproductive discussions and disputes, and end up feeling empty. This is sometimes combined with a sense of being a fake, someone who fools others.

Psychodynamic theory has a developmental perspective on personality. This perspective is that the person grows and develops as a person in close relationships with others, significant caregivers and close relatives, based on their genetic equipment and temperament. The concept of the ego (Freud, 1961) is central to the integrated theory model outlined in the previous chapter (Kernberg, 2016). The ego constitutes the strategic agency of the personality, and maintains the person's connection to reality, harmonizes the relationship between external and internal impulses and has a synthesizing function in the personality as a whole (Gullestad & Killingmo, 2019). The ego plays on a number of functions, personality traits or ego functions in the execution of these tasks, which to the individual run unconsciously or automatically as partly conscious actions or choices. A level of ego-strength and a number of personality structures should have reached a degree of maturity for a patient to benefit from FGAP. A person with central ego functions that are less well developed or who is involved in intrapsychic conflict will respond to inner or outer stress in a rigid, stereotypical way. This person only has a few solution strategies at their disposal, none perhaps being well adapted to individual situations that arise.

Clinical example

Steve, a member of the demonstration group, is an example of such a person (see Chapter 5 and appendix). He has moderate internal conflicts around autonomy and domination/submission, which appear in interpersonal situations as a reluctance to follow the lead of another in a tight situation, for example when solving a task at work. Steve frequently perceives wishes and suggestions from others as demands for submission. He also easily feels dominated or controlled. The internal conflicts therefore influence his experience of himself and of others. He easily feels exploited and weak, while he perceives others to be dominant and strong. Others see him as being a stubborn and self-sufficient person who likes to lead and decide what to do, but who quickly withdraws if things are not done his way (rigidity of behavior).

Steve harbors a moderate degree of personality pathology. A person with less rigid personality traits would adapt more flexibly to the situation by seeing the problem from different points of view, choosing one of the possible solutions and acting on that. They also feel worthy as a person when others find solutions that are different from theirs.

Personality traits and ego functions

Many human traits are dimensional phenomena that exist to a greater or lesser extent in everyone. FGAP, however, poses specific challenges which make some factors more important than others. Patients should, for example, generally have some ability to adapt, to handle conflicts and to regulate affects. Personality traits and ego functions should also not be too rigid or too deviant, which they can be in a highly deficient development, or if characteristics are too involved in intra- or inter-systemic conflicts (Killingmo, 1989). Some of these properties are described below. They partially overlap.

Identity

A person with a good identity has a sense of who they are in the moment and over time. They can experience themselves as consolidated, have a feeling of what they like and dislike, and know their values and their short- and long-term goals in life. They also have nuanced, realistic experiences of how and who the people closest to them are, and therefore have an ability to describe them and themselves in a complex and precise way. An impairment of identity is referred to as an identity diffusion, which is found at the other end of the dimension, where identity is fragmented and there is a degree of loss of sense of reality. A patient should have a relatively well consolidated identity to benefit from FGAP.

Object relations

The term "object relations" is often used in psychodynamic theory to refer to a person's relationships with other people in the "outer world". The term is also used to describe an "inner world" of object relations, of internalized *representations* of the self and other objects, as described in the previous chapter. A person with good object relationships is able to establish and maintain close, stable and satisfying relationships with other people. At the other end of the scale are those who have unstable relationships, who do not become attached to anyone, or who solely socialize with people who are useful to them. They can, however, have stable pronounced dependency relationships with their parents. One of our research studies found that the majority of patients with moderate to well-integrated object representations achieved satisfactory improvement within 20 hours of group treatment. It also found that patients with more personality pathology often required longer-term therapy (Fjeldstad et al., 2016; see Chapter 9).

Attachment style

Attachment theory incorporates psychological, evolutionary and ethologic principles. British psychiatrist and psychoanalyst John Bowlby's (1968, 1973, 1980) theory of how children internalize their experiences with caregivers proposes that early attachment experiences form the prototype for later relationships outside the family. His work was continued by Mary Ainsworth, who observed the reactions of young children over many years in situations where they were alternately separated from and reunited with their mother. Attachment theory and self-psychology (Kohut, 1984) are related to the development of object relations theory. They emerged as a part of more recent relational models in psychodynamic theory

(Greenberg & Mitchell, 1983; Pantone, 2013), there being a close relationship between attachment theory and interpersonal theory (Horowitz & Vitkis, 1986; Benjamin, 1974; Henry et al., 1990). All psychopathology is usually manifested in some form of "disturbance" in interpersonal relationships, such as frequent "breaks" in social attachments (Sullivan, 1953a, 1953b; Vinogradov & Yalom, 1993; Leszcz & Malat, 2012). The close connection between these theories is reflected in the interpersonal interactions that arise and develop in most types of group psychotherapy. These interactions arise and develop almost irrespective of the therapist's theoretical orientation, or whether they are actively explored in therapy. Patients should have some ability to attach to each other if they are to benefit from psychodynamic time-limited group therapy. Patients' anxieties and ambivalence around closeness or intimacy, and their consequent avoidance of others, should therefore not be too strong.

Defense mechanisms

Defense mechanisms are structured and automated psychological functions. They are embedded in the personality and can affect feelings and overt behavior in characteristic ways. The function of defense mechanisms in the ego's execution of its moderating function between a person's inner and outer demands and needs is important (Rapaport, 1951). Defense mechanisms are activated more or less unconsciously, to regulate tensions that arise in association with intra-systemic or inter-systemic conflicts. A person with a satisfactory personality development will have a diverse set of defense mechanisms of varying degrees of maturity at their disposal. A well-integrated person will therefore have a register of differentiated defense mechanisms, and therefore have a greater chance of avoiding an uncontrolled and at worst psychotic regression (decompensation) when challenged by painful external or internal circumstances such as loss of close relatives, personal illness, work conflicts or major financial losses, than a person with a more poorly integrated identity.

The way in which different authors classify defense mechanisms within psychodynamic theory shows convergence. Some items may, however, be weighted differently. Research studies have also demonstrated a significant link between pre-treatment functional levels of defense mechanisms and treatment outcome (for example, Bond & Perry, 2004).

It can also be argued that patients, if they are to benefit from FGAP, should have access to more mature defenses and should not, when under stress, rely too heavily on the use of more primitive defense mechanisms. Perry (1990, 1993) and Perry, Lingiardi and Ianni (1999) have defined seven clusters of defense mechanisms, from the most mature (altruism, humor) and gradually, stepwise, moving toward the most immature defenses such as splitting, projective identification, primitive idealization and acting out, some examples giving a dimensional view of the maturity of defense mechanisms. A selection of specific defense mechanisms is presented here.

```
Mature to intermediary level
   Anticipation
     Sublimation/humour
       Suppression
         Isolation
           Reaction formation
             Displacement
               Primitive defense mechanisms
                 Omnipotence
                   Idealization/devaluation
                     Denial
                       Projection
                         Splitting of self and other
                           Projective identification
                             Primitive idealization
                               Acting out
```

Figure 3.1 Degree of maturity of defense mechanisms (in descending order).

Affect tolerance and control

Affect tolerance indicates that a person *has* emotions and is able to experience them, their qualities and strengths. Some people seem to have a poorly developed repertoire of affects, and seem to totally lack contact with their emotions or can not find words to describe them. This is a syndrome Sifneos (1973) called *alexithymia*. Patients should have at least a moderate level of affect tolerance to benefit from FGAP.

Affect control describes the ability to regulate impulses and affect and to ensure a satisfactory adjustment to inner tensions and demands from the outside. This implies flexibility in the use of defenses and/or coping strategies. A person who uses socially acceptable ways of expressing aggression shows good affect regulation. Someone who has frequent "blowouts" as a response to even minimally stressful events shows the opposite. FGAP patients should have a moderate impulse control, particularly of aggression, and should not be prone to acting out, because the *development of affect control* through therapy often requires more time than FGAP allows. Frequent outbursts of aggression in a group can also easily create general insecurity and conflicts in group relationships. This can easily lead to the retraumatization of vulnerable patients, which can not be repaired, and relationships can not be re-established because of the limited time available.

Moral values

Patients in FGAP should have some internalized values and ideals (see superego integration; Freud, 1961). They should function in a way that is more or less consistent with these standards, and respond with a certain degree of guilt when they do not. These qualities are perhaps more important for patients in group therapy than in individual therapy, constructive relationships between group members being an important therapeutic factor (Lorentzen et al., 2018). This may be even more important in short-term therapy, because of the problems associated with limited time.

Narcissism

Narcissism is about self-love. It springs from a child's necessary and natural sense of omnipotence and grandiosity, which good parents usually mirror and confirm. This wonderful feeling of being at the "center of the universe" is, according to Kohut (1968), the foundation for the development of a healthy personality structure. The positive response of one or more empathetic and loving caregivers leads to the internalization of this feeling by toddlers. The child will then gradually, in interaction with those around them and in the face of the realities of life, develop a more balanced and nuanced perspective of self and others. The simplified presentation of a successful integration of self and object representations given in Chapter 2 is contingent on and runs parallel to a normal development of narcissism (self-love). This is another example where the sum of positive and negative experiences with significant caregivers must be mainly positive if internal *representations* are to be successfully integrated. Unempathic responses and excessive or deficient mirroring from central caregivers over a period of time can later cause narcissistic problems, which is reflected in a spectrum of symptoms and dysfunctional personality traits. How these are manifested and how they are evaluated will be described in more detail in Chapter 4.

Mentalization

The faculties of introspection and self-observation have, from an early stage in psychoanalytic theory, been considered to be important qualities that a patient should possess if they are to benefit from psychodynamic therapy. The ability to interpret one's own or others' behavior as expressions of internal mental states is often called a person's ability to mentalize. Expressions of mental states include feelings, attitudes and particular ideas, assuming that the person has some contact with their own cognitive and emotional life (affect tolerance). A similar concept is the "ability to see psychological connections", for example between aspects of one's own person or inner conflicts and overt behavior. The term is, however, also used to refer to the connection between central features of oneself as an adult, and early traumata or persistent undue influence from early caregivers (the psychogenetic perspective).

Reality testing

An ability to test reality entails an understanding that there is something that can be called *an objective reality*, which most people will perceive relatively similarly and therefore can confirm the existence of. This ability includes being able to differentiate between one's *subjective reality* of inner desires, dreams and fantasies and the world "out there", which includes the subjective realities of other people. Human behavior is heavily inflicted by norms and value judgments. This can make it more difficult to agree on what is "reality" or "truth", or make relationships in psychology seem more random. This seems easier in physics, where most people seem to accept that the apple falls *downwards* when it is "let go of" by the tree, and that the earth moves around its axis. The ability to test reality is not a purely objective function. It must be assessed against the backdrop of the person's intelligence, education, degree of psychopathology and cultural, spiritual or political affiliation.

A patient's reality testing ability should be relatively intact for them to achieve some degree of structural change through FGAP.

Motivation

It is also important that the patient *wants to change* and is *willing to invest* the time and effort that therapy requires. It is therefore important that the therapist/interviewer, as mentioned earlier, carefully explores the patient's doubt and ambivalence about group psychotherapy. There is often a high correlation between what somebody wants and what they are capable of. There are, however, many examples of patients with assessments that show they should benefit from FGAP refusing to attend group psychotherapy. This can be due to many causes. A research study showed that 19 patients, who initially agreed to attend group therapy, changed their mind in the few weeks in which they had to wait for the group to start (11% of those who were to begin). When asked why, four said they had started in some other therapy, six said that they had a strong ambivalence to the therapist or the group format, and three had changed jobs and had practical difficulties in participating (Lorentzen et al., 2013).

Level of personality organization (PO)

The psychiatrist and psychoanalyst Otto F. Kernberg (1975, 1984) developed an early model for grading levels of personality organization (PO). The model distinguishes between neurotic, borderline and psychotic PO, which are abbreviated to NPO, BPO and PPO, respectively. He also designed a semi-structured interview for determining a patient's PO (Kernberg et al., 1981). The model is based on object relations theory, which I described in the previous chapter. The level of integration in his first model was based on just three domains. *Sense of identity*, the scale being between consolidated identity and identity diffusion, degree of *maturity in the use of defense mechanisms* and the *ability to test reality*. Patients with NPO have a stable ego identity, use more mature defense mechanisms and have a good ability to test reality. Patients with BPO have a greater degree of identity diffusion and use immature defense mechanisms more. Patients with PPO also have an impaired ability to test reality. The model was later developed through research and clinical experience to five levels of PO, by differentiating between a high, moderate and low level of borderline PO (Clarkin et al.,2016).

Patients who may benefit from FGAP have a normal, a neurotic or a high level of borderline personality organization (BPO). Patients with high BPO will be able to establish relationships with others. These are, however, often characterized by dependency and frequent conflicts (stormy). Many may also have a moderately developed superego functioning, i.e. an ability to empathize and to feel guilt. These functions may also be slightly impaired. Many will also have moderate control of aggression (toward self or others), but may exhibit bursts of verbal aggression or actions of high risk taking (unprotected sex, occasional uncritical use of drugs).

How a patient's level of structural PO is assessed and how a distinction is made between patients with higher, moderate and low organization BPO is described in the next chapter.

Social conditions

An overview of a patient's social conditions is an integral part of an assessment of psychological problems and mental disorders. How an assessment is carried out is described in more detail in the next chapter. I here briefly emphasize that candidates for FGAP should have reasonably stable living conditions, housing and finances. They should have at least a small network of family and friends and be engaged in some kind of work or education. Stability and structure in these areas give patients the opportunity to invest their energies in therapy and a potential change process. A relatively active social life, private and at work or college, challenges and activates the patient on some of the issues, and their role in interpersonal situations. They can therefore explore and scrutinize this for the six months in therapy. A final point is that these arenas offer numerous opportunities for trying out and developing any new interpersonal skills learned in therapy, and can represent a training ground for testing out or working through some of the central issues from group therapy. Treatment therefore becomes an addition to a life lived, and not a major occupation because everything else in life has stopped.

In summary, patients should have a normal, neurotic (NPO) or borderline personality organization (BPO) at a high level to benefit from FGAP. They also should have a relatively good sense of identity, an ability to test reality, have a limited degree of attachment anxiety and social avoidance and be prepared to interact and communicate. They should also have a limited impairment in superego functioning, have moderate affect tolerance and control and exhibit a limited use of immature defense mechanisms. Patients with psychosis, organic brain syndrome, severe personality disorders, major suicide risk, substance addiction or who are in a severe crisis, are not usually suitable for FGAP.

Chapter 4

Evaluation of patient suitability for Focused Group Analytic Psychotherapy

Overview

A summary of the patient characteristics and other factors that can be used to identify patients who may benefit from Focused Group Analytic Psychotherapy (FGAP) was given in the previous chapter. This chapter moves on from this and provides a more comprehensive description of how patients are assessed and how information is obtained from them. The interview is the most important tool in the evaluation of patients with mental health problems/disorders. Psychometric measures including questionnaires have, however, also become quite common in use in assessing patients. Biological tests can also be carried out, but there are very few that can directly indicate specific mental disorders. A thorough somatic check is, even so, always recommended to rule out underlying somatic disorders. The primary goal of the assessment is to obtain information on the psychosocial condition of the patient, psychosocial condition also encompassing many of the factors targeted by FGAP. An assessment is to first determine whether psychological treatment is a desirable option for a patient, and then determine whether FGAP is a suitable treatment for that patient.

The question of whether FGAP is a suitable treatment for a patient can be answered by the following. The patient's level of personality organization (PO) should firstly be determined by assessing *key* personality domains. A circumscribed *treatment focus* should then be able to be formulated that expresses central aspects of the patient's symptoms and interpersonal (problematic) behavior. This should be rooted in a psychodynamic case formulation, which concludes with a psychodynamic hypothesis of the links between the vulnerable aspects of the patient's personality (predisposition) that have been shaped by unfortunate factors (emotional neglect, trauma, loss) during the patient's development, precipitating events (stressors) and the clinical resultants (symptoms and problems). A clinical diagnosis should finally be given and a graphic profile of the patient's main interpersonal problems should be drawn up based on a self-report questionnaire.

There are many methods that can be used to evaluate and assess patients. I have, however, found the above procedures to be well suited to clinical practice, primarily because they meet the following requirements:

DOI: 10.4324/9781003216377-6

Assessments are to be of high quality and cover aspects that clinical experience and research have shown to be relevant to therapy. Interviews are also to be organized such that trust in the therapist and the treatment can be developed from the very start of the process, this being primarily achieved by the emotional needs of the patient being addressed. Clinical interviews therefore begin with an exploration of the patient's current symptoms and problems, structured (diagnostic) interviews, psychological tests and questionnaires being carried out at a later stage. The patient's faculties of self-reflection and of connecting psychological events with their feelings and behavior should not only be activated, but also developed and strengthened in evaluation interviews. A well-informed clinician should be able to carry out an assessment in three to five hours.

Information from interviews and questionnaires

Information on the patient can be obtained from a number of sources. Interviews with the patient, however, yield the most important information, this sometimes including initial interviews in which a spouse or other family members participate. Interviews take different forms, the context and the interviewer's background and preferences often determining the ultimate form of the interview. I will, however, present three interview prototypes here that can be used to determine whether treatment is needed, and whether the patient can benefit from FGAP. The three prototypes are the clinical interview, the psychodynamic interview and the structured diagnostic interview.

The traditional clinical-psychiatric interview can be viewed as being an attempt to achieve an objective, descriptive, approximately "atheoretical" clinical-psychiatric version of the medical examination. This approach first gathers information and then reflects upon and discusses the case, finally drawing conclusions based on more specific psychological theories, and possibly a biopsychosocial frame of reference (Falkum, 2008; Engel, 1977). The clinical interview, which is usually the most important part of the assessment, often also contains key elements of the psychodynamic interview (Gabbard, 2004; Cabaniss, 2013), where the interviewer's theoretical orientation is psychodynamic. The *inter-subjective perspective* is, however, found in both types of interviews. This perspective requires interviewers to ask themselves how their presence and behavior, their responses to the patient's information, rhythm, activity and the way they structure the interview, affects the patient. Interviewers should, in other words, ask themselves to what degree is what the patient reveals of themselves influenced by the context, or whether this mainly can be seen to be representative of the way the patient usually is.

A central element of the FGAP assessment is the "Inventory of Interpersonal Problems" Circumplex questionnaire (IIP-C; Horowitz, Rosenberg, Baer, Ureno & Villasenor, 1988; Alden et al., 1990). This questionnaire is a standardized, internationally used psychometric test in which patients score themselves on a scale of 0 to 4 for different types of problematic interactions with others. More information on this test is presented later in the chapter (see also Chapter 8, "Clinical quality assurance").

Interviews and the IIP-C questionnaire usually provide the therapist with enough information to make a decision on their need for treatment, and whether the patient can be helped by FGAP. The two methods can also provide enough information for the assessments that are recommended prior to FGAP – recommended assessments being the grading of key personality domains, a psychodynamic case formulation, establishment of a treatment focus and a clinical diagnosis. The level of personality organization (PO) can also be assessed from the information obtained from the clinical/psychodynamic interview, if the interview includes relevant questions that relate to the ego-functions and the personality traits required by a PO assessment (see, e.g., information on different ego-functions presented in this and the previous chapter of the book; see also Appendix 3, Clinical anchor points). A structured interview, which is briefly presented later in the chapter as an example of a *diagnostic interview* (STIPO-R; Clarkin et al., 2016), can also be conducted. It is, however, a more time-consuming alternative.

Types of interviews

The clinical interview

The interview is the most important element of a standard psychiatric examination, and is focused on obtaining information on four areas of the patient's life – their background, their developmental and life history, their somatic and psychiatric medical history and their present status. Interviews are often begun by encouraging the patient to open up, and by inviting them to give an overview of their current problems. How did the problems start and how did they develop? Did they start suddenly or more gradually? What brought about the patient deciding to be examined? Were the symptoms triggered by specific events, or did the symptoms appear without any clear cause? Once a picture of current symptoms and ailments has been formed, the interviewer can move on to asking about past problems. Has the patient experienced any symptoms or signs that could indicate mental illness? Has the patient experienced any physical disorders? How has the patient's somatic health in general been? The interviewer can, once this has been completed, turn to other background information and the patient's developmental and life history. The interviewer can start by asking the patient about the people and family around them such as grandparents, parents, siblings and extended family? Has the patient experienced the death of anyone in this circle, and what was the cause of death? Are there any psychological problems or somatic illnesses in the family? Where does the patient come from, how were conditions in the offspring home, where did the patient grow up, and how was their childhood? Did they experience loss, divorce, the absence of a parent or particularly frightening periods in their childhood? What kind of schools did the patient attend, and what type of practical training, higher education and work experience does the patient have? The interviewer can also ask patients to look back and say how they see themselves in their schooldays and early and late adolescence? How do they spend their free time, and what areas of life interest them most? The interviewer can then ask questions about past and present relationships, girlfriends/boyfriends, cohabitants/spouses and whether the patient has children.

The interviewer (often a therapist) is looking, through asking these questions, for factual, biographical information on family, friends, education, work and background, and circumstances around birth, early childhood, childhood and later development. They are at the same time also looking for *who* the patient is, *their* personality and any events and relationships that may have influenced them and their development. The interviewer therefore remains alert throughout the interview to *how* the patient responds, the *way* a story is told, the words used and how the patient values and ranks the importance of the areas of information they present. Aspects and nuances of the patient's responses contain information about the patient and how they act in context. Responses can also contain information on how they usually appear to others and on the *patient's feelings*, whether displayed and directly expressed, or absent, suppressed, pushed away or neglected.

The interviewer can gradually, once this information has been obtained, turn the focus of the interview to asking the patient about *their experience* of the people, events and relationships they mentioned in the narratives from their life. How do they reflect on important events, choices made by their family, choices they made themselves and on life in general? Important patient characteristics such as their view of life, personal values, their ability to reflect on the links between events and people, specific patterns of behavior of themselves and others, their own emotionality and the quality of their sense of reality can emerge through this.

A rich, detailed picture of the person's current and past life is created by the interview process. This picture includes whether they have succeeded in meeting important challenges in life, the factors that have influenced their development and the underlying family and social conditions that have shaped the patient's person and life so far.

A well-conducted explorative interview can also strengthen the alliance between the interviewer and patient, with trust and bonding growing, allowing the patient to open up and reveal more shameful information. The patient should also develop better contact with or discover new aspects of themself during the interviews, as the interchange proceeds.

The psychodynamic interview

A psychodynamic interview is carried out by an interviewer who has some knowledge and training in psychodynamic theory and practice. A key characteristic of the method is that the interviewer "tunes in to" the here-and-now experiences of the interview, a skill which this training gives. This stance was described by one of Freud's early students as "listening with the third ear" (Reik, 1972). The method involves focusing on the feelings or reactions that arise in the interviewer when directly interacting with the patient, and exploring these feelings and reactions as potential reflections of aspects of the patient's unconscious, internalized relational world. Information of the patient's internal state can also be obtained through the interviewer's empathic attunement with the patient, and with other persons who appear in the patient's detailed descriptions of close relationships or with feelings the patient has about themself.

It is very important that the person who conducts a psychodynamic interview has a theoretical pre-understanding and practical experience. This provides the interviewer with the skills they need to register and evaluate psychological phenomena, in particular psychodynamic phenomena such as the patient's disposition for transference reactions, the use of psychological defense mechanisms and of internalized self and object representations. Evaluations are often carried out by the interviewer deliberately entering the patient's field of experience, to check whether the patient can register to the interviewer in the here-and-now any of the feelings, attitudes or responses that they register with other persons in the world at large. The interviewer's insight into his own behavioral patterns and dispositions for countertransference reactions may inform the interviewer whether they are subject to devaluation, idealization or projective maneuvers by the patient. The interviewer therefore, through their interactions with the patient, indirectly obtains valuable additional information. The information the patient presents about themself usually only includes aspects of their personality that they are aware of. The therapist's experiences from direct interaction with the patient can therefore correct patient provided information, including the patient's opinions on personal motives and intentionality in interchanges with others, or the ability to regulate emotional intimacy/distance to others. This will allow the interviewer to register attitudes and other aspects of the patient that are a part of the patient's unconscious, but which are important in the treatment context. It can also allow the interviewer to register a range of personality traits that are often imbedded in intrapsychic conflicts or attachment styles within the framework of psychodynamic theory. Interviewers can also test their hypotheses of the patient's relational faculties through being an "interacting observer". The interviewer can refer to contradictions (confrontations) or make suggestions of latent meanings (trial interpretations) in the patient's statements, and through this gain an impression of the patient's self-observing and self-reflective abilities.

Active questioning and entering the "interactional field" as a collaborator can lead to increased patient anxiety, which can, in turn, give the interviewer an impression of the patient's anxiety tolerance, and can allow the patient's readiness to work on their irrational reactions in the group to be tested.

Combining the two ...

The clinical interview and the psychodynamic interview are usually combined. The extent and the way in which they are combined is, however, often dependent on the interviewer's training, experience, interests and preferences. For example, a clinical interview can include elements of the psychodynamic exploration in the here-and-now situation. A clinical interview can alternatively solely focus on obtaining fact-oriented, biographical information – a more comprehensive psychodynamic interview being carried out after the clinical interview has been completed. The interviewer's approach in a dynamic interview is often less structured and more laid back. This gives the patient an opportunity to take greater control of how they present themselves. This can, however, lead to greater anxiety in some timid, depressed or dependent patients, as it is less clear what is expected of them.

The information obtained in the traditional clinical interview on the patient's development history, central relationships, relevant problem areas and symptoms of mental disorder can be used to describe the patient's personality, key personality traits and important personality resources. Patient characteristics can also be evaluated indirectly through using detailed descriptions of *how* the patient behaves in relation to third parties. The information obtained in interviews can also be used in the outlining of a treatment focus, and to rate central ego-functions (psychological structures) that are considered to be important in FGAP selection. Detailed exploration of the patient's relationships with close family members, friends, romantic partners and current or former spouses provides enough information to formulate a plausible hypothesis of the patient's sense of identity, quality of object relations, defense mechanisms, affect regulation, moral values and reality testing abilities. The patient's reflections in interviews on their relationships and other key aspects of their life, provides furthermore insight into the patient's ability to mentalize (psychological mindedness) and ability to empathize with others, as well as their use of psychological defense mechanisms and their sense of reality. Hypotheses can then be formed of the extent to which repetitive patterns are caused by underlying destructive, stereotypically poorly integrated self- and object representations that are almost compulsively lived out, by comparing conflict episodes with examples of solution attempts. This again provides information that allows hypotheses to be formulated on the patient's level of structural personality organization, ego-strength, and ability to adapt and resolve conflict, this providing the basis for an assessment of whether the patient has the ability to utilize FGAP.

It is an advantage that psychodynamic information can be obtained in different ways. Therapists can have different professional backgrounds, practical/theoretical training and clinical experience. Phenomena and patient characteristics can therefore often be conceptualized differently by professionals with different theoretical backgrounds. Parallel runs may therefore become more visible where phenomena are described from slightly different angles. This is one reason why I have covered both the clinical and the psychodynamic interview comprehensively.

Most treatment sites and practitioners have, furthermore, developed their own procedures, and therefore use interviews and measuring instruments that target and are quality assured for the population of patients they treat.

The diagnostic interview

The third interview prototype is the *diagnostic interview*. This interview prototype has become more widely used in clinical work in recent decades. This is probably due to a strong increase in the volume of research in the field, to this research calling for stronger conceptual rigor and to this showing that there is a great need for reliable and valid measures and data. There are many interview types. These are often fully or partially structured, and target specific characteristics such as clinical diagnosis, self-esteem, quality of object relationships, depth of depression or ability to regulate emotions. *Structured* interviews always contain a specific number of questions that cover the phenomenon or traits that are to be evaluated. This ensures that most of the aspects are covered in the assessment, and leaves less to chance. Less experienced interviewers can also extract the information required from an interview, as less inference is required from the answers. Data obtained by different interviewers from structured interviews also usually have a higher degree of correspondence (higher inter-rater reliability).

Structured Interview for Personality Organization (STIPO-Revised)

I will briefly describe the revised edition of the Structured Interview for Personality Organization (STIPO-R; Clarkin et al., 2016) as an example of the structured diagnostic interview. The interview form is based on Kernberg's early work on borderline patients (Kernberg, 1975, 1984), which includes his structural interview (Kernberg et al., 1981), a clinical method devised to cover the most relevant aspects of the psychiatric assessment of patients. Clarkin et al. (2016) have continued Kernberg's work and created a semi-structured interview for use in research and clinical work. This interview form allows the grading of personality organization to be increased from three to five levels: normal, neurotic and high, moderate and low levels of borderline PO. This increase was achieved by increasing the number of underlying domains, so making the scale for PO assessment more sensitive.

The interview consists of 55 questions which result in a numerical expression (graded from 1 to 5) of resources/pathology within six important domains of personality functioning, the domains being identity, quality of object relations, maturity of defense mechanisms, tolerance and control of aggression (affects), moral values and degree of pathological narcissism. All of these domains are relevant when considering the suitability of a patient for FGAP. The complete STIPO-R interview and scoring sheet are available at https://www.borderlinedisorders.com

Many therapists find structured interviews to be too time-consuming in a busy clinical situation. I will therefore present a shorter, more *clinician-friendly version* that is more suitable for clinical practice. Those not acquainted with Kernberg's object relations theory may find it useful to review the questions in STIPO-R for the domains. The questionnaire can also be useful in the training of new, more inexperienced therapists.

Clinical assessment of level of personality organization (STIPO)

This method uses information from the clinical/psychodynamic interviews to carry out a dimensional mapping of personality organization. Based on the information that informs each domain, the therapist first scores (on a scale of 1 to 5) the quality of the patient's sense of identity, quality of object relationships, maturity of defense mechanisms, aggression tolerance and control and moral values. The assessment is then compared with the stepladder of the clinical anchor system *for these five domains* (Caligor et al., 2018; see Appendix 3). Scores are adjusted where necessary. The score for each domain is then entered into the corresponding column in the table for the five levels of personality organization, normal, neurotic, and high, medium and low levels of borderline organization (see Table 4.1).

(The table is reworked from Caligor et al., 2018: the domains aggression and narcissism are added, reality testing is omitted).

The table provides an overview of the degrees of pathology within different levels of PO. Scores for domains increase from 1 to 5 when moving from normal to low borderline PO, the level of personality organization decreasing as the degree of pathology increases.

The mean score (average) of the domains gives a dimensional assessment of the patient's PO level, and indicates whether the PO is normal, neurotic or borderline high, medium or low (1–5). Patients with normal and neurotic levels of PO and high levels of BPO will be suitable for FGAP (average scores between 1 and 3). It is important to note that this BPO label is used in a much broader way here than in a diagnosis of "borderline personality disorder".

This method is more pragmatic, time-saving and clinically applicable than a structured interview (STIPO-R), because the information required has already been obtained in the clinical/psychodynamic interviews.

A short presentation of the domains (personality structures) and brief suggestions of how relevant information can be obtained are given below.

Identity includes a person's sense of self and of others, and the person's capacity to invest in and pursue long-term goals. It includes the *ability to invest* in work, study and leisure pursuits, and the degree to which the person is *effective*, has *ambitions*, *thrives* and shows a *continuing interest* in these areas. It is important that the interviewer asks the patient about their ambitions and goals, and evaluates the correspondence between these and *actual results*.

Self-esteem (sense of self) is characterized by the degree of cohesion and continuity. Self-esteem can be evaluated by asking the patient to describe themself as a person: "Can you quickly describe yourself so that I can get a vivid and nuanced picture of who you are?" The *description of the self* can then be estimated from the patient's answer based on superficiality/depth, ambivalence/stability, cohesion at present and over time, taste/opinions, intimacy/distance and ways of regulation (can appreciate oneself or depends on the admiration of others).

Table 4.1 Level of personality organization (PO). Suitable for FGAP: levels 1–3

	Normal PO 1	Neurotic PO 2	High 3	Moderate 4	Low 5
PO Score				Borderline Personality Organization (BPO)	
Rigidity of personality	None	Mild-moderate	Moderately extreme	Extreme	Very extreme
Identity	Consolidated	Consolidated	Mild-moderate pathology	Moderate-severe pathology	Severe pathology
Object relations	Deep, mutual Mature	Deep, mutual Repression-based	Some mutual Splitting- and repression-based	Need-fulfilling Splitting-based	Exploitative Splitting-based
Defense mechanisms					
Aggression	Adequate, episodes of anger and verbal expression appear to be appropriate to the situation	Relatively good control, deviance limited to inhibition, minor self-destructive behaviors or occasional verbal outbursts	Moderate failure in control, deviance include higher-risk behaviors, self-neglect, frequent outbursts, hostile control of others	Poor control, more serious if self-directed, often hateful toward others, frequent threats to hurt self or others	Little or no control, pervasive tendency toward severe, lethal expression of aggression. Frequent hateful, sadistic abuse and/or physical harm to self and others
Moral values	Internalized, flexible	Internalized, rigid	Uneven/inconsistent, mild pathology	Mild-moderate pathology	Severe pathology
Pathological narcissism	No narcissistic features. Good social and occupational functioning	Some narcissistic features, impaired close relations, but able to sustain friendships. Some troubles at work	Significant narcissistic features, chronic disruptions in intimate relationships, needs admiration from others, signals troubles at work	Severe narcissistic features, more extreme than above, overt hostility, self- or other-directed. Exploitative	Severe narcissistic features, with addition of paranoia, severe aggression, ruthless exploitation and lack of concern over own aggression

Reworked from Caligor et al. (2018) (the domains aggression and narcissism are added, reality testing is omitted).

Evaluation of patient suitability for FGAP 53

Representation (sense) of others can be assessed by asking the patient to describe a relationship with a person who is close to them, and evaluating whether the description provides a coherent or more fragmentary picture of the person, whether it is superficial or more in-depth, and whether it signals ambivalence and possibly a variable experience of the other. Useful information can also be obtained by asking about the images of and feelings the patient has for the other person.

Quality of object relations is evaluated based on interpersonal functioning, capacity for intimacy and the person's inner working models for relationships (friendship). It is useful to begin by establishing whether the patient has such relationships, and how many persons the patient considers to be close friends or acquaintances. The interviewer can then ask whether there is a sense of closeness in these relationships, whether the relationships are stable over time and whether they are limited to the private sphere or extend to colleagues in the work situation.

Intimacy and sexuality with a close partner (girlfriend/boyfriend/partner/spouse) are assessed based on the degree of intimacy, whether intimacy is mutual, whether it is a combination of intimacy and sexual activity, whether intimacy is limited by sexual inhibition or whether sex and love are interrelated.

An assessment of the internal investment in others is based on the degree to which relationships are characterized by self-centeredness, boredom, dependence, openness/closeness, exploitation or empathy.

All the information required to evaluate these dimensions can spring from a detailed questioning about past and present relationships, and from subsequent dialogue that engages both patient and therapist in a mutual exploration of and reflection around the material that is shared by the patient.

Defense mechanisms (see Figure 3.1 in Chapter 3) can be evaluated according to whether they primarily are flexible/adaptive and repression-based (mature) or more splitting-based (immature, primitive). Some of the defense mechanisms mentioned below do not appear in the prototype presented in Chapter 3, but can readily be included in this.

Mature defense mechanisms include anticipation, sublimation/humor, repression, displacement, flexibility, perfectionism, regression, reaction formation and isolation.

Primitive defense mechanisms include paranoia, primitive idealization/devaluation, splitting (for example black and white thinking), projective identification, denial, acting and narcissistic fantasies.

The therapist can obtain many clues and ideas about the patient's repertoire from the relationship stories the patient shares. Clues and ideas can also be obtained from how the patient responds when the therapist explores and comments on specific aspects in the patient's narratives.

Aggression: tolerance and control. The therapist usually gains a good impression of *if* and *how* they handle their own and others' aggression, from the narratives and relational stories the patient shares. Does the patient experience aggression at all? How much aggression can the patient tolerate/mobilize, and to what degree is the patient able to express or react adequately in a socially acceptable way? The evaluation must be based on the context of the events presented, the degree of provocation involved and the potential aftermath and consequence of the patient's reaction. The issue can also be explored by asking the patient directly how angry they can become. Is their repertoire limited to verbal outbursts, can they sometimes throw a cup or a dish on the floor, and has anger manifested as a physical attack on a person? It may also be relevant to ask, based on relational stories, whether the patient in some cases likes to inflict pain or suffering on others, enjoys seeing others' pain or suffering (emotionally or physically), whether they often want revenge or to hit back and whether they feel neglected or badly treated by others.

Patients may also *direct aggression toward themselves* through neglecting their own nutrition or health care needs and by engaging in different forms of high-risk behavior, self-harm, suicidal thoughts or in repetitive suicide attempts. Patients may also be asked directly whether they often feel bad about themselves when others succeed, as a possible covert expression of hostility or envy.

Moral values (superego-functions). These can also be assessed from relational stories, which the therapist explores and reflects, often in concert with the patient. Does the patient appear to have internalized values and ideals that govern behavior and relationships with others, or do values and ideals appear to be weak or lacking? Are there signs of unethical and antisocial behavior? Does the patient appear to be concerned about moral values or actions? Do they have the ability to experience guilt, or does the feeling of guilt arise only where there is a risk of being caught in the act? Does the patient tend to deceive other people, to constantly engage in illegal activities or to exploit other people or situations if the opportunity arises?

A dimensional assessment across these five domains can be combined, to determine the patient's level of personality organization, and whether this is normal, neurotic or borderline high, medium or low.

These first five domains, even though they are overlapping, constitute individually structuralized processes in the personality. Pathological narcissism, however, covers a wider phenomenon that may affect all of the five personality domains, the extent of this being dependent on severity.

Narcissism. Hartmann (1964) defined normal narcissism as the libidinous investment in the self, which is popularly called self-love. I provided a simplified description of the self in accordance with Kernberg's (1975) object relations theory in Chapter 2. I will now take a step into his metapsychology, in which he describes the self as an intrapsychic structure consisting of representations of self and others, with associated affective coloring. I quote:

> Self-representations are affective-cognitive structures reflecting the person's perception of himself in real interactions with significant others and in fantasied interactions with internal representations of significant others, that is, with object representations. The self is part of the ego, which contains, in addition, the object representations mentioned before, and also ideal

self-images and ideal object-images at various stages of depersonification, abstraction and integration. The normal self is integrated, in that its component self-representations are dynamically organized into a comprehensive whole. The self relates to integrated object representations, that is, to object representations which have incorporated the "good" and "bad" primitive object representations into integrative images of others in depth; by the same token, the self represents an integration of contradictory "all good" and "all bad" self-images derived from libidinally invested and aggressively invested early self-images.

(Kernberg, 1975, pp. 315–316)

Normal narcissism reflects the libidinous investment in the self. Positive and negative sources of emotions also, however, explain the paradox that the integration of love and hate is a prerequisite for the ability of normal love.

This also means that normal narcissism springs from the integration of self- and object representations into complex "whole" structures, and that affective coloring contains both positive and negative (merged) aspects, with an overweight of the positive. Poorer integration means that the person is more marked by more primitive "all good" or "all bad" self and object representations, and more primitive aggression.

Pathological narcissism may, because of its superior position, affect every structuralized personality domain included in STIPO-R (identity, object relations, aggression, defense mechanisms and moral values). Narcissistic persons may therefore show increasing signs of disturbances in the perception of their own identity and in the perception of others. This presents problems in both accomplishment and well-being at school, at work and in leisure activities. A poorer quality of object relations leads to frequent problems in relationships with others, which is reinforced by deficient affect tolerance, less aggression control and frequent use of more primitive defense mechanisms including exploitation. Failure in these areas is often obscured by a more inflated or grandiose self-presentation, leading to a behavior toward others that gradually may become more unpleasant or directly harmful (Lingiardi & McWilliams, 2017; Kernberg, 1984).

It is beyond the scope of this book to provide an exhaustive description of the different clinical manifestations of narcissistic disorders. I can, however, refer the interested reader to other key literature (e.g., Rothstein, 2018). A number of central aspects of pathological narcissistic features will, however, be covered in the scale below of increasing levels of narcissistic pathology.

The degree of pathological narcissism can also be assessed on a dimensional scale ranging from *normal*, which corresponds to a young person's natural pride in having accomplished something, to more *pathological* forms that are more apparent in people with a *neurotic, borderline* and ultimately *psychotic* personality organization. Here, I will mainly cover the characteristics of patients who are suitable for FGAP, i.e. patients with a degree of pathological narcissism which is compatible with that of persons belonging to the three highest levels of personality organization (PO).

- The first stage (1) is characterized by an absence of pathological narcissism and there is good social and professional functioning. Persons in the first stage have a stable, good self-esteem and can describe themselves and a close partner in a coherent, nuanced way.
- The next stage (2) is where a person exhibits some narcissistic features that impair intimate relations, but have the ability to sustain friendships over time. Some may have difficulties in occupational functioning, but usually have the ability to sustain meaningful engagement in a primary role.
- In the third stage (3) a person is showing more significant narcissistic features, such as being dependent on the admiration of others, having chronic conflicts and disruptions in intimate and social relationships. These may also involve exploitation or hostile control of their partner, subsequent difficulties in maintaining intimate and social relationships over time, often also significant occupational difficulties (in advancing, lack of responsibility or chronic functioning below level of ability); there may often be severe fluctuations in self-esteem, maybe related to the failure to live up to self-standards, feelings of envy and a preoccupation with comparisons with others.

Sufficient information to determine whether a person can be placed on one of these three levels will usually appear during a standard clinical interview, if enough time is spent on eliciting detailed relational narratives, and the patient is invited to reflect on the information, and if inconsistencies and discrepancies are explored by the patient and the therapist together.

- As persons move toward the more pathological pole of the scale (stages 4 and 5), they can be characterized by the presence of more severe aggression toward self and others, exploitation of others, a lack of guilt or remorse and even paranoia with serious affection of the patient's sense of reality.

Assessing more pathological narcissism can be challenging. This is partly due to many of the most seriously disturbed not usually presenting themselves to a psychotherapeutic practice. Readers with an interest in pathological narcissism assessment can refresh their knowledge by reviewing the questions that Clarkin et al. (2016) recommend in an assessment. The STIPO-R Questionnaire is available at https://www.borderlinedisorders.com

Questionnaires, patient self-report (psychometry)

Structured diagnostic interviews are widely used within mental health services. Standardized questionnaires and patient *self-reports* are also used to obtain a quantitative expression of important aspects of a patient's personality, disorder, resources and pathology. The patient's subjective world is always important in assessment and therapy. Most problematic aspects of a personality or a disorder are, however, often unconscious and hidden from the person. Self-report scores, which are based on the person's subjective perception of themselves, therefore provide little insight into these important unconscious and hidden aspects. Standardized questionnaires and patient self-reports can, however, be used in the course of a treatment to monitor change in, for example, subjective suffering (symptoms) and interpersonal problems. I will now describe one I have found to exhibit great utility in both clinical work and research.

Measuring interpersonal problems (Inventory of Interpersonal Problems)

Interpersonal problems are a frequent complaint of patients that seek help, including those seeking psychotherapy (Horowitz, 1979; Horowitz et al., 1988; Fjeldstad et al., 2016). Horowitz et al. (1988) were struck by the absence of a systematic method for recording types of interpersonal problems. They therefore developed a comprehensive questionnaire (127 items) of things the patient "had difficulties doing" or "did too much of" in relationship to others. The instrument proved to be sensitive to change, and is widely used to monitor if and how patients change during and after therapy. Alden et al. (1990) developed the instrument further based on the ideas of interpersonally oriented theorists (Carson, 1969; Leary, 1957; Sullivan, 1953a, 1953b). Interpersonally oriented theorists are concerned with people's tendency to repetitively use typical interpersonal behavior patterns (traits) that are associated with key aspects of their personality. Sophisticated geometric methods have shown that the best model for capturing people's distinctive features is a two-dimensional circle (circumplex), variables positioned circularly around two orthogonal dimensions. One dimension is domination versus submission and the other is self-sacrifice versus hostility (Benjamin, 1974, 1984; Kiesler, 1983; Lorr & McNair, 1963; Wiggins, 1979). Sub-scales have been validated against an established measure of interpersonal dispositions (Strack, 1987).

A patient's interpersonal behavior is depicted around a circumplex by placing the features that are most closely related to each other together. Variables that end up on the opposite sides of the circle are negatively correlated, and variables that end up at 90 degrees to each other (orthogonal) are unrelated. All variables are therefore spaced evenly around the circle in an exact circumplex. Statistical methods should, however, be used to verify whether this occurs in real life in each case.

The circle clearly shows the patient's perception of their interpersonal problems within the eight sub-scales represented.

Alden et al. (1990) improved the measure further and reduced the number of items (statements) to 64, 39 of these beginning with "It's hard for me to…", and 25 being about "things I do too much of". Examples of "Its hard for me …" items include "It is difficult for me to receive instruction from people who have authority over me" and "It is difficult for me to show other people that I love them".

Examples of "things I do too much of" include "I am too aggressive toward other people" and "I too often let the needs of others go before my own". Each link is scored on a scale of 0 (= "not at all") to 4 (= "extremely"), IIP-C consisting of eight sub-scales (see Figure 4.1). A total score (average for all subsections) and a score for each sub-scale is calculated.

What do the numbers mean?

The patient's self-report results give an average value for the 64 points and for each of the eight different sub-scales. The values are often compared with so-called norms for specific groups in the population, such as non-clinical samples (people who do not have mental disorders), or values recorded for outpatients or hospitalized patients. I have included in Appendix 2 an example of normative values from a Norwegian non-clinical sample. A patient's profile can therefore be compared with the profiles of other patients, and with the profile of an "average person" from a normative sample, for example a non-clinical sample.

What do the different sub-scales represent?

The interpersonal circumplex (IIP-C) represents the patient's subjective experience of interpersonal problems within the areas of dominance, vindictiveness, reservedness (coldness), social avoidance, lack of assertiveness, exploitation, self-sacrifice (overly nurturance) and intrusiveness (Alden et al., 1990; Horowitz et al., 1988). The information is collected by a patient answering a questionnaire

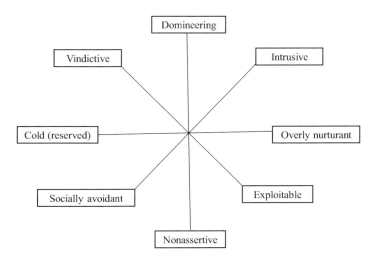

Figure 4.1 Interpersonal Problems. Eight sub-scales of the IIP-Circumplex. (Alden et al., 1990).

they receive in the evaluation, each sub-scale being represented by eight specific items. Detailed information on the patient's perception of how they habitually behave toward others is obtained through this. Some aspects will be recognizable by others. Others are based solely on the patient's subjective experience.

Domineering (assertive)

People who score themselves as being dominant often perceive themselves to be self-assertive. They may, however, also easily feel controlled or directed and react with aggression, resistance or stubbornness. A potential strength is that this person may have a talent for leadership. Another is that they can be a model for those who are too submissive.

Vindictive (focused on own needs)

People who perceive themselves to be vindictive are often focused on their own needs and have problems with distrust or suspicion of others. They often care less about the needs and welfare of others, and can often want revenge when offended. A possible strength may lie in their ability to take care of themselves. They can also be role models for those who are too focused on others (exploitable). Those who score high on vindictiveness often lack close relationships, and more frequently end up in quarrels with others.

Cold (reserved)

Reserved people can have difficulties feeling or expressing affection or love for another person, and may frequently seem cold. Many lack social relationships and may strive to associate with the leader or others in a group. They can also easily become too critical of others.

Socially avoidant (inhibited)

Socially avoidant people can easily feel anxious or embarrassed when among others, and often struggle in social relationships. They find it difficult to express feelings and often expect to be judged or criticized by others. Their strengths may include an ability for introspection and to manage on their own (independent).

Nonassertive (less self-assertive)

Submissive people often find it difficult to disclose and assert their needs, and often let others' needs take precedence. They can feel discomfort if given a role of authority and often have difficulties being direct or assertive toward others. They can be good team players and also good role models for more domineering persons. They often, however, lack self-confidence and are dissatisfied with many of their relationships.

Exploitable (focused on the needs of others)

Exploitable people are often focused on the needs of others, and may have difficulty expressing anger. They are afraid of offending others, are often somewhat gullible, and have a tendency to be exploited. An advantage is that they easily get along with others and they can, through the warmth they show, be role models for those who are too vindictive.

Overly nurturant (warm)

Overly nurturant people can be warm and caring. They can, however, have difficulty making room for themselves or take time to talk about their problems. Their bids for close contact and their warm concern can sometimes scare off those with a higher level of attachment anxiety. Their kindness is often a strength, and they can be role models for those who are evasive or reserved.

Intrusive (uninhibited)

Intrusive people can often be too direct and uninhibited in their approach to others. They are often too self-revealing and attention-seeking, and may sometimes have difficulties being alone. A strength is that they sometimes can energize a group and be well suited to being leaders. They can also be positive role models for the inhibited or submissive, and for those who are too focused on their own needs.

Use of IIP-C in the FGAP evaluation

Figure 4.2 presents the scoring diagram for the eight sub-scales. Examples are given for three demonstration group patients – Mary, Elsie and Steve (see also the Appendix).

Comments: Mary's interpersonal problems profile appears to show that she perceives herself to be more socially avoidant, more submissive (less assertive), exploitable and more overly nurturant than others. She also feels to some extent more intrusive. Elsie also perceives herself to be more avoidant and less assertive than others, but at the same time gives herself high scores for domineering and intrusive, and she also indicates that she feels more reserved than others. Steve scores lower on all the sub-scales than the norm values for the non-clinical population. He believes that he does not have more interpersonal problems than anyone else in *any* of the areas.

More detailed information on the three patients is presented in the Appendix. Mary and Steve are also mentioned below under "Psychodynamic case formulation" (Mary) and "Treatment focus" (Mary and Steve).

Clinical diagnosis

Clinical diagnosis is, in the Norwegian mental health system, based on the International Classification of Diseases (ICD-10; World Health Organization,

62 Evaluation of patient suitability for FGAP

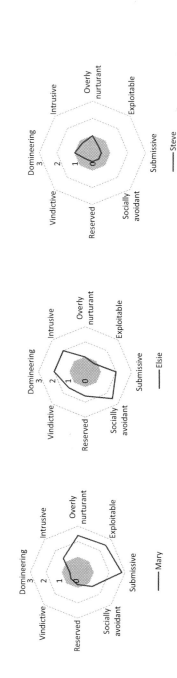

Figure 4.2 IIP-C- Profiles of Mary, Elsie and Steve from the demonstration group. Persons from non-clinical samples will usually rate themselves within the gray area of the graph, which approximately represents normative values (see appendix 2).

1992), soon to be replaced by the next version (ICD-11; World Health Organization, 2018). The classification provides a diagnosis for the symptom picture (mood disorder, anxiety disorder, eating disorder), but also registers whether the person has a personality disorder (PD). PD diagnosis is used if the person has presented rigid and deviant personality traits in a number of areas, if there has been a significant functioning impairment and/or a high level of subjective suffering over time and if there are no other diagnoses that can better explain the condition. A similar system was developed by the American Psychiatric Association called the Diagnostic and Statistical Manual of Mental Disorders. A number of revised editions have been published since the 1980s, the last being the fifth (DSM-5; American Psychiatric Association, 2013). There are a number of structured interviews that point to specific diagnoses in these diagnostic systems. An example is the Mini International Neuropsychiatric Interview (MINI-PLUS; Sheehan et al., 2002).

These diagnostic systems are descriptive and categorical and use inclusion and exclusion criteria to decide whether a patient should be given a diagnosis. Diagnoses are dependent on a number of inclusion criteria being met and there being no exclusion criteria. Patients can therefore be diagnosed with multiple symptom disorders and personality disorders (PD). Diagnosis is primarily based on *phenomenology*, persons receiving the same diagnosis if they and/or the "disturbances" seem to share specific characteristics, such as types of symptoms. The diagnosis alone can therefore often be too "superficial" and not cover aspects of the disorder or the personality that are targeted by a particular form of treatment such as FGAP and most other psychodynamic therapies.

The *relationship* between the patient and the therapist is invariably of central importance to treatment in psychodynamic therapy. The idea that a patient suffers from *several* personality disorders appears, in this context, to be an absurdity that creates distance between the two collaborators. A person has only one personality. Their personality can, however, be flexible and adaptable (well functioning), and can be characterized by a diversity of traits (see "Personality", Chapter 3). I refer those interested in personality diagnostics to *The Psychodynamic Diagnostic Manual* (PDM-2; Lingiardi & McWilliams, 2017). This manual provides criteria for different personality types or styles, and contains a specific axis (the M axis) which allows a dimensional assessment of mental functioning based on psychodynamic theory.

The last editions of both DSM-5 and ICD-11 contain alternative, dimensional models for characterizing and grading personality pathology (Section III, DSM 5, 2013; ICD-11, 2018), thus indicating a mentality change within the editorial committees of the traditional categorical systems. I consider this convergence within key diagnostic (taxonomic) systems to be a sign of increasing support for the assessment of a patient's level of personality organization, as advocated in this book.

I will briefly, to conclude this section, mention that the essence of the personality pathology in DSM-5 Section III is covered by the domains "disturbances in the person's relationship with himself" and "problems in the person's relationship with other people". The "Self" is represented by the "identity" and "self-direction" sub-domains and interpersonal functioning is represented by the "ability to empathize" and the "ability/wish for intimacy". All of these are rated on a dimensional scale. A structured clinical interview based on the model outlined above has been developed to assess the "level of personality functioning" (Bender et al., 2018). I can recommend, to those wanting to read more about this, a paper that compares this interview with STIPO-R (Kampe et al., 2018).

Psychodynamic case formulation

The psychodynamic case formulation represents an attempt to describe and integrate all central information on each patient, and to this formulate a psychodynamic hypothesis (summary). A psychodynamic case formulation is prepared before therapy starts, and constitutes a useful tool in the therapist's planning and implementation of treatment. The formulation attempts to explain the patient's psychological distress and problems (the clinical form of expression) in terms of the interplay between predisposing (vulnerability in personality) and precipitating factors (stressors). Inferences about potential mechanisms that can explain ("cause") the development of mental disorders and/or symptomatic behavior are based on a biological (heredity/temperament), psychological/psychodynamic and/or sociocultural frame of reference. There are many models for "mapping" individual patients in this way (Eells, 2011; Cabaniss, 2013; Gabbard, 2004). I have in this book, however, used a traditional psychoanalytic approach for editing patient information (Messer & Wolitzsky, 1997; Lorentzen & Høglend, 2002), which I outline below.

Areas to be covered in a psychodynamic case formulation

The full psychodynamic formulation is not shared with the group. The treatment focus, which should be closely linked to aspects of the psychodynamic hypothesis is, however, usually presented by each patient and shared with the group at the start of the first therapy session. The full psychodynamic formulation can be shared and discussed with the patient before the therapy begins, even though the

Table 4.2 Template for formulation of a psychodynamic hypothesis

Surface phenomena (resultants)	Precipitating factors (stressors)	Predisposing factors (events) (personality-vulnerability)	Attempts to integrate (mechanisms)
Symptoms	×	Early childhood	Biological
Symptomatic behavior	×	Puberty	Psychological
Avoidance	×	Young adult Adult	Sociocultural

patient may not agree with all aspects. Parts are frequently reformulated during the therapy course as new information emerges.

A good psychodynamic formulation seeks to elucidate all the areas mentioned in the template, and gives the premises for the psychodynamic hypotheses. It links the clinical picture (surface phenomena) that brought the patient into treatment, with the predisposing life events that characterize the personality (rigidity and/or vulnerability) and also with the precipitating factors (stressors). The "conclusion", which consists of hypotheses that include biological, psychological and sociocultural factors (mechanisms), should consist of a brief description of the patient that explains the clinical picture and provides therapy guidance. It can also include predictions of the course of treatment and a potential prognosis (Kassaw & Gabbard, 2002; Gabbard, 2004).

Clinical example

I will use the information about Mary to give an example of a psychodynamic case formulation. She is a 39-year-old married teacher, has two boys aged six and seven and is a member of the demonstration group presented in the Appendix.

Reasons for referral: Mary has suffered several depressive episodes, the first being after the birth of her second child. These episodes have caused short periods of absence from work. She attributes the depressions to her having to bear too much of the responsibility for the home and children, as her husband weekly commutes and is away during the working week. She asked her GP to refer her to a specialist, to find a solution to her problems.

Clinical ("surface") phenomena

Symptoms: moodiness, frequent depressions, irritability, somatizations and a shaky self-image.

Symptomatic behavior (interpersonal): Mary feels easily controlled, her husband is somewhat domineering, and she easily feels irritated and angry with him. However, she mostly ends up feeling discouraged and guilty after conflicts. She now and then appears somewhat rigid and stubborn at work, and may sometimes be a little too strict with students. At home she can frequently lose control and shake her boys roughly when she feels they quarrel too much. At school she has control of her negative emotions, most of the time.

Avoidance: she keeps some distance from others both at home and at work, to control her irritation and anger. She tries to avoid conflicts by withdrawing, but often gets headaches and neck/shoulder pain.

Precipitating factors (stressors)

She feels she has sole responsibility for the home and children. She also sometimes thinks that her job is too demanding, both pedagogically and in the setting of limits for undisciplined students. She has also recently lost contact with the previous principal when he retired, and misses him. He trusted her and let her work on her own, delegated tasks to her and was supportive and warm. Her new principal is, however, more demanding and authoritarian. Two parents had criticized her some time before the last referral at a school parent/teacher open meeting. They claimed she had been unreasonable and too strict with their children.

Predisposing factors (vulnerability)

Mary is the second oldest of five siblings and grew up on a small farm. The family's finances were poor during her childhood, but they never lacked food or clothing. Mary's mother has always been anxious and resembled Mary's grandmother, who had once been hospitalized for a "nervous breakdown". There was some abuse of alcohol in her father's family, and one of his brothers hanged himself as a youth. They never talked about this at home. Her father was short-tempered and often exploded over trifles when she was a child. He also had long periods in which he was sulky and silent. He never missed an opportunity to criticize Mary, and seldom praised her. All the children had to work on the farm, and there was little time for play and fun. Her mother took it for granted that the children participated in the daily activities of the farm, as she had done in her childhood. An older brother was her father's favorite and was invited to accompany him everywhere. Everything her brother did was good, according to the father. The mother left all important decisions in the home to the father, and usually abided by what he decided.

Mary was almost surprised when her father allowed her to attend high school when she was 16 years old, which meant she had to move out of the family home and to a nearby town. After leaving home, she changed from being "kind and obedient" to becoming more rebellious. She was in opposition to teachers, often threw herself into discussions with peers and became assertive and a know-it-all. She also easily felt wronged, angry or humiliated if she didn't have the last word. Occasionally she would stay away from high school on the day after such events to "lick her wounds". She had a couple of good friends at school who were also "in disarray", but eventually began to spend time with a group of slightly older adolescents who partied. She was uncritical of her use of alcohol, indulged in unprotected sex with random contacts, and visited her family less and less often. Finally, she passed her exams with moderate grades, but could have done better if she had not been so engrossed in her group of friends and at odds with her teachers.

Mary, shortly after high school graduation, moved to Oslo and worked for a few years as an assistant in a nursing home. She made some new friends at work and in a social club, calmed down and gradually adopted a more stable life. She eventually returned to school, re-took and improved some of her subject grades, and decided to study to become a teacher. The period in which she studied to become a teacher was relatively stable. She enjoyed the curriculum and was happy with the company of her small network of friends. She also engaged in a short love relationship, but did not seriously connect with anyone until she met Hans, a fellow student, about six months before her final exams. She became pregnant after three months, and wanted to get married, but felt "badly treated" and "used" when he hesitated. The pregnancy ended in a miscarriage, but they did finally marry in a rush. Both also passed their final exams. The marriage has had its ups and downs, and a good deal of bickering. She has tended to fluctuate between being critical and unhappy and feeling easily offended, wronged and ill-treated. Her husband has been more patient and accommodating, but has also tried to control her. Having children has mainly been positive for the marriage, although disputes over how the children are brought up have been frequent. They both share an interest in the outdoor life, films and music, and can sometimes enjoy going for a walk or to the cinema or a concert together.

Personality

Mary was timid, submissive and afraid of authority as a child. She never protested, even when she had to do things that she did not like doing. She was obedient and conscientious until she, in puberty, became more rebellious and critical of others. She became more self-assertive, got involved in discussions and easily reacted with anger if she did not get her way. She was somewhat self-righteous and showed disrespect for other people's views, something that annoyed many. These traits persisted into adulthood, when she learned to suppress both the need to dominate, win disputes and to protect herself from being hurt by creating distance from the people around her. She is in touch with her irritation and angry feelings. There is, however, frequently "friction" between her and others, despite her efforts to control these feelings. She has largely managed to control herself, but also has a tendency to signal dislike by avoiding contact, through sulkiness and use of irony. She has experienced more and more bodily "aches" over the years, probably with a psychological background.

Psychodynamic hypothesis

Information on the characteristics of her caregivers and her own relational competence nurtures the hypothesis that Mary's inner world of self and object representations is characterized by a lack of early positive affirmation, anxiety and that she has been the target of unpredictable outbursts of aggression. This manifests itself in unstable self-esteem, vulnerability in relationships and a relatively high need for affirmation, support and care. These are only met to a limited extent, because she distances herself from others. Her inner representations are also colored by her father's poorly controlled rage. At puberty, she tried to become less needy by becoming more self-sufficient and independent. Early father identifications and insecurity as a person, however, led her to become more rebellious and aggressive, others therefore avoiding her. Some of her anger is also directed toward herself, this leading to somatization, poor self-esteem (self-hate) and depression. She has relatively large conflicts around domination and submission and feels easily controlled, which makes her feel worthless. She has a strong expectation of being rejected if she clearly expresses who she is, and she uses distance to protect herself from this. This expectation of rejection is, however, partly irrational and is governed more by her inner world than by the reality of the people around her. The mechanisms behind her problems are mainly psychological, although information about her father's problems, and the suicide and alcohol abuse of family members could support a hypothesis that there is a genetic disposition to bipolar disorder (mainly depression) in the family.

An overall evaluation

The therapist, after conducting clinical and psychodynamic interviews and assessing the patient's level of PO, has a wealth of information and is nearly ready to decide who might benefit from FGAP. Patients suitable for FGAP should be at the normal, neurotic or high borderline level of PO. The review of the domains on which the PO is based, furthermore, gives clues of which traits are particularly affected by pathology. I have, in this chapter, presented the Inventory of Interpersonal Problems-Circumplex (IIP-C) and have described the additional information that follows from this and the psychodynamic case formulation. I will therefore conclude this chapter with a description and two clinical examples of treatment foci. However, before I do this, I would like to share a few thoughts on how the psychodynamic therapist can reflect on the clinical material collected so far.

Information springs from different sources, including the patient and therapist and also third parties such as other family members or the referring physician. Information can therefore easily contain contradictory information. The diversity of sources also, however, provides an opportunity to further explore dynamic connections with the patient.

The IIP-C profile is mainly based on the patient's conscious beliefs. Central aspects of the patient's repetitive, dysfunctional relationship patterns may therefore not be represented. The strength of using profiles is that they are likely to express the problems the patient perceives to be greater for them than for others. This therefore represents behaviors that are undesirable (ego-dystonic) and which the patient might want to change. The profiles may, however, be influenced by subjectively colored thinking such as idyllisations, symptoms, wishful thinking or exaggerated self-critical thoughts. The profiles will usually express at least *some true features* that can also be verified by others. A sensitive and trained therapist will, however, often capture a number of the same traits and attitudes during the psychodynamic interview. Patients are reminded, through encouraging them to reflect on contradictions, that there are aspects of their behavior that are visible to others, and that impact how others in and outside the group relate to them. The therapist can therefore, in this way, successfully expand the patient's scope of understanding (insight) already during the evaluation interviews. This information may enable the therapist to form new hypotheses that point to the patient's unconscious self and object representations, and how these are organized and emotionally colored.

Treatment focus

The dialogue between the patient and the therapist also provides an arena for together finding a *focus for the therapy*. It is important that the therapist uses his or her total understanding of the patient as a person and actively proposes a treatment focus that is central and relevant to the assessment. It may, at the same time, be vital that negotiations between the patient and therapist result in a consensus. The focus of treatment will therefore include elements that are conscious for the patient, and elements that have more or less unknown branches to the patient's unconscious. The therapist's attempts to explore parts of the information can stimulate a patient to reflect, but also points attention forwards and awakens their interest in more latent aspects of their psyche. This can include affective and cognitive expressions or overt behavior, with ramifications for the patient's neurotic, rigid personality patterns, which in turn are rooted in poorly integrated self and object representations. The goal is to gain greater insight and new experiences through encounters within and outside the group, so that relational patterns that create or maintain difficulties in relation to one's self and others can be changed.

The therapist should, during the discussion of treatment focus, also explain to the patient why and how the proposed treatment can be helpful. The explanation should be based on knowledge from research and clinical experience, and should be formulated in a language that is meaningful to the patient.

It may be useful to base this discussion on problems that the patient struggles most with, and that may have prompted them to seek help. These problems are usually composite, and include symptoms, problems in relationships and negative experiences of themselves.

I will illustrate examples of treatment foci through two clinical vignettes of Mary and Steve in the demonstration group. Details of their backgrounds and assessments are given in Chapter 5. Appendix 1, in which all eight patients in the demonstration group are presented, does, however, give a more complete description of the premises behind these formulations.

Clinical example 1 – *Mary, 39 years*

Treatment focus: Mary and the therapist, after exploring and discussing all the data, decided that the focus of her therapy should be on recognizing and problematizing her tendency to avoid and distance herself from others. It was also emphasized that she, despite her IIP-C profile showing that she perceived herself to be low on "domineering" and high on "avoidance", was in contrast at times being somewhat controlling and rigorous toward her students, her children and her husband. She should therefore, during treatment, try to understand how she uses these behaviors to protect aspects of her inner world, and explore how they affect others' behavior toward her. She was instructed (through being given behavioral tasks) to more often convey her own wishes, feelings and boundaries to the other members of the group. This included her wish to be seen and cared for. She was also to acknowledge others when they expressed similar feelings, and regularly ask for feedback from the others on how they perceived her. It was emphasized that these aspects of her personality were probably related to repeatedly becoming depressed and to her somatic pain.

The next example illustrates that patients with a tendency to act out (instead of feeling, thinking and reflecting) may also be suitable for FGAP, if the destructive behavioral pattern is carefully explored in advance, and given a central position in the patient's treatment focus.

Clinical example 2 – *Steve, 28 years*

Treatment focus: Steve had been able to acknowledge, during the evaluation and the discussion of his IIP-C, that he sometimes perceived himself to be weak and inferior to others. At other times, however, he felt that others "were stupid" and saw himself as belonging to "a higher league". These feelings were frequently activated if he did not have the last word in a discussion or when he did not feel sufficiently appreciated for something he had accomplished. He would then become offended and wanted to "hit back". He also, during the evaluation, had accepted the therapist's suggestion that his frequent break-ups in relationships were linked to "a fear of being abandoned".

A number of aspects of his problematic attitudes (self-sufficiency, wish for revenge and devaluation of others) were explored and finally defined and placed at the center of his treatment focus as aspects that he should try to change during therapy. It was predicted that the interpersonal conflicts he reported from his life situation would also occur in the group. It was also predicted that he might then be tempted to leave the treatment. The therapist emphasized that this happening would be a call for him to remain calm and ask for help to explore in detail what was taking place.

Steve's *behavioral tasks* were to practice a more "laid back" stance, observe and listen to other members of the group and try to understand how they were thinking and feeling (mentalizing). He was to report when he felt offended, but to remember that we all live in a subjective world which is characterized by differences in backgrounds, development and choices.

Steve is an example of a patient who is assessed to have a high-level borderline PO. His case illustrates a number of important issues that I would like to briefly comment on.

Impairment in domains that constitute Steve's PO mean that his treatment is threatened by his tendency to act out instead of feel and reflect. This tendency is partly due to a reduced reflective functioning/mentalizing capacity, combined with poorer control of aggression and greater use of primitive defenses, his shaky self-esteem and compensatory fantasies of superiority adding to the problem. If, during the evaluation, the therapist and the patient agree that this destructive pattern of behavior is a key factor in the patient's pathology, then this can be designated the treatment focus, as in Steve's case. The technique of exploring behavioral patterns that can jeopardize therapy, and the prediction that these will be activated in the treatment, has been referred to as being an "inoculation" (Whittingham, 2018) – a word borrowed from immunology. The patient informs the group of a situation that can occur in the group, before it occurs. The group is therefore prepared and can say, when it happens "Now you are there", "Now it is happening again", "Let's take a closer look at this".

Steve's case is an example that illustrates the importance of the therapist working prior to the group starting, to make such patterns ego-dystonic, i.e. "undesirable to the patient", by making the patient aware that they are creating and maintaining problems not only for themself, but also for others. The person may, in addition to needing help with their tendency to act out, also need help with other issues such as an increased vulnerability, attachment anxiety, problems of affect control and self-esteem regulation. Group therapy offers each patient a unique opportunity for support and feedback from other group members, including the therapist. This support, combined with a thorough preparation for the group including "inoculation" may enable many patients, including those with more personality pathology, to break vicious circles of problematic behavior and initiate a constructive developmental process that can continue even after the therapy has ended.

It is important for both the patients described above that the therapist, through comments, demonstrates that he understands and confirms that the patient's problems are shaped and colored by "events from their background/upbringing/development". At the same time, the emphasis during therapy should be placed on the *patient's responsibility* to use the *opportunities for change* in the here-and-now situation.

Chapter 5

Establishing and composing the group – introducing the demonstration group

This chapter discusses establishing the group. Establishing includes the final preparation of the patients, the contract between the therapist and the patient and the overall focus of the group. I will also introduce eight patients who have each been assessed and brought together in a group I call the *demonstration group*. The results of their evaluations are presented in a table, to help readers quickly get an overview. The table includes the patients' name/age, reasons for referral, clinical diagnosis, IIP-C self-report results (Alden et al., 1990), therapy focus and level of personality organization (Table 5.1). IIP-C scores and important personality domain scores (identity, object relations, defense mechanisms, affects, moral values and narcissism) are also presented in Figures 5.1 and 5.2. The patients were selected to illustrate typical patients who can benefit from FGAP, and also to show that the group's potential to promote change can be increased by including patients who both match and challenge each other. The chapter concludes with a set of guidelines on composing FGAP groups.

The eight patients are not real persons. Their stories are largely composed. I have, however, been working in this field for more than 45 years and specific patients often come to mind when I discuss my work. I have also in this time, however, learnt to be very careful to anonymize and change details about patients who come to mind, to maintain confidentiality. If anyone feels that they recognize themselves in these patients, then I would say to them that despite all of us being unique and having our own, distinctive character, we have more traits and problems in common than we sometimes like to think.

Some patients need extra preparation

The evaluation process normally fully prepares patients for therapy. A treatment contract can therefore be made at the end of the evaluation.

Some patients can, however, benefit from extra time with the therapist. Finding and evaluating enough of the right patients to make up a new group often takes time. A patient might therefore have to wait a few weeks after evaluation before a group starts. It can, however, be beneficial that the therapist maintains some contact with the patient and that the patient has at least one extra individual

DOI: 10.4324/9781003216377-7

Establishing and composing the group 73

Table 5.1 Demonstration group patients

Patient	Reason for referral	Clinical diagnosis	IIP-C Interpersonal problems, self-report	Therapy focus	Level of personality organization (PO)
1. Mary, 39, teacher, married, two sons – six and seven.	Frequent depressive episodes leading to sick leave. Irritability and somatization. Sometimes shakes her children hard. Wants specialist help.	Recurrent depression. Some personality pathology, but no PD.	More avoidant, nonassertive, exploitable, overly nurturant, intrusive and less domineering than others.	Observe her own social avoidance and withdrawal tendency. What is she avoiding or protecting herself from? Communicate her wishes, feelings and boundaries to others to a greater degree.	Identity 2.5 Object relations 2 Defense mech. 2.5 Aggression 2.5 Moral values 2 **Mean 2.3** Narcissism 1.5
2. Henry, 36, priest, married, a daughter and a son – four and six.	Sleep problems, wakes frequently at night. Doubts his faith and ability to be a priest. Self-blames for issues at work, thinks others are angry with him.	Depressive episode, moderate. Dependent PD and traits from Avoidant PD.	More avoidant, nonassertive, exploitable and overly nurturant, less domineering and intrusive than others.	Should practice commenting on things he does not like. Should take some time to himself each session, especially when he disagrees, but should also share more tender wishes and longings. Ask for feedback from other group members.	Identity 2 Object relations 2.5 Defense mech. 2 Aggression 2.5 Moral values 2.5 **Mean 2.3** Narcissism 2
3. Emily, 28, accountant, cohabitant, no children.	Panic attack tendency with somatic symptoms. Usually manages to calm down. Fears large groups and people. Afraid that cohabitant will leave her (jealousy).	Panic attacks with agoraphobia (mild). Mixed PD. Some obsessional, paranoid and dependent traits.	More concerned with own needs (vindictive), and more domineering, intrusive but also more nonassertive than others.	Become more nurturant and exploitable by getting in better touch with needs and tender, loving feelings. Take more responsibility for her aggression and challenge her "sense of entitlement" – a right to get more attention than her partner.	Identity 2.5 Object relations 2.5 Defense mech. 3 Aggression 3 Moral values 2.5 **Mean 2.7** Narcissism 2

(Continued)

74 Establishing and composing the group

Table 5.1 (Continued)

Patient	Reason for referral	Clinical diagnosis	IIP-C Interpersonal problems, self-report	Therapy focus	Level of personality organization (PO)
4. Doris, 41, auxiliary nurse, married, one son – ten.	Frequent depression, often feels tired and takes to bed. Frustrated with herself. Wants to do something about this.	Recurrent depression.	More overly nurturant, exploitable, nonassertive and socially avoidant, but also more reserved (cold) than others.	Who has the responsibility for conflict situations? Distinguish between her and others' input. Ask others more about what they need, before confirming them. Take her irritation and anger seriously and share it with the group.	Identity 2.5 Object relations 3 Defense mech. 2.5 Aggression 2.5 Moral values 2 **Mean 2.5** Narcissism 2
5. Steve, 28, taxi driver, unmarried, no children.	Dissatisfied with life, sometimes plagued by feelings of emptiness and meaninglessness. Easily enters into conflicts with people, quarrels. Suicidal thoughts when drinking.	No symptom diagnosis. Borderline PD. No PD.	Lower scores than others on all sub-scales. Controlled and wants to maintain a socially acceptable facade.	He got in touch with his feelings of inferiority during the evaluation. Also feels he is a little better than others and is easily offended. Longs for closeness, but is afraid of being abandoned. Becomes self-sufficient and isolates himself. Should explore these feelings. Potential for acting-out is predicted (inoculation).	Identity 3 Object relations 3 Defense mech. 2.5 Aggression 3 Moral values 2.5 **Mean 2.8** Narcissism 3

Establishing and composing the group 75

6. Anny, 43, nurse, divorced, new cohabitant, daughter – 22.	Referred due to a depressive episode. Often has feelings of guilt, shame and anxiety after having left her husband a few years before referral.	Depressive episode, moderate. Avoidant PD.	Sees herself as more nonassertive, domineering, cold (reserved), avoiding and intrusive than others, and less overly nurturant and exploitable.	Explore different, contradictory aspects of herself. Try to get hold of a better integrated and true picture of herself. Learn to distinguish between assumed and real expectations of others, and her own needs and longings. Practice setting boundaries to others.	Identity 2.5 Object relations 1.5 Defense mech. 2 Aggression 2.5 Moral values 3 **Mean 2.3** Narcissism 2
7. Elsie 36, secretary, divorced, new cohabitant, son of eleven from previous marriage who lives with them.	Suffered in recent years from unspecific anxiety in social situations. Easily feels criticized and avoids places where there are many people. Wants to be referred to a specialist.	Social phobia. Avoidant PD.	More domineering, intrusive, avoidant and nonassertive than others, but also less exploitable.	Focus on her labile self-esteem, explore how this affects her experiences in the group. Should report when she thinks she is domineering and when she feels criticized. Ask for feedback on how others perceive her.	Identity 2.5 Object relations 2 Defense mech. 2.5 Aggression 2 Moral values 3 **Mean 2.4** Narcissism 2
8. Frank 43, auditor, divorced. No children.	His life has "stopped". Operated for cancer 13 years ago. Is cured, but fears relapse. Has gradually withdrawn from friends and family. Wants to "connect back with life" again.	Dysthymia. Mixed PD, dependent and paranoid traits.	Sees himself as more cold (reserved), avoidant and exploitable than others, but less domineering, intrusive and vindictive.	Challenge his feeling of being a victim. Ask others how they feel. Explore in the group how his anger, envy and bitterness affect others. Make contact with and restore contact with family and former friends.	Identity 2.5 Object relations 3 Defense mech. 3 Aggression 3 Moral values 2.5 **Mean 2.8** Narcissism 2.5

76 Establishing and composing the group

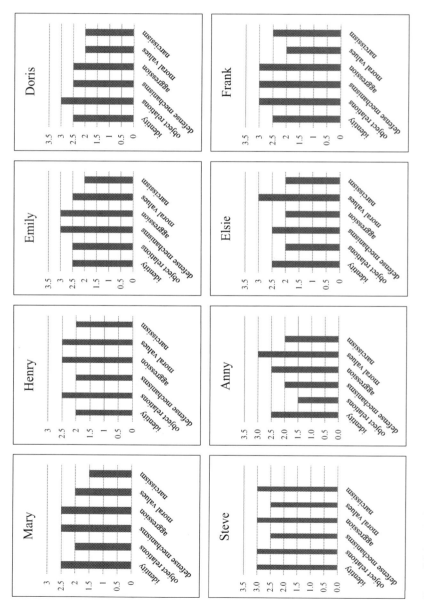

Figure 5.1 Level of personality organization (PO), structural dimensions.

Establishing and composing the group 77

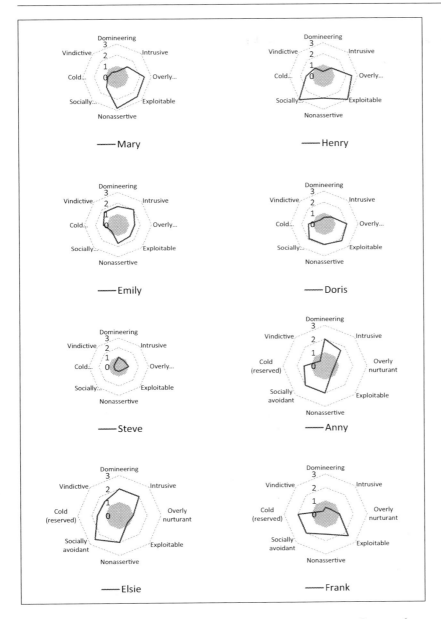

Figure 5.2 IIP-C profiles of all patients in the demonstration group. Persons from non-clinical samples will usually rate themselves within the gray area of the graph, which approximately represents normative values (see appendix 2).

session just before the first group session. This is particularly true for patients who show weak motivation or ambivalence to entering a group. It can also be beneficial for patients who the therapist believes poorly understand their therapy tasks. This extra session can also be used to check whether any important issues remain to be discussed or whether new problems have emerged and need to be clarified.

I have often seen the motivational work of previous evaluation sessions come to fruition in these extra sessions, and ambivalent patients become ready to start therapy. This might be due to the growth of an emotional bond between the patient and therapist during these interviews, which leads to optimism and positive expectations in the patient that the therapy could be useful. Both can be important to patients quickly entering a treatment mode, which is desirable in FGAP.

Patients who tend to withdraw and break off therapy when group interaction starts to "heat up" may also benefit from an extra session. Some patients have a history of "self-sabotaging" previous therapies and may have repeatedly broken off close relationships, often during crises and in affect. A solution to this, as in the case of Steve (see Chapter 4), could be to make this destructive behavior the focus of the therapy. This, however, requires the patient to acknowledge the pattern as a key factor behind their problems. The therapist must then also consider whether the patient, with the group's support, can manage to stay in and work with the situation when "the heat is on".

The therapy formally starts at the moment the patient shows up for treatment. The vast majority of patients have, however, started their own process and preparation for therapy during the assessment. Exchanges with the therapist, which include exploration of their life history and the patient scoring different aspects of their relationships with others, can activate important problem areas in patients before the group begins, an internal process therefore starting "there and then". Explorations may also stimulate and sharpen important patient faculties in therapy, such as getting in touch with emotions, the ability to reflect on psychological connections and increasing internal life awareness. The patient is challenged time and time again to scrutinize themselves in their encounters with the therapist's observations, these not always matching the patient's perception of themselves.

Contract between patient and therapist

A contract is entered into when the patient accepts a place in a group. It can be written or oral, the details being more or less thoroughly worked out. The contract should include information on practical aspects such as time, place, duration, session frequency, total duration of the treatment and possibly the total number of sessions. It should also contain information on financial terms. Some therapists like to include a few words on the group's general goals and want patients to sign contracts. Others, including myself, limit themselves to providing this information verbally and to the patient's verbal acceptance of the group requirements. Each group member should, however, provide their written consent if the therapist wishes to make audio or video recordings of group meetings. There must be a justifiable reason for recordings, such as therapist supervision, or that the group is part of a clinical trial (informed consent).

The group usually consists of six to eight patients and one to two therapists. Each session lasts for 90 minutes and is ended by the therapist at the scheduled time. The group meets once a week unless holidays prevent this. The number of meetings in a course is usually 20, and they are held over a period of around six months.

The patient must usually accept a set of rules. The most common rule is that the patient accepts "the rule of confidentiality", and does not divulge any information on fellow patients to anyone outside the group. Most therapists also emphasize the importance of attending all sessions and of being on time. Patients who are unable to attend must inform the therapist of this as soon as possible.

Groups are "stranger groups". Patients should therefore not know each other before the group begins, and should not meet otherwise outside the group during the course period. The therapist cannot, for reasons of confidentiality, check that a patient does not know the other group members. It can therefore occasionally become clear at the first session that two patients know each other. The relationship between the two patients must be explored there and then and, if this is more than superficial, one must leave. The patient who leaves can hopefully join another group.

Rules should be clear, well founded and not be presented in an authoritarian manner. This is important to the development of the treatment culture atmosphere in the group, this atmosphere ideally being as accepting, including and caring as possible. The therapist should "expect" but not "require" all group members to attend all sessions. It is, however, almost inevitable that patients during the six months are from time to time unable to be on time or to attend. The therapists should also share some of their positive experiences with group therapy, including research results, to create positive therapy expectations.

A contract involves mutual obligations. It is therefore natural to also describe the role and responsibilities of the therapist. The obligations of the therapist are usually implicit and embedded in the role of their profession and training. Therapists must therefore comply with all laws and professional ethics guidelines, including keeping their professional knowledge up to date. I often limit myself to saying that I will do my utmost, through applying my professional knowledge, experience and skills, to help patients understand and solve the problems that have brought them into therapy.

Overall group objectives

The overall goal of FGAP is that the group should, as far as possible, assist the individual patient to reduce symptomatic distress and subjective suffering, to improve problematic perceptions of themselves and others, and to achieve a better ability to function. All of these elements underlie an improved mental health. The main focus of the group is on transactions and interactions between group participants, including with the therapist – in the here-and-now situation. Emphasis is placed on exploring and understanding dysfunctional, individual and interpersonal patterns. These are often rigid, problematic, repetitive, and often create or sustain the individual's problems and symptoms. Developing an open and safe treatment culture allows this exploration, the emphasis being on understanding how each patient behaves toward others. The group tries to provide patients with "corrective emotional experiences" through support and through exploring these patterns under the guidance of the therapist (Alexander & French, 1946). Patients should also be encouraged and supported in attempts of trying out new, more appropriate interpersonal strategies.

Each patient introduces themselves *in the first session* and describes their treatment foci and their goals for the treatment. This is the start of patients becoming acquainted with each other. This information and the relationships and experiences that grow over time out of communication and interactions provide leads and material for contributing to each others' change processes. Group therapy, however, contains a paradox that the therapist and the group must navigate. This paradox is that all group members are responsible for developing and maintaining a mutually constructive and respectful treatment culture. Patients are, however, also expected to expose their more dysfunctional patterns of behavior, so that these can be worked with. A fundamental responsibility of the therapist is to protect the individual patient through their role, their knowledge of the treatment needs of each patient and their experience with the subject and the group method. This responsibility is acted through interventions (see Chapter 7) and through decisions about who can or cannot participate in the group.

All patients have a treatment focus and therapy goals, these all falling within the group's overall goals.

Demonstration group

I will briefly, using a table and two figures, present eight patients who have been evaluated and found suitable for FGAP. The table outlines the patients' reasons for referral, clinical diagnoses, interpersonal problems, treatment focus and personality domains (identity, object relations, defense mechanisms, control of aggression, moral values and degree of pathological narcissism), these domains being the determinants used to assess the patients' level of personality organization (PO) (see Table 5.1). The domains (STIPO-R, clinical version; reworked from Caligor et al., 2018) and a self-report of the patients' interpersonal problems (IIP-C; Alden et al., 1990) are presented graphically below (see Figures 5.1 and 5.2).

More detailed information on each patient, such as background, developmental history, personality, history of somatic and mental/psychological disorders and a psychodynamic case formulation, is presented in the Appendix. This is provided to allow the reader to further scrutinize the clinical material.

Group composition guidelines

We now come to how the therapist "composes" or assembles a group, which I will discuss using the patients presented. I would, however, like to first make some general comments on group composition, and then end the chapter with a discussion of the demonstration group.

Patients are deliberately selected because it is acknowledged that different constellations of people and their characteristics influence group atmosphere or the culture of treatment in different ways. It is also acknowledged that poor selections can make a group less effective for some or most of the patients. I would like to illustrate this with two group constellations. The first group is made up of eight anxious, severely depressed patients with serious psychomotor inhibitions. They were diagnosed with "depressive disorder, episode of moderate to serious strength" and their personalities were characterized by traits such as "submissiveness" and "social avoidance". The second group brought together eight patients with severe personality disorders, all with traits of dominance, lack of empathy and poorly controlled aggression. It is easy to imagine that the interactions in these two groups will be very different, and that the therapists will face nearly directly opposing challenges in trying to activate, stimulate and control the members.

It is a widely held clinical truism that *time-limited* groups are most effective if the patients are similar and exhibit some kind of homogeneity. Homogeneity can be in patients exhibiting similar diagnoses or the same clusters of symptoms. Empirical research has shown that different time-limited psychodynamic treatments are effective for patients with problems or diagnoses such as pathological grief (Piper et al., 2001), burnout (Sandahl et al., 2011) and eating disorders (Tasca et al., 2006; Tasca et al., 2012). I, however, do not know of any good studies that have shown that the outcomes for patients with these diagnoses, treated in short-term groups, are equal or superior to outcomes in long-term groups.

Homogeneity is also based by others on the assumption that the causal factors behind mental health problems are equivalent. For example, that there is a homogeneity between patients that have been subjected to traumatic childhood events such as physical violence, sexual abuse or loss of caregivers. It is therefore believed that the "common fate" of the members of such a group means that they start to interact more quickly and then build cohesive groups. Group members with similar experiences might also make it easier to spot evasiveness or other forms of resistance during the therapeutic work. It might, however, also make it more difficult for individual patients to claim a special position in the group. The efficacy of such groups has been documented (i.e. Lundquist et al., 2006). The claim that the "causal" connection between trauma similarity and group treatment efficacy is, however, based more on clinical experience than research evidence. There is no evidence that time-limited groups that are considered to be "homogeneous" based on similar clinical diagnoses are more effective than groups of patients with a greater variety of clinical diagnoses (mixed or "heterogeneous" groups). It should, in this respect, be noted that patients diagnosed with a specific symptom or personality disorder using ICD-10 or DSM-5 often, from a psychodynamic point of view, have very different personality structures and dynamic conflicts (Lingiardi & McWilliams, 2017). Fjeldstad et al. (2016) found that patients with a higher level of personality organization (PO) changed more in a time-limited therapy than patients with more personality pathology. This study therefore provides some of the rationale for recommending that patients included in FGAP have a higher level of personality organization (normal, neurotic and upper level borderline).

The *Noah's Ark principle* (MacKenzie, 1990), which also has acquired a certain status in the group analytic tradition, addresses the need of a patient to find someone in the group who is familiar to them (similarity) and someone who, due to one or more characteristics, they experience as being challenging (difference). The principle is based on the Biblical story of Noah and that he was to have *two of each* species, one of each gender, on the ark. This is used as a metaphor for patient inclusion in a psychodynamic group and the *composition* of this group. The principle "appreciates that both commonality and difference are vital to psychological development, for while *the foundations (and maintenance)* of a person's self depend upon the experience of safety gained through an encounter with *sameness*, the *development of self*, of identity, grows out of an encounter with *difference*" (Barwick & Weegmann, 2018). Commonality can help prevent anyone feeling isolated or alone. Difference, however, maintains that patients must interact with people who are different from themselves, to create greater opportunities for learning and change. A more spontaneous or impulsive person can activate the more withdrawn and elusive, and a more distant and self-sufficient person can be "warmed up" by those who may be too preoccupied with the needs of others. Tensions will, however, may certainly arise between the more dominant patients and those who are less self-assertive or even self-effacing.

The value of heterogeneity is twofold. It partly lies in *direct stimulation* through communication. It also is indirectly in the confrontations that patients experience with their "opposites", those they may want to or try to change. These opposites can also act as models that a person can imitate or identify with. Interpersonal theory (Sullivan, 1953a, 1953b) supports the argument that domination by one part in an interaction can lead to greater submission of the other. It also supports the argument that the withdrawal and emotional distance of one can provoke the other to withdraw, rather than react with increased concern and care. These interactions are examples of situations that therapists hope will be activated in a group. All participants in a group are a part of an interactive field in which aspects of the participants' relational patterns are constantly activated in the here-and-now situation. The therapist and other group members will, however, at times lean back to clarify, reflect on and discuss what is taking place. All group members can express their opinions and feelings about an event, spontaneously or when invited to do so by the therapist.

Many therapists also want to include patients of different ages in a group, to activate themes from different life stages. My opinion is, however, that the age range in a *time-limited* group should not be too wide. Life themes can easily become too diverse. Groups could therefore, for example, be for patients aged

18–25, 20–40 and 40–60. It is also important to include both genders to activate gender-related tensions. The overall group experience is enriched where participants have a range of life experiences, such as a range of civil status (single, divorced, married), and where some participants are parents. Patients who are suitable for FGAP have a certain level of personality resources (ego-strength), like some awareness of their inner life, contact with emotions and ability to reflect on psychological issues. There is often enough time in a long-term group to develop such faculties, for example, to train patients in reflective functioning or affect tolerance and control, and for patients to develop these faculties through observing, interacting with and imitating others who exhibit more of them. The FGAP therapists have less time at their disposal, but can also, in some cases, work on these qualities with patients during a longer, extended evaluation period.

Some therapists are reluctant to include patients who are too prone to acting-out instead of feeling and reflecting. This is understandable, as it can lead to unsuccessful therapies. It can also have a negative impact on group climate and reduce the opportunity for other patients to improve. The tendency to act out often appears in a patient's relational histories, and in destructive affective outbreaks, frequent use of immature defense mechanisms, numerous break-ups in relationships and possibly also dropping-out of previous therapies. These events can be explored in more detail during the evaluation, the best solution being that the patient and therapist agree to include the dysfunctional pattern in the patient's treatment focus. Whittingham (2018) calls these preparations "inoculation", which is a term borrowed from immunology. If a patient at least partly acknowledges these sides of themself as troublesome and wants to change them, then there is a chance that the alliance with the therapist and the group relationships may prevent the patient from leaving the group *if and when* the potentially destructive situation arises.

Discussion of the composition of the demonstration group

I will now share some thoughts on why these eight patients were included in the demonstration group, based on the guidelines outlined above.

The homogeneity of the demonstration group is primarily ensured by all patients having a *treatment focus* that includes one or more dysfunctional relational patterns, and that these are associated with the problems or symptoms they sought help for. These patterns are likely to be activated through interactions and communication, and can then be explored, understood and potentially changed. The patients were also carefully selected to ensure that their level of personality organization is fairly good, this also representing a homogeneity (Clarkin et al., 2016). Those with a normal, neurotic or higher level of borderline PO are most readily helped by FGAP. They have a certain level of ego-strength and interpersonal skills and a greater ability to work constructively with their own and others' dysfunctional patterns within a time-limited period. This does not, however, mean that these patients have fewer problems or suffer less from symptomatic distress.

There are discrepancies between how all patients in the demonstration group describe their interpersonal behavior using IIP-C and how they appear in their narratives of their close relationships. This goes particularly for Steve, Emily and Anny. Exploring these in the here-and-now mode will lead the exploration to the latent factors that sustain these problems, and lead to occasional "dives" into the patient's psychogenetic history. Patients are given behavioral tasks such as "to be more supportive", "to disclose more tender feelings" or "to show appreciation for openness in others". These tasks will challenge their defensive attitudes and mobilize underlying emotions. All patients will find someone similar to themselves in one way or another in the group. Some, for example, handle conflict situations by feeling guilty and blaming themselves (Anny, Doris), others hold the other part responsible (project), react with distaste or anger (Steve, Emily), withdraw (Henry, Mary) or even alternate between withdrawing and blaming others (Elsie, Frank). Patients also always find models of behavioral patterns that differ from theirs in one or more ways, as shown by the participants' IIP-C.

The thorough FGAP evaluation serves as a "preparation for therapy". Patients are prepared by being constantly encouraged in the evaluation interviews to elaborate and qualify feelings with examples from current or past relationships and situations. They are also encouraged to reflect on and link events in their history. This stimulates or initiates a process of acknowledgement, the objective being to become better acquainted with aspects of themselves. This is perhaps most evident with Emily and Steve. Emily became more open through the evaluation to the idea that her anxiety was due to other things than the fear of panic attacks, and through this gained a more explorative and accepting attitude toward her internal life. Steve also seemed to become less "self-sufficient", and could let go of some of his need to be for example "problem-free" and "supernormal" by acknowledging that he was afraid of being dependent on a woman, while at the same time longing for a relationship.

I would like to conclude by emphasizing the importance of a pragmatic attitude toward composing and starting groups. It is important to get a group going *when* the patient needs it. Patients can drop out or find alternative treatment options if they have to wait too long for a group to start. Better group compositions can, of course, be achieved in larger institutions or at clinics that base their treatment on differentiated group programs, due to a higher number of referrals. A therapist in a private practice will, however, also be able to increase the potential for good groups by starting several groups at the same time, or by continuously having at least one short-term group with a set termination date. This gives the opportunity to recruit new patients while the first group is running. Another option is to collaborate with other practitioners who can refer and take over patients, and also recruit a network of GPs who can refer patients on specific indications. Recruiting patients to "stranger groups" in more scarcely populated parts of the country will always be a problem, as many patients will know each other. A possible solution might then be to attend group therapy in a nearby town.

Chapter 6

The group process

If you paint with a broad brush, it can be said that the group process consists of the sum of all that happens between the participants in the treatment group, including the therapist. This applies to everything that happens both during a specific group session and from session to session, as long as the group lasts. The group starts with the first group meeting, that is, when the therapist(s) and the patients meet at the appointed time in the designated place, and start working within the overruling objective of the group. Strictly speaking, one could say that the process started earlier, because the patients and the therapist usually already will have developed emotional bonds during the evaluation process. In addition, the evaluation may have activated problem areas that some patients have started to work on. Many will also have envisioned what their role in the group will be, and perhaps also had fantasies about how the other members of the group will be.

In most groups with a designated leader, and where members meet regularly to work on specific tasks, some kind of process will be initiated, for example that the participants start communicating and interacting. In many forms of group therapy, however, these processes are not directly commented upon. This is, for example, most often the case in theme-oriented groups (i.e. psychoeducation) or in some forms of group cognitive behavioral therapy (GCBT). Although the content may vary from one session to the next, each session follows a set program, according to a given treatment manual.

In FGAP, on the other hand, the process between the participants is of the utmost importance, both because it discloses and reflects the patients' central psychological problems and because the interactions themselves constitute a necessary resource influencing and promoting change in the individual patient.

In this chapter, I will try to sketch this process, by pointing out both what elements it consists of, how it is formed and how it evolves and changes over time. The point of departure is *closed groups*, that is, groups where all patients begin and end at the same time, with the consequence that everybody follows the entire course of treatment. The task is challenging because many aspects of FGAP affect the group process and will therefore already have been covered in other chapters. The presentation may therefore some places seem somewhat incoherent, but I will start by trying to gather some threads, while referring to other chapters where the

DOI: 10.4324/9781003216377-8

process is discussed. I then give a more general overview of important elements that also characterize the process in FGAP. Thereafter, various therapeutic factors of significance for change follow. In conclusion, I give a more detailed description of the framework that constitutes the short-term group's developmental stages or phases. This is crucial to understanding the phenomena that take place at different times in the life of the group. The framework also provides central and necessary guidance for the therapist when questions arise about how she should intervene in a given situation.

The process of Focused Group Analytic Psychotherapy

FGAP has an overall psychodynamic perspective on the therapeutic group process, and this should be reflected in the treatment culture being developed. Through the collaboration in the group, the therapist wants both to engage the patients in a psychodynamically oriented exploration of the individual's treatment focus and partly to develop a culture of treatment that is specifically adapted to the patients admitted in this group. The interest in this exploration has already been tried to be stimulated during the evaluation. The therapist's interventions will be described in a separate chapter, but it would be impossible to describe the process without elaborating on how the therapist continually and consciously builds and develops a specific treatment culture that involves all members of the group.

An important task for the therapist is to provide didactic input. It may consist of suggestions or instructions on how patients can behave in the group, such as being as open as possible and putting aside self-censoring attitudes as much as possible. In addition, the therapist models an analytical attitude in her relationship with individuals, in interpersonal transactions and with the group as a whole. The invitation to be open will, to some extent, pave the way for transactions where several of the group members engage. Eventually, the individual's more typical, problematic relationship patterns may also manifest as transfererence reactions. This provides opportunities for a psychodynamic exploration of motivational systems, such as desires, effects and impulses, as well as conflicts and defense strategies, and how these collectively influence behavior in the patient's relationship with himself and others.

Group analytic views on the therapy process

Foulkes saw communication as central to the therapeutic process. The essence of his view was that the group participants, through conversation, achieved an ever better articulated and deeper form of understanding in the sense that communication led to more latent aspects of relationships that had not immediately been associated with the manifest content of the interactions. This activity involved all members of the group, and Foulkes saw this collective pursuit as a contradiction to the psychoanalyst's "interpretation" of a phenomenon's underlying meaning (Laplanche & Pontalis, 1988). Again, this highlights the opportunities offered by the group to mobilize the therapeutic potential that other group members represent. Foulkes was also concerned about the development of a free group discussion in group analytic psychotherapy by the group members freely associating with what was happening at all times. The ideal was to develop a working group (Bion, 1961) where the group engaged in each patient's core problems, which through this method became more visible in the group. However, the process in FGAP will appear to be relatively structured and controlled, through the individual patient having their treatment focus and possibly also through increased activity on the part of the therapist, for example, by proposing more latent meaning behind transference elements that are manifested in the group. However, the therapist's activity will vary, because he also wants to mobilize all the participants in the group in the treatment work.

An important mechanism that also contributed to the insight and change that can be achieved in the group, Foulkes called "ego-training-in-action" (Foulkes, 1977). This means that the patient, who in the group may be constantly stimulated to act, manages to postpone this and instead reflects and searches for meaning in the transactions. The new experiences that insight through analysis and testing of alternative relationship strategies represent can over time lead to new responses from the others in the group, which opens up opportunities for new learning and leads to modification of past behavior.

Group-specific group factors

It may also be of interest to briefly repeat the group-specific (therapeutic) factors described by Foulkes. He emphasized that by considering how others in the group behaved in interpersonal situations, the individual patient was given opportunities for *socialization* through the group. He also appreciated the social learning opportunities the group provided by allowing the patient to directly try out new interpersonal strategies. An important factor is the *mirror phenomenon*. The group situation has been compared to a mirror hall, where an individual is confronted with different aspects of his social and psychological character through the reactions of others. Perhaps the individual may also become better aware of how aspects of their own body language are included in the communication. Foulkes also noticed what he called the *condenser phenomenon*, where a sudden discharge of deep and primitive material or of a collection of associated thoughts in the group could take place. The *chain phenomenon* was characterized by its own distinctive free-flowing group discussion similar to the individual's free association, a kind of "chain reaction", where each member contributed an important and idiosyncratic link to the chain. The communication in the group is characterized by both "dynamic matrix" and "foundation matrix". While the latter is based on a common biological and cultural background, "dynamic matrix" represents a created but potentially intimate network developed by the members of the group. All participants speak and understand the language, but interpret and interpret in accordance with the *resonance* or reverberation of the topic being addressed in themselves, thereby constituting an activating factor.

The therapy process is formed by several elements

In individual therapy, the process is more straightforward, and many of its key elements are captured by the concept of the "therapeutic alliance", which according to Bordin (1979) consists of an emotional *bonding* between the patient and the therapist, a certain consensus about *the goals* of the treatment and about what *tasks* the patient must take in order to achieve these goals. In a group, the situation is more complex, as the patients will to a greater or lesser extent also engage and interact with the other members of the group as well as in the group format itself (the group as a whole). The group atmosphere is experienced as a product of everyone's contribution, and the therapist must therefore take into account principles that apply to the dynamics of small groups when he understands what is happening (Burlingame et al., 2013; Lorentzen et al., 2018). MacKenzie (1997, p. 15) has provided an overview of many of the factors research and clinical experience have demonstrated the importance of. Some of them are presented below, such as what the patient and therapist bring into the group, the importance of therapeutic factors, the group's developmental stages and how interaction and multidimensional feedback interact, including therapeutic alliance and group cohesion.

Many of these elements can be found in the description of the process within groups of different theoretical backgrounds, although they may have originated from one of these. Therapeutic alliance, for example, comes from psychoanalytic theory and is often referred to as the working alliance, that is, the patient collaborates with the therapist to explore the background for the patient's symptoms and disorder (Horvath & Luborsky, 1993). Theories of group developmental stages are central both in studies of small group dynamics, in treatment groups (Brabrender & Fallon, 2009) and in systemic theory (Durkin, 1982b), while the concept of "therapeutic factors" is derived from many types of clinical groups and is not least colored by psychoanalytic/interpersonal theory (Sullivan, 1953a) and existential psychology (Yalom, 1980; May, 1994).

What do patients and therapists bring to the therapy?

Both patients and therapists bring with them qualities that are characterized by socio-demographic conditions, such as ethnicity, age, gender, family relationships, education and social class. If the differences in, for example, age, ability level, education or social background are too large, this *may* inhibit the development of an analytical culture or at least require longer than is possible within the FGAP's time frames. Everyone also has their own developmental history, which has been embedded in unique relational patterns, interpersonal skills, self-perception and views of others. In FGAP, a certain heterogeneity in the composition of groups is recommended, with regard to, for example, gender and different types of personality styles and symptom expressions. However, it is emphasized that everyone should have at least one co-patient they can recognize themselves in, and others who can be models for different types of relationship patterns than their own; that is, the group should be assembled according to the so-called Noah's Ark principle (see Chapter 5). Most professionals will probably agree that some homogeneity in terms of ego-strength (see Chapter 4) or resource level is desirable. In this way, everyone will be able to develop in parallel and avoid the group having to use all its resources to help a small number of patients. However, some heterogeneity is also desirable in the FGAP, despite the fact that the time limititation may give less opportunity for exploration of differences.

The notion of inequalities between people presented above may appear to be on a collision course with what Foulkes argued through his concept of the matrix of reason (described in Chapter 2), where he points out how similar people are just because of a common biological, social and cultural background.

Foulkes contrasted what the individual brought with him to the group (foundation matrix) to the dynamic matrix, which encompassed what the group itself developed over time, and became its accumulated experience and history, the group as a whole. He used the image of a network that consisted of all individual mental processes, the psychological medium in which they met, communicated and interacted, to describe the group as a whole. He also emphasized that the processes were transpersonal, that is, they reached the core of each individual. Another thesis was that the group was more fundamental than the individual, a statement he possibly made to distance himself from Freud's early theories, where instinctual satisfaction was portrayed as the most important, while the meaning of the object was sharply dimmed. Although Foulkes as a clinician was concerned with the individual patient, it struck me while working with FGAP that the significance of the individual's personality (character) has been too diminished among many of the successors. This may have resulted in many making a slightly too quick and superficial evaluation of the individual patient's problems and personality, possibly also in a poor planning of the individual patient's treatment. I have therefore tried to emphasize the individual more, not least that the patients bring different characteristics to the group, which means that they may also need different approaches in the treatment. Despite similarities, humans develop on the basis of different genetic, temperament-based dispositions as well as environmental influences for particular individuals. Through the interactions in the group, some of the relational qualities rooted in the individual's primary network, consciously or unconsciously are activated constituting the multiple transferences (distortions/projections) manifested in the interactions among group members. It is precisely these transactions that the therapist wants the group to stop by and explore. This may clarify aspects of the individual's attachment style (to the primary object) and more or less elaborated relationship patterns to other members of the family group, which may be of importance in creating interpersonal problems and maintaining mental suffering.

Patients seeking help also often bring with them previous experiences of treatment, which can affect their expectations in both a negative and a positive direction. The therapist, in turn, will influence the therapy both through his professional role and the status it provides, and by his personal qualities, family background and sociocultural history. In addition comes the therapist's theoretical orientation and professional experience. Tensions arising from differences in experiences or perceptions are easily activated in the meeting between the parties, which in turn can be growth-promoting and relationship-developing, depending on how they cope and develop further.

Interaction and multidimensional response (feedback)

The group is a microcosm of numerous interactions involving many. This means that group therapy offers an environment for "real" relationships to a greater extent than individual therapy. When the individual patient presents his or her personal problems, this is often done with more anxiety in groups than in individual therapy because of the concern for the other's reactions. A positive and accepting group atmosphere therefore results in a more active self-exposure earlier in the course of treatment. The other patients are often affected by and take after those who are more open. In a short-term group, it is obvious that time must be shared in order for everyone to have some time, which makes it more important, and for some easier, to speak. Increasing development of group cohesion and explicit group norms will contribute in the same direction. Exploration of the individual's problems depends on a mutual commitment and a mutual interest in understanding each other's problems in the group. Therefore, in addition to the therapist's response, patients must also consider the reactions of fellow patients. These mean that there is a richer access to alternative views in a group compared to individual therapy. Patients' mutual involvement usually starts early in the process. First, the feedback can be strongly colored by the sender's own problem areas. Gradually, the responses will become more objective, both because responses from multiple participants provide a greater nuance of views, and because patients, by developing increased security and autonomy, are able to reject comments that are perceived as too foreign.

The interactional environment thus makes the group a more challenging and varied learning situation than is usually encountered in individual therapy. Despite this, many patients who fail to open up in individual therapy will "melt" because of the supportive, but persistent pressure other group members exert through expectations that everyone should convey something personal. From the beginning, the therapist works on how the individual patient relates to feedback, and both tendencies to reject or to swallow everything that is said should meet with the same exploratory interest. Destructive polarization of "power" is often calmed down by fellow patients commenting empathically "from the sidelines". The fact that critical events involve multiple actors is also the most complicated part of the group model. Individual patients may also, like the therapist, become the focus of other members or the entire group's rejection and criticism, thereby making a potentially harmful experience. Groups are potent media!

The group process often accelerates or is supported by the so-called therapeutic factors, which constitute a separate area of research in group psychotherapy. Several of the factors are considered to constitute mechanisms behind change (Bloch & Crouch, 1985), but many are overlapping and will interact in a dynamic interaction, making it more difficult to understand the significance of the individual factor. I have mentioned many of these factors on and between the lines above and will elaborate on the significance of the factors in the next section.

Therapeutic factors

The historical background for research on therapeutic factors is discussed in Chapter 9. Here I only include what is relevant in contemporary clinical practice and especially FGAP.

Irvin D. Yalom (b. 1931), an American psychiatrist inspired by interpersonal psychoanalysis (Sullivan, 1953a, 1953b) and existential psychology (May, 1994), has a central position among those who have done research and written about therapeutic factors in group therapy (Yalom & Leszcz, 2005). Although he recognizes that the factors may be closely interwoven in a dynamic process, he has separated them to study them individually. He emphasizes that not everyone is equally important, and that the significance of the individual factor varies with the type of group, clinical population, target setting and group context. After interviewing 20 patients selected by their therapists because they had successfully completed therapy, Yalom's research group originally found 12 categories of factors, which were transferred to a 60-paragraph questionnaire. Patients were then asked to rate these items according to their significance. The factors have remained almost unchanged since Yalom (1995) did his first study, and I present the 11 factors presented in the last edition of this book (Yalom & Leszcz, 2020). The factors are briefly defined and commented on:

1. Instillation of hope. This often happens when someone tells fellow patients that they have previously received good help through group therapy, by referring to good results from research by the therapist, or by the patients themselves discovering new opportunities for change. This factor can be useful because many seek treatment in a phase characterized by resignation, pessimism and low self-esteem.
2. Universality. Patients recognize themselves in others and thus feel less isolated or alone.
3. Imparting information. Co-patients and therapists sometimes come up with recommendations, advice and information about mental disorders and psychodynamic relationships.
4. Altruism. The factor entails a desire to help others and the patients find that it gives pleasure that what they say can mean something positive to others.

5. The corrective recapitulation of the primary family group. Group participation provides opportunities to relive and understand what it was like to grow up in your own family. The patient meets in the group others who can recall close family members and thereby better see and understand their own difficult sides. Many may perceive the group as more benevolent and accepting than the family and receive a "corrective emotional experience" (Alexander & French, 1946), which can lead to change for the individual. Distortions that are rooted in misinterpretation of one's own and others' motives are reduced, and patients gain a more realistic view of what happens in interpersonal transactions.
6. Development of socializing techniques. The group becomes an arena where you can learn from other people's behaviors and try out new ways to relate to others and themselves.
7. Imitative behavior. This means taking after others. One can imitate and try out behaviors that one sees in others, which can eventually lead to attitudes or traits becoming one's own (identification). This is the same as Corsini and Rosenberg (1955) called "spectator therapy", and which others have called temporary learning.
8. Interpersonal learning. Through interaction, feedback from others, reflection and increased self-understanding lay the basis for changing inappropriate behavior. Freud called the irrationality of human behavior transference as it manifested itself in the therapy situation.
9. Group cohesiveness. A simple definition of this is "all the forces that hold a group together" or "how attractive a group is to its members". This is possibly one of the most important factors in groups, and it will be discussed in more detail in the next section and in the chapter on empirical research (Chapter 9).
10. Catharsis. This really means "purification by expressing their feelings". There is a difference between crying in a single room and doing it in a group. The therapeutic in the situation will be conditional on the patient feeling cared for.
11. Existential factors have gained a central place in Yalom's writings (Yalom & Leszcz, 2020). The experience of the authors is that many patients consider these factors highly, while therapists tend to underestimate them. It may be that patients through discussion in the group get better contact with important aspects of life and to a greater extent take these seriously. The themes may be, for example, individual responsibility and freedom, the inevitability of death, the consequences of honesty and falsehood and the importance of purposefulness as opposed to chance and destiny.

I think all of these factors are important in group psychotherapy, a little depending on the type of groups and patients involved, and possibly also what phase one is in for each therapy. The awakening of hope, altruism and universality are often called the "supporting factors". They were identified relatively early and considered to be particularly important for hospitalized, somewhat demoralized patients. However, I believe that these factors are also important in FGAP, especially in the early phase of therapy, as uncertainty about whether one will be accepted in the group and anxiety about rejection may be stronger. The factors are often also a necessary prerequisite for the patients to gradually dare to disclose vulnerable sides of themselves so that interactions and group cohesion develop. Group cohesion is an important factor, which is also a prerequisite for patients to relate to each other and to become more open and personal, which also includes exposing vulnerable and shameful relationships. An important part of this is being able to share emotions (catharsis), which gives life to interactions and depth to relationships. From a psychodynamic point of view, it is of course important that patients gain insight into their own conflicts and dysfunctional interpersonal patterns, and that this insight is used in trying out new ways to relate in and out of therapy. Part of the core of FGAP is to achieve greater self-understanding, which, in Yalom's form, comes under "interpersonal learning". The same factor is also important in the work on the treatment focus the patient has prepared, and the desire is that the interaction can be corrective, even emotionally. Corrective recapitulation of the primary family group will only partially be possible in a time-limited therapy, but this is also a factor affecting the patient's treatment focus, as this often has roots in relation to the primary family. Imitative behavior is a precursor to identification (and internalization), a factor traditionally considered central to psychoanalysis. By observing others, it becomes possible to look for attitudes as well as behavior and thereby develop social techniques. The interactional aspect increases the opportunities for interpersonal learning, which, together with self-understanding, is closely related to "working-through" in psychoanalysis and Foulkes's concept of "ego-training-in-action". Group cohesion, which is described in more detail in the next section, is the group-specific factor that correlates most strongly with a positive treatment outcome (Burlingame et al., 2011; Lorentzen et al., 2018). It is important to work actively to develop cohesion at an early stage in the group, especially in short-term groups. However, group cohesion can vary by hour and over time, for example, under the influence of negative, critical events. One of Yalom's factors that may be less important in FGAP is providing information, a factor that points more toward psychoeducation. This does not prevent patients from frequently stating much appreciation of advice from fellow patients and therapists.

Therapeutic alliance, group cohesion

The therapeutic alliance between patient and therapist is the strongest predictor of treatment outcome in individual psychotherapy (Flückiger et al., 2018). In group therapy, the relational conditions are more complex and complicated, although the alliance between the individual patient and the therapist also plays an important role for change here (Lorentzen et al., 2004; Joyce et al., 2007). Usually, it is the patient's assessment of the alliance that is most strongly associated with outcomes (Horvath et al., 2011). However, group cohesion is traditionally seen as a more central factor in the group, defined as the sum of all the forces that hold the members together. Cohesion has been described in previous literature as a feeling of belonging to the group, of being accepted and of being involved in something important. Here, too, patients' assessment of cohesion has a stronger correlation with a positive outcome than the therapist's assessment. However, recent research (Johnson et al., 2005; Krogel et al., 2013; Burlingame et al., 2011; Bakali et al., 2009; Lorentzen et al., 2018) points out that cohesion can be divided into different qualitative aspects: positive affiliation, positive cooperation and a negative reaction. These aspects arise between the group's actors (structural elements), that is, between individual patients, between patient and therapist and between individual patients and the group as a whole. This creates the opportunity to investigate the relationship between the individual relationships and outcomes. A separate questionnaire, Group Questionnaire (Krogel, 2009; Krogel, Burlingame et al., 2013), including a Norwegian version of this, "Questionnaire on the group" (translated by Lorentzen et al., 2016), is described in more detail in Chapter 9.

In a group where the degree of cohesion is strong, security is also much higher and offers completely different opportunities for working with sensitive, personal material than is possible in a newly established or unsafe group.

Groups developmental phases (stages)

In a closed group, the group process is the same for everyone. Several clinicians and researchers have observed and described a nearly similar progression, especially in closed, time-limited groups, where the group appears to go through certain stages or phases (Brabrender & Fallon, 2009). It seems as if the group at each stage is gathering *on specific interactional tasks*, which in turn appear in *typical forms of behavior*. The FGAP emphasizes four phases: engagement, differentiation, interpersonal work and termination, all of which are distinctive and present specific challenges for the individual patient, for the group as a whole and not least for the therapist. These challenges must be addressed in order for the group and patients to have optimal development conditions (MacKenzie, 1997, p. 43; Lorentzen, 2014). During the initial phase, supporting factors are often strongly mobilized. However, one can expect a more challenging attitude during the differentiation phase and in the interpersonal work phase, while repair attempts and the desire for other members to "take back their projections" often manifest themselves more strongly in the termination phase. By this is meant that reconciliation occurs by the fact that several participants take responsibility for contributing to critical events that have occurred along the way, while in the current situation they placed all the responsibility on the other.

The rationale for using the developmental stages of the therapeutic work is derived from system theory, where it is argued that events at one level will affect other levels. This means that the development process in each patient will go in parallel with the development process that the group as a whole is going through. Therefore, it is important that all patients participate at every stage.

MacKenzie (1997, p. 44) has prepared a detailed overview of the group's developmental stages that includes the group's and individual's task, focus for boundaries, threat to individual members and possible solution attempts for the individual and group at each stage of the process. However, I think such a form can easily seem constructed and normative. I therefore present a simplified edition that will hopefully provide greater scope for exploring unconscious (underlying) driving forces in patients and the group. However, some of the tasks and challenges MacKenzie describes are mentioned during the different phases (Table 6.1).

Opening (engagement, 2–4 sessions)

This is the phase where members meet for the first time, introduce themselves to one another and begin to become acquainted. Each member already has some connection to the therapist. I therefore welcome everyone to the first meeting and ask the patients to introduce themselves to each other. This includes, in addition to names, that they also tell about why they are in the group, a brief background story, but most importantly, they inform the group about the treatment focus they have worked out with the therapist. Patients often seek early advice on how to relate to the other patients or the group, and the therapist must take a more active role. The "threat" to the individual patient may be a fear of not being accepted and included, but on the contrary being rejected by the others in the group. The solution to this is that despite the anxiety, the patient dares to take the challenge and show or present something personal to the others. Ideally, each patient should recognize themselves and experience that some of the others have similar problems as themselves, for example, experience that others may also have anxiety in association with others (universality). In this phase, it is a challenge for each patient to become part of the community and overcome the fear of being isolated. The group's task and challenge consists of starting the development of a group identity and building group cohesion.

The therapist has many tasks in this phase. Firstly, it is important to keep an eye on each group member. At the same time, work begins on establishing the

Table 6.1 Overview of the group's stages, their duration and characteristics

Stage	Duration	Characteristics
Opening, engagement	Two to four sessions	Feeling of community "What happens here is something special". Anxieties about belonging in the group
Differentiation	Two to four sessions	Assert oneself and find strategies for handling of tensions, to open up, build cohesion
Interpersonal work	8 to 12 sessions	Confrontation and introspection: work with own and others' dysfunctional interpersonal patterns
Termination	Two to three sessions	Loss and separation: to have received enough in therapy and life. Everyone is responsible for oneself. What have I learned?

group's boundaries with the outside world and promoting the development of cohesion, both of which are important elements of the group's treatment culture (Burlingame et al., 2002; Burlingame et al., 2011; Lorentzen et al., 2018). The therapist promotes group norms and strengthens the group's external boundaries by emphasizing that "what happens here is unique and different from what happens in other social situations". He or she stimulates interaction by emphasizing that it is perfectly okay to express thoughts and feelings as they emerge in the situation. Such statements and comments such as "what happens in the group stays in the group" can reinforce the norms presented in the initial individual conversations. By stimulating interaction between group members, pointing out similarities and differences and asking others what they think, the therapist builds group cohesion. The therapist also displays attitudes and presents specific types of questions or comments and models the behavior that can be fruitful in an exploratory group. Further development of a psychodynamic treatment culture is underway. In this phase, participants must be protected, statements should be redefined if someone is strongly criticized or attacked and patients should be calmed down or stopped if they almost immediately present too much, highly personal and highly emotionally charged information. Early in therapy, supportive therapeutic factors are particularly important, such as acceptance, universality ("we are all in the same boat"), instilling hope, and altruism, which means that patients feel they can mean something to each other. During the early stages, the therapist wants to ensure membership and commitment to the group and the other patients. It can also be important to look for reactions to what it is like to be in and expose themselves in the group, not least to address ambivalence and negative expectations. Another central theme is the growing recognition of the group as a unique place that has its very special rules, different from ordinary social situations. Comments like this coming from the therapist will strengthen the group's external boundary (toward the outside world).

The group's task in this phase is solved when all members are determined to participate, and when everyone has participated in discussions and shown some of themselves at least to some extent. Patients must feel and decide that they want to belong to the group and that they want to work with themselves (change). Important keywords may be that they have an experience of community, and that they have experienced that what is happening in the group is something special and different from what is otherwise experienced in social situations.

Differentiation (2–4 sessions)

Unlike in the previous phase, where equality was desired, patients often feel the need to assert themselves as unique individuals. They go from having a common atmosphere to positioning themselves a little more in relation to each other and may be thinking: "we are not so equal", "my problems are bigger (or smaller) than the problems of NN", "there is something I don't like about that man" or "it was an exciting girl!" Such thoughts may lead to a little more assertive behavior and a desire to express one's own unique character. Some may point out that there are differences between themselves and other members.

The therapist's authority is also sometimes questioned, which may be reminiscent of a kind of "youth rebellion" that occurs mostly for the sake of the rebellion, although there is also an opportunity for patients to help define group norms. In this phase, the atmosphere can become more negative and confrontational when disagreements and potential conflicts emerge. The threat to the individual may now be the fear of getting into conflict with other members or the therapist, and the challenge is to dare to assert themselves and stand out as different, but also to allow others to do the same. This applies not least to exposing your own problematic sides, which can often be colored by soreness, anger or shame. The group's challenge is to develop strategies to collaborate despite differences or disagreements between team members, and to educate patients in a collaborative culture where problems are openly discussed despite conflicts.

The therapist's most important tasks are to follow developments in the group and with each group member. Work on developing group cohesion and group identity continues. In addition to maintaining and further developing the group's boundaries to the outside world, the therapist is also aware of the boundaries around each patient and between the different patients who interact. The therapist continues to stimulate exploration of interactions within the group through comments and questions, recognizes that there are many subjective realities and even tries to demonstrate that fruitful dialogue is possible, even in situations where the individual is subjected to criticism or involved in disagreement.

This stage may have therapeutic potential for many because the two central tasks the group has, namely learning to address problems in a positive confrontational way and developing enough confidence in the group to be able to talk even if one disagrees with others, are central problems for many, especially neurotic and disabled patients.

The group challenge is solved when team members can work together despite contradictions and differences, and when patients feel safe enough to both expose vulnerable, shame-stricken sides by themselves and to confront other patients with problematic sides they disclose in the group.

Interpersonal work (8–12 sessions)

In the group, an increasing capacity to be both supportive and confrontational has gradually developed, which provides opportunities to explore relationship patterns and problematic behavior. The individual patient is now more able to disclose more negative and controversial aspects of himself and confront others with their less desirable traits, as they appear in the interactions in the group. The challenge for patients is to be self-observant, reflective and to accept the implications of establishing relationships. Patients have gradually taken on more responsibility for the group work, and it is expected that they will explore the problems that brought them to the group. The individual is now more frequently inquiring into sides of himself and is confident enough to disclose more personal qualities in the group. The process of strong emphasis on the individuality that started in the differentiation phase is thereby consolidated. The tool is partly introspection and partly feedback from the others in the group in the form of reflection and confrontation (mirroring). Individual behavioral or relational patterns and potential distortions in interactions are also subject to collective exploration within the group. The group is now able to address the problems of its members in a more direct and pervasive way and its main task is to address and work constructively with the problematic interpersonal patterns of the various patients. However, many have a constant fear of not being understood, and it can be daunting to be open about vulnerable personal problems. However, the personal nature of the material can also increase the degree of closeness between the members, which in turn gives rise to an examination of the relationships within the group. An increasing sense of intimacy may arise; sometimes it is also romantically colored, which in turn can activate anxiety and possibilities for rejection, with subsequent loss of self-esteem. During the process of understanding relationships, themes such as autonomy and over-involvement are activated, and relationships that are associated with dependency and control may be touched upon during this work.

The main task of the therapist is to support patients in opening up, stimulating interaction, recalling the treatment focus if necessary, continuing to build and develop tolerance for differences between self and other and to convey values of openness and equality. It is important to work in the here-and-now by drawing attention to what is happening in the group and limiting the time spent on stories about things happening outside of therapy.

Signals that can show the therapist that the group is actively in this phase are that patients can alternately between being both disclosing and confrontational, that they can focus on their own and others' dysfunctional interpersonal patterns and that there is a relatively safe and supportive, exploratory atmosphere.

Termination (2–3 sessions)

Ending is a particularly important part of the closed short-term group because all participants end at the same time. This magnifies and intensifies the experience, and this in turn can activate feelings about previous endings, breaks, separation and loss. The emotional strength can be partly attributed to the intensity that has developed in connectedness during the time the group members have spent together. Many patients in a group often try to "forget" this phase, which increases the therapist's responsibility to bring the end to the path. The threats to the individual patient can, among many others, consist of one or more of the challenges outlined below:

- Patients may feel that they have not had enough back from joining the group, just as they have not had enough out of life.
- They are reluctant to end relationships with people they have met through the group, which has been of great importance to them.

- For some, past loss experiences may be activated at the upcoming end.
- Patients are confronted with the fact that they must again manage on their own, without the support of the group.

All of these themes have strong existential undertones and are important in the maturation process. The intensity of the termination phase will often be directly related to the time the group has spent together. However, this does not prevent the termination process from also being highly emotionally charged in a time-limited group, if successful, and if the therapist and other group members have made an effort to engage emotionally with each other.

Participants must now manage on their own, as they had to before the group started. This can lead to isolation and loneliness. Some solve this by internalizing and thus taking the group with them, by recognizing or accepting the loneliness and loss, or by mobilizing new or old human resources. The task and the challenge for the group members is to be close and open up even if they are to separated and manage on their own. The therapist's most important task is to "keep the members in the termination phase", possibly exploring comments such as "it will be nice to be able to do something different on Tuesday afternoon" as a possible expression of trivialization or denial of possible loss. How each member experiences the ending should be clearly stated in the group, not least because everyone experiences it differently. The focus of attention is the parting with the others in the group, while at the same time the therapist also contributes to the patients becoming more concerned with the "outer group", i.e. the conditions at home. A successful conclusion is characterized by the patients accepting responsibility for themselves, while recognizing the importance the group, therapist and other members have had for them.

This model of the therapy group's developmental stages allows the therapist to orientate himself in the process. As a leader, therapist and interacting member of the group, the therapist will continuously be involved in strong emotional transactions that may challenge his ability to reflect. When the therapist "leans back" at certain intervals, this framework provides clues to understanding the interaction in the here-and-now situation, while at the same time helping the therapist to intervene to bring the group forward.

A clinical example

I conclude this chapter with a clinical example that shows the interaction between some of the patients in the demonstration group early in the phase of interpersonal work.

In one session, it was pointed out that Mary seemed to be distancing herself and switching off contact with the others in the group, and Emily, one of the other patients, then kindly asked what she was concerned about. Mary then replied quite annoyed that Steve had interrupted her in the middle of a sentence. Steve was a young man who could often be too active and unresponsive, and who among other things had as a treatment focus to develop a more expectant, listening and empathic side. Mary had said before the interruption that she felt her husband had let her down by handing over all the care of the house and the children to her. In response to her claims to have been interrupted, Steve steps up and denies angrily that he had been rude to her. Henry, who has a problematic relationship with conflicts and anger and therefore quickly becomes submissive or evasive in situations where this occurs, immediately begins to explain that Steve did not really interrupt, but that he had been eager to tell something positive that had happened at work. The example is a typical sequence from a group in which three patients, in a row, through what Foulkes called a free-floating group discussion, "commented on one another" and at the same time exposed some of the behavioral pattern they agreed to work with in the group (treatment focus).

The therapist, who has been quietly observing the group for a while, has recorded how Steve sweeps Mary aside when she talks about being let down by her husband. The therapist is also struck by how Mary's annoyed response "scares" Henry out on the field to cover up signs of conflict and anger. She then remembers that Steve's relationship with his father was partly characterized by his father's traveling a great deal and partly neglected Steve even when he was at home. As a 16-year-old, Steve had almost declared war on his father after the father had asked Steve's grandmother, whom Steve had strongly associated with, to move out after living with the family for many years. Dad died suddenly while Steve was in the military, without any reconciliation between them. The therapist wonders if Mary's story has created an imbalance in Steve's inner relational world, where painful feelings associated with self-object representations that linked father and him together were suppressed and denied. The therapist then decides to stop at this sequence. She knows it is not obvious that those involved are aware that everyone's focus is being affected, but finds that the group is confident enough to work on what has happened. The intervention can be simple: "Let's stop a little; here I think something important is happening!" The others are invited to reflect on and explore the sequence where everyone has been affected (transpersonal perspective). Based on the manifest, everyone is invited to explore the "underlying", which is related to several of the patients' focus and relational history. The sequence in the group can be recapitulated and provides potentially great opportunities for what are called "corrective emotional experiences" (Alexander & French, 1946; Palvarini, 2010; cf. corrective relational experience: Buchele & Rutan, 2017). By starting from what happened here-and-now in the group, and by downplaying the negative aspects of aggressive oubursts, by defining them as communication attempts, an atmosphere of wonder, reflection and exploration can be created at best. And if similarly more or less stereotypical, dysfunctional plays from the individual are constantly met with interest and understanding, the opportunities for mutual learning also increase. This contrasts with an almost automatic rejection of one another's views, which would lead to an escalation of conflicts and "retraumatization" of those involved. The prerequisite for change is of course conditional on patients and therapist being open and accessible to new impulses and through this learning something new.

Chapter 7

The therapist in Focused Group Analytic Psychotherapy (FGAP)

Much has been written about the importance and responsibilities of the therapist in the chapters in this book on the history of group therapy, the description of psychoanalytic and group analytic theory and in the discussions of evaluation, selection and preparation of patients. The importance of the therapist's role is also emphasized in the chapter on the therapy process. I will, however, in this chapter describe FGAP therapist roles and responsibilities that have not been covered earlier in the book. There are similarities between the role of the FGAP therapist and the role of the therapist in other types of group therapy. I therefore, for didactic reasons, sometimes compare the role of the FGAP therapist with the role of the longer therapy group analyst (GA).

Leadership role in FGAP: responsibilities and tasks

The following are central FGAP therapist tasks:

- To create and maintain the structure of the group and to understand and intervene constructively when boundary incidents occur
- To initiate and facilitate the development of the group process and to engage each group member and the group in this
- To be the foremost representative of an analytic attitude, and, through this model, to demonstrate and explain to the group members how to relate to each other, and to promote the quick development of an analytic treatment culture
- To work with meaning creation through translation and interpretation

The therapist's function as a model is crucial in the tasks specified above. The therapist should accept all communication as valuable, be directive in a moderate way and contribute to the translation, clarification and interpretation of preconscious and unconscious material, so that group members can learn something about themselves and the others. The therapist also makes him or herself available to the group as a transference object, and is willing to comment on the relationships that develop between them and the patients and make them the subject of

DOI: 10.4324/9781003216377-9

analysis. The therapist should lead, but also should to some extent be led by the group. The therapist should also stimulate interactions and *be present in a controlled way*. One example of this approach is not utilizing the group as an audience for personal, narcissistic gains. The therapist should, ideally, leave much of the exploring and teasing out the meaning of transactions in the group to the group members but should, when this does not happen, place events in the correct psychodynamic perspective.

Both the FGAP and GA therapist have three key roles, namely as the *dynamic administrator* of the group, as a *therapist* and as a *group member* (Behr & Hearst, 2005).

The therapist as the dynamic administrator of the group is responsible for creating the group's structure, and the boundaries that separate the group from other social situations. This includes deciding who joins or leaves the group, and maintaining the structure or what one can call "the group analytic situation". The physical conditions define the space where the group meets. There are, however, also psychological dimensions that define the group's psychological structure and boundaries. A patient who suddenly and quietly leaves the room during a group session is, for example, from one perspective just a person opening a door and leaving. This action is, however, within the psychological space of the group, a highly charged communication which has an impact on all who are left behind. It touches a number of "boundaries"; boundaries between talking and silence, between being inside and outside the group and between commitment and indifference. The crossing of a boundary such as this also creates a highly charged communication which can generate strong feelings and fantasies in the other group members. Such an incident should therefore be explored and discussed in the group, to make sense of what occurred. Absence, both physical and mental, may also have a similar effect. A group member who regularly arrives late or leaves early, or who introduces mainly trivial topics that are void of emotional involvement or connection with the problems that brought the patient to therapy, may also have a strong impact.

Boundaries also exist *within* the group, for example between patients and the therapist, and between individual group members (MacKenzie, 1997). Patterns such as slightly intrusive, unempathetic or hostile inputs or interactions represent boundary crossings, and can be easier to spot early-on in FGAP than in GA within the matrix of interactions and communications of the individual members, because FGAP is more directive. Such patterns can be contextually triggered, but often express typical personality traits of the patients, thus making "work in the boundary areas" an especially important tool in time-limited therapies, as time is scarce.

There are similarities between the roles of the GA and FGAP therapist. The FGAP group is, however, closed, all patients starting and ending at the same time. GA groups are "slow-open", with patients leaving the group when treatment is considered to be over, and new patients being admitted individually or in pairs. Both the GA and FGAP therapist engages all group members in the process, helps develop the process and uncovers meaning in transactions. The differences between the two therapies such as in the time perspective, use of treatment focus, the use of thinking in stages and working in the here-and-now mode means, however, that *different types of input* are required. I will elucidate this further in later sections, and cover aspects such as the therapist's stance, the supportive-interpretative dimension and the therapist's interventions. I will also provide some guidelines on how the therapist should intervene in FGAP, and illustrate this with clinical examples.

The therapist as a *group member* abandons the role of administrator or interpreter, and comments more as an equal to the other group members.

The roles of the therapist are intertwined, but are described separately here for didactic purposes. Considerable responsibility is, even so, linked to all roles. Therapists should therefore always place great emphasis on maintaining a reflective and controlled presence, but should not allow this to prevent them from being open and genuine.

The therapist as leader and authority

Foulkes's understanding of the importance of mobilizing the group's therapeutic potential, and of engaging and involving all group members in the therapeutic work, is the strongest element of his work (Foulkes, 1977). He therefore downplayed his role as an authority figure, renaming the therapist "conductor", depicting the therapeutic group through this as an orchestra, the therapist's role being to get the participants to "play together". The same applies to FGAP. Interactions and feedback from the other group members play an important role as corrective factors in this active interpersonal therapy. Some professionals have, however, interpreted Foulkes's stance as being one in which he "relinquished leadership and authority" (see, e.g., Karterud, 2015). Those who have sung in a choir or played in a band know that the conductor is the "boss". Conductors, however, while being required to faithfully follow the intentions of the composer, also have the opportunity to add their own interpretations and personal taste. My understanding of Foulkes's metaphor is that therapists should, through their personality, knowledge, skills and authority, strive to mobilize and activate *all members* of the group (orchestra) and through this optimize interactions and communication to "create" as much mental growth as possible. It is therefore hard to believe that Foulkes, when faced with a "locked situation" in a group of prolonged, oppressive and unproductive silence or open, destructive fighting, would passively let time go by without intervening. This view also seems to be shared by other authors who have discussed Foulkes's relationship with authority and leadership (Hutchinson, 2009; Behr & Hearst, 2005).

The therapist has a clear leadership role in FGAP, not least because the limited time available requires a focus on how time is spent and shared. The therapist must also actively keep patients within their treatment focus, so they make an early start on the change process and therefore have the greatest chance of achieving their therapy goals. The group must also be actively led into the here-and-now mode, which requires the therapist to take active responsibility for maintaining a focus on interactions *in*, rather than outside, *the group*. The analysis of emotionally charged interactions in the group provides a greater potential for emotional insight and new learning than reported narratives brought from outside the group. This does not, however, mean that outside events are unimportant. It is, however, important in FGAP that the therapist keeps each patient and the group "on track" toward their treatment goals. The therapist should also, however, understand that exploring each patient's treatment focus may expand and deepen the problem complexes that appeared to be most urgent early in the treatment. The initial treatment focus may therefore need to be adjusted along the way. It should not become a straightjacket!

Challenges for the FGAP therapist

The short-term perspective is key in FGAP and in the therapist's behavior. There is less time for each patient to open up, to attach to the therapist and others, to work with resistance, to attain insight and through this to work through conflicts and problems. The therapist's active role in promoting each patient's and the group's progress through the stages of development (see Chapter 6) help make aspects of the role of leader more salient, and so make FGAP a more structured treatment than GA.

Higher level of activity

A short-term therapist must think quickly and combine the ability of introspection and reflection with action. This does not mean that the therapist should be zealous or domineering. They should, however, use their faculties to make the right strategic choices and do what is necessary to advance the process for each patient and the group, based on the overall treatment goals and the framework. This implies that therapists should *avoid* long periods of inactivity, that they are *active* and are willing to *interpret or share* their hypotheses of what is happening in the group and that they *avoid appearing unresponsive or "unknowing"* when they are not.

Work in the here-and-now mode and within the treatment focus

The stories that patients *bring to the group* may be emotionally charged, may be connected to treatment focus and therefore may to a certain degree be relevant to and capture the interest of the group members. The extent of such narratives must, however, be limited in a short-term group. Material linked to the patients' treatment foci and which emerge as problematic relationship patterns in the group should instead be prioritized. Patients in crisis, for example, should be given the time to discuss urgent problems. The group may also, sometimes, need "lubrication" if the level of emotionality drops, which can be stimulated by giving room for emotional episodes from the patients' lives outside the group.

The therapist must also determine how to prioritize group members and decide whether working with an individual patient or at a group level (at a specific point in time) is most important. A further dilemma can be how far a theoretical discussion of a topic should be stretched before the therapist points out that those involved in the discussion seem to lack emotional commitment.

Less time to repair ruptures of the therapeutic alliance

There is often too little time to solicit reactions from everyone. The therapist should therefore try to assess how interventions are perceived by all group members. It can also be difficult to "turn the clock back" and repair any ruptures that occur. Comments on the negative traits of individual patients should therefore be presented in a supportive way, or should be addressed to a subgroup or the group as a whole if several patients are involved. The quality of the therapeutic alliance and the strength of cohesion in the group will often determine how comments are received.

Focus on group structure and boundaries

The "boundaries and structure focus" approach originates from systems theory (Bertalanaffy, 1968), and has been subsequently adopted by systemic and psychodynamic group therapy (Durkin, 1982a, 1982b). Time-limited therapies usually are more structured than longer therapies. The therapist is therefore more active in time-limited therapies in exploring boundary phenomena, as it is important to quickly capture the characteristics of the person. Patients soon discover, when they begin to talk about themselves in a therapy group, that talking about themselves in this group is different from communicating in other social contexts. This discovery confirms the patient's perception that there is a boundary around the group. The individual patient and the therapist also have boundaries, and there are interpersonal boundaries, boundaries around subgroups and inner (intra-psychic) boundaries in the group context. The therapist can therefore question, for example, how each member relates to the group as a whole? Whether all group members see themselves as part of, or whether some see themselves as being outside, the group? Do some patients often arrive late, rushing into the room and interrupting? Do some patients stay away when they realize they are late? How do patients relate to the therapist's boundaries? Is the therapist often interrupted in the middle of an intervention? Do patients often continue to talk after the therapist has announced that the time is up? Are there patients who seem to be engaged in lively discussions in the waiting room, but become silent as they enter the room and take their seat? Are there patients who always seem to address only the therapist, or who always talk as if the therapist were not present? Do some patients treat other group members as advisors or an audience? Do some have such strong internal boundaries that they always show a "poker face" and convey little about what is going on inside them?

Greater attention to termination

Experience has shown that the limited time factor can often have a structuring effect on the individual patient's development process. The rate of a patient's progress through the therapy stages seems, however, to be controlled by both conscious and unconscious forces in patients. These forces include, for example, ego-strength, type of defenses, degree of traumatization and type and degree of psychopathology. There is, however, often a great variation between patients. At one extreme is the patient who wants to go in to therapy, but who quickly regresses to a helpless, dependent state shortly after therapy begins. This type of patient may need a longer or a different type of treatment than FGAP, and may therefore have to be taken out of the group. Good evaluation and selection will, however, hopefully make this a rare occurrence. This type of patient may be able to continue in the group if they receive individual therapy conjointly, and also possibly use medication. The other extreme is the patient who "never really starts in therapy" and goes "untouched" through the different stages of the process, therapy for them being an intellectual exercise.

Most patients will, however, become involved in the process. Many will also be reluctant to end the therapy as it approaches, and therapists should therefore remain alert to and remind the group of the upcoming end. They must also understand that patients have their own unique ways of dealing with termination and separation, so that these can be analyzed in the final stage of the therapy. The therapist may sometimes, based on a patient's history, early gain insight in how a specific patient approaches therapy termination. He may then also have taken this into account during therapy, and tried to strengthen a patient's defenses or actively encouraged them to improve their social network.

The stance of the psychodynamic therapist. Objective perception or transference?

The therapists' influence is made up both of what he or she says and does (interventions, technique), and who and how they are as persons (Wampold & Imel, 2015). It is therefore important that therapists know something about how they are and how they affect or are frequently perceived by others when working with transference reaction, such as in FGAP. This can help the therapist achieve a more accurate understanding of the patient's ways of dealing with given situations. An example might be that a patient perceives the therapist as strict, critical and somewhat judgmental. This can be due to the patient's experience being colored by "transference", and by the patient seeing the therapist through lenses colored by experiences with central caregivers in their upbringing. The patient's impression can, however, also be a precise and objective observation of the person and be similar to the impressions of the other members of the group. Impressions are often based on a combination of the two. A therapist with some of these traits may more easily activate the patient's own object representations having similar qualities, which will in turn contribute to a distorted experience of the other. Other group members can also activate a patient in the same way. It is often also important in an interactional, interpersonal context such as FGAP, that therapists admit to their idiosyncrasies having an impact on others, as this makes it easier for the patient to take responsibility for "their part" in episodes and the ambiguities that arise. Therapists that are open about their potential impact on others may also appear to be more genuine and honest in their interactions, most patients being familiar with the therapist's habitual ways of communicating.

The therapist's opinion will often, despite the therapist's attempts to be non-dogmatic, be given *more weight* than those of other members of the group. This underlines the additional responsibility the professional role of therapist brings, the role including professional knowledge, agreement to provide assistance and offering themselves as a transference object.

The therapist's behavior and therapeutic activity can influence the effect they have as model and activator on the development of the treatment culture and attitudes that can facilitate a group process given below (see also Lorentzen, 2014). Therapists should, therefore, through their stance:

- Convey that the therapy has a structure, and that there is an expectation that patients work primarily with their treatment focus and issues associated with it.
- Encourage patients to put self-criticism aside and expect them to communicate what they think and feel as this emerges. The therapist may emphasize that there is a difference between a therapy group and ordinary social situations.
- Maintain an expectation that patients engage in what others say or do, and that group members are active participants in and not passive recipients of treatment. Patients are at the center of the group and are therefore constantly confronted with situations that they must actively deal with. The group, in this way, becomes a practice arena for the development of interpersonal skills.
- Encourage patients to explore themselves and the group, including their own and others' unpleasant feelings. The therapist demonstrates, by accepting and encouraging statements that would not be tolerated in ordinary social situations, that the direct communication of personal feelings and experiences is desirable in the group.
- Use the group situation to demonstrate that interactions represent the meeting of subjective worlds, and which everyone can learn something from. Statements from one member to another can have a strong projective feel, but provide information and are therefore important.

- Show interest in the patient's subjective impressions of the therapist and other group members, and occasionally point out the similarities between these and the patients' relationships with others in their lives.
- Place greater patient and therapist focus on the "here-and-now situation" in the group than on the patient and significant others outside the treatment situation ("there-and-then").

The balance of support and interpretation (confrontation)

Therapists' interventions can be placed on a dimension that extends from "very supportive" to "very interpretive". This spectrum may not, however, include all technical approaches. No standard recipe can be given for how therapists should behave in any situation. It is, however, important that therapists continually assess whether the mix of supportive and interpretive strategies is balanced and meets the patients' and the group's needs at that point in time. A quality measure of group progress could, therefore, be that interventions lead to *increased collaboration* in the group, and to the maintenance or further development of positive cohesion/alliances between group members. This may be particularly true for the bonding part of the alliance (Bordin, 1979). Time-limited groups often do not provide enough time for extensive repairs to the therapeutic alliance, or other group relationships (Krogel et al., 2013). These dimensions are therefore more important in short-term than in longer-term therapies.

Some research shows that supportive techniques also may be important in the treatment of more well-integrated patients (Kernberg et al., 1972). I include some points below to distinguish between supportive and more confrontational (interpretative) therapy, which I have adapted to the framework of FGAP (MacKenzie, 1997):

- A certain degree of *neutrality* is important in both models. The therapist, however, feels freer in the supportive model to express acceptance, respect and sympathy. In the interpretive model, the therapist only leaves a neutral position if this is necessary to secure the therapeutic alliance.
- Therapist style in the supportive model will be more conversational. There should, however, be no prolonged periods of inactivity or lack of answers to direct questions in any of the models. A certain level of goal-directedness in dialogue is important in both models. The patient should also be reminded at regular intervals of issues that relate to their treatment focus.
- Techniques for improving self-esteem may differ. The therapist may, in the supportive model and in a crisis, try to increase the patient's self-esteem through direct encouragement (i.e. through awakening hope and the recognition of progress). Self-esteem is expected, in the interpretive therapy, to improve as functional ability and insight improve.
- Anxiety can be treated in different ways. The therapist may, in the supportive model, try to comfort and calm the patient, while the therapist in the

interpretive model will primarily want to explore and understand the anxiety in light of the transference.
- Defenses are also treated differently. The therapist is more reluctant to interpret defenses in the supportive model, unless these are immature and destructive. Defenses should, however, in the interpretive model be seen in the light of transference, this including understanding the function it has for the patient.
- Transference should in both models be understood, translated and interpreted. Working with the negative transference will be more important in the supportive model, positive transference being left unaddressed. All aspects of the transference should, however, be actively explored in the interpretative model.

As mentioned previously, the therapists' measure of how well the group is working is based on the quality of the alliance with each patient and whether there is a positive working atmosphere in the group. An interesting point is that (unlike individual therapy) groups provide opportunities to receive support from fellow patients. This is a major advantage when relationships between the therapist and one or more patients falter. Other group members can then provide enough support for the alliance to be restored and for the positive group work to continue.

Guidelines for interventions in FGAP

The therapists' activities are traditionally made up of *observation*, *reflection* and *intervention*. These take place alternately and partly overlap. Much was written about how this should be done in the manual on the study of differences in the effects of short-term and long-term group analytic psychotherapy (Lorentzen, 2014). Some of the guidelines presented in that book were inspired by ideas from *A Workbook of Group-Analytic Interventions* (Kennard, Roberts, & Winther, 2000) that for a large part is concerned with the practice of more traditional, *long-term* group analytic therapy. In the following, however, I will focus more on how the therapist should observe, reflect and intervene when practicing FGAP, which is a *more structured and directive therapy* than the short-term therapy described in the original research manual (Lorentzen, 2014).

The therapist should, therefore, keep an eye on the framework of the therapy (see Chapter 2), this for example being made up of the therapy contract, treatment focus, time frame, stages of the process and work in the here-and-now. These aspects constitute the terrain that therapists move around in when observing, reflecting and intervening. It is therefore important to have the best possible overview and grasp of this. Many believe that conducting short-term therapy is more demanding, and that acquiring good skills and abilities to more intuitively intervene in a productive way demands more training and practice than conducting a long-term therapy. I think this could be true, and I also believe that a personal short-term therapy could be beneficial for new therapist in training to acquire competence in FGAP. I will end this section by referring to the study by Hilsenroth et al. (2006) that shows that practicing short-term psychotherapy is essential to becoming a better therapist and achieving better outcomes with patients.

In the following, I will briefly comment on how the therapist observes and reflects, and then go on to describe different ways of intervention, again with particular emphasis on those most central for FGAP, which will also be illustrated with clinical examples.

Therapist observation

The ideal in traditional group analytic psychotherapy is that the therapist observes the interaction in the group with what Freud called a *"free-floating attention"*. The therapist should therefore have a "bifocal" orientation, keeping an eye on both the individuals and the group, so experiencing that individuals, statements, interactions and emotional outbursts alternate in the foreground of what he observes, against the background of the rest of the group.

The *selective* capture of material (statements and interactions) is more desirable in FGAP. Observation is therefore possibly more "directed" and is to a greater extent based on the therapist's understanding of the treatment focus, stage of therapy and specific knowledge about the patients.

Therapist reflection

Kennard and co-workers (2000) recommend that the therapist questions his observations before he intervenes. This is fundamental and is relevant in all process-oriented, exploratory groups. I would like, however, to again emphasize that the FGAP therapist should *reflect in a more focused way within the therapy framework*, and be alert to material that relates to the group's objectives, the individual's treatment focus and the stage the group is in. Examples of questions could be as follows.

What is the state of the group?

How high or low is the activity level and degree of emotionality in the group, and what themes are affected? Are group members interacting or are they talking over each other? What types of emotions are prominent?

What processes are contributing to the activity?

Do members continue a conversation that started in the waiting room? Did something special happen in the group in the last session that was taken up again in today's session? Do you see repetitive patterns in single patients that relate to their treatment focus?

What is the group not talking about?

The group often fails to comment on important events in the group, such as members being absent, important incidents in the last session, e.g. a member revealing intimate details of their life.

Is the state constructive, destructive or neutral?

Is the group locked or is it moving in a positive direction? Are any group members under attack or pushed into a scapegoat role?

Would it be advantageous to change this state?

The answer to this is "yes" if the group is locked, if a member is attacked or abused, if there are long and unproductive silences, or if the group struggles or is going in circles without anyone in the group intervening. The next questions then could be: Is it possible to change it? What interventions could be effective?

A therapist who has an understanding (hypothesis) of what is happening in the group can describe and interpret the behavior he experiences as resistance against change. The therapist must therefore, based on this, decide whether to approach the whole group, subgroups, a single member, or a combination of these. The therapist should, however, approach the constellation that is most likely to bring about a positive change. If a therapist begins to feel powerless and out of hypotheses about what is going on, then the therapist can share these feelings with the group and ask others for help. If they can not help, then the therapist could take responsibility for the group being locked and interpret this as meaning that all or some of the members in the group feel they are not being helped, supported or understood and that they are dissatisfied with the therapist, which may sometimes help, "opening up" the communication. A more directive intervention could be to suggest a round in which everyone reports on where they feel they are in relation to their treatment focus. This intervention is not directly exploratory, but an invitation to "go back to the start".

Is the time ripe for an intervention?

The question of "timing" is more relevant in time-limited therapy than in longer-term therapy. The therapist will, in longer-term therapy, often wait to see what patients bring to the group. The short-term therapist will, however, often intervene early in the therapy to quickly stimulate interactions, build cohesion and develop a treatment culture. Patients must therefore be helped to "find their place" in the group, in which strategies for collaboration and for exploring themselves and each other must be jointly developed. The therapist must keep an eye on what is happening and help the individual patient and the group progress through the therapy. Interventions are therefore particularly important if the process seems unproductive or locked, or if the group is going in circles.

I would like to emphasize that I have included this list on how to reflect for didactic reasons. What is written here about *reflection* is therefore not categorical. Most therapists will, as their levels of experience and practice increase, internalize many of the faculties and skills I describe, and will increasingly "intuitively" read the group and have access to helpful interventions. Some therapists may have a natural talent for influencing others. See, for example, Strupp and Hadley's study (1979) which showed that college professors and trained psychotherapists achieved nearly equal results in treating students with problems. There is, however, ample evidence that suggests that most of us need training and practice to improve as therapists.

I decided a few decades ago to learn to play jazz, and was fortunate to train for a year with a well-known Norwegian jazz pianist. I incorrectly thought before this that pianists who improvise "play by ear", and are free to strike any key they want in a sequence they find suitable. He taught me numeracy, and the encoding of chords by numbers in the notation. I also learned, however, that you could not play ad-lib. Each piece is played in a key, and each key has a set of chords that support and harmonize with the melody of each song and that forms part of the framework that you must remain within. I also learned that the more jazz you listen to, the better you become at improvisation through internalizing material that can be used when needed. I once asked my teacher how many pieces he knew. He replied, "All the standard songs". "How many are there?" I asked. He replied, "About 800!" He was not only an eminent pianist, arranger and composer, but also a modest and pleasant man. So I believed him. He also said that when he was young he had attended seminars with well-known musicians, many from the United States, in which they went in detail through the harmonization of a piece each day. When the day was over, the participants were asked to go home and practice it in all of the 12 keys!

I am not a brilliant improviser. I do, however, know quite a few pieces and can let myself go a little more when playing and finding chords that belong in the framework. I've also become less afraid of playing wrong notes, unlike when I was seven and my teacher rapped me over the knuckles because I hadn't practiced.

Most readers have probably realized the point of this story. Practicing, knowing the framework and not worrying about being the best helps performance. We can, without being maestros, still do a lot of good in our work and not least enjoy what we do!

Therapist interventions: overview

The interventions that a therapist makes to stimulate, model and promote the activities of group participants can, for didactic purposes, be categorized for example as below (Roberts, 2000; Lorentzen, 2014). The communication process is, however, in the real world more complex. The therapist's interventions include verbal elements, but also non-verbal elements such as variations in voice, tone and strength. Information is also conveyed through different forms of mimicry, gestures and posture. Our objective is that patients expose their problematic relationship patterns to allow interventions from other group members, to enable the "therapeutic factors" (see Chapters 6 and 9) to be effective and the therapy goals of each patient to be achieved. Interventions are made in FGAP to demonstrate and influence aspects of the individual's treatment focus by, for example, uncovering key underlying conflicts, so that patients can understand more about the driving forces and consequences of their own behavior, and so that a process is initiated that can run during the course of and continue even after the therapy is over.

It is helpful to remind ourselves that a large proportion of interventions in a well-functioning group are made by the other group members. Their comments give the individual patient new perspectives, their spontaneous responses often being better received than the therapist's filtered, clinical comments. Patients often receive surprising remarks from fellow patients that challenge their accepted and often fixed opinions and views of themselves. These comments are often direct, but often balanced by the group mobilizing strong support through identification with and empathic understanding of other group members.

1. *Maintenance of structure.* Central dysfunctional features of patients often appear when the group's structural boundaries are exceeded. These boundaries are determined by the group's framework, for example the room the group meets in, the time factor (the total duration of each session and therapy), the tasks assigned to patients in therapy and the group's rules. Other examples include that participants should not meet outside the group and that sensitive information from the group should not be disseminated. Boundary violations (physical or psychological) can for example include that a group member is always late, that a member gets up and walks around the room during a session or seems to use the session for other purposes such as eating or checking their phone. The therapist, who is also a dynamic administrator and is responsible for maintaining the group's structure, starts the intervention by drawing attention to the violation, and encourages group members to comment and reflect on it. The patient involved may immediately feel criticized and negate the event. It is then important to show the group that the therapist's intention is to make visible and explore the intra-psychic correlates of the behavior of those involved, including interpersonal implications and consequences – and not to criticize the patient.
2. *Open facilitation* is an intervention that is aimed at moving the group forward. It is not based on any particular therapist hypothesis. Nor does it openly refer to any specific unconscious level of understanding.
3. *Guided facilitation* encompasses all remarks that are not "open," but which demonstrate that the therapist has a hypothesis on which they base their questions, inquiries and shared observations.
4. *Interpretation* (of content and form) consists of verbal interventions by the leader to name feelings or opinions that are latent in the group as a whole,

in interpersonal transactions or in what individual members say or do. This includes Freud's goal of psychoanalysis to "make the unconscious conscious".

5. *"No immediate response"* is where the therapist is silent and refrains from saying or doing anything. This silent time is spent observing the group, feeling into a previous action and reflecting on what is happening. Long periods of inactivity should, however, be avoided. The therapist should respond to direct inquiries with at least "I don't know" or "I'll have to think about it". It is, however, important that the therapist returns to events later on.
6. *Action* encompasses all physical activity emanating from the therapist during group sessions, such as leaving their chair to close a door or window or touching another group member.
7. *Self-disclosure* is any statement made by the therapist that relates to their private thoughts or feelings, or that deals with their external world, and which does not fit into any of the other categories.
8. *Modeling* refers to all activities that involve an implicit intention that they should be assumed and become part of the repertoire of the group or members. This includes, for example, expressing compassion and the modeling of an analytic questioning attitude when a group member is struggling with unpleasant feelings. There are many models in groups, because patients have ample opportunity to capture and use the behaviors they see in fellow patients, such as solution strategies or modes of expression.
9. *Staying with the focus*. This includes everything the therapist says to bring the patient back to the treatment focus after wandering away from it. It can also include the therapist's attempts to reformulate the patient's impressionistic, global and distanced interest in a vague topic to something that is personally relevant, emotionally charged and that have a potential connection with the therapy focus.
10. *Switching to the here-and-now*. The therapist addresses stories from present or past that are brought to the group, to turn the patient's attention onto how past events may be manifested in the here-and-now interactions in the group.

Examples of specific types of interventions in FGAP

There are few or no differences between interventions in long and short-term group therapy such as "open facilitation", "no immediate response", "action" or "self-disclosure". The FGAP therapist must, however, at all times pay attention to the framework of the therapy. Facilitating comments should, as far as possible, be related to the treatment focus, the group's treatment goals and here-and-now interactions, and so should any therapist self-disclosure. The importance of "maintaining the structure" and of actively using boundary phenomena to clarify behavioral patterns in individual patients was described earlier in the chapter. I will therefore limit myself here to providing examples of guided facilitation, interpretation, modeling, staying with the focus and switching to the here-and-now. The four different stages are also important parts of the framework (described in Chapter 6); interventions varying considerably with the stage the group is in (opening, differentiation, interpersonal work and termination).

Guided facilitation

This intervention suggests that the therapist has a hypothesis that resonates with or points toward a psychodynamic theme at the individual or group level. An example of a guided facilitating intervention (which are common in the opening phases) may be the therapist's comment on two patients who gaze at each other during the first sessions. They can be searching for a soul mate to feel more secure in this new situation. The therapist may, to find the right words to describe an observation and to promote the development of group cohesion, for example suggest that they seem to feel a fellowship and to be looking for support from one another. The two may quickly be joined by others, who swiftly form a subgroup that others join. This intervention emphasizes that one is not alone in the group (universality) and that one's feeling of safety may increase.

Patients in another group may, for example, complain that they are not able to open up, others in the group expressing dissatisfaction because they are unable to use what they learn in the group in their day-to-day lives. A guided facilitation in the differentiation phase could be: "I wonder if this dissatisfaction and self-criticism reflects a disappointment with me, that you feel I have not given you enough help to find your way in the group". This intervention is based on the hypothesis that patients shy away from criticizing and confronting the therapist, which is not uncommon at this stage. The therapist could also point to the future:

> In the first few sessions there was a lot of talk about "being in the same boat", and that a number of you had similar problems. I wonder if, by taking all responsibility upon yourselves individually, that you are shying away from what is actually a group task: that we must jointly find ways to explore similarities and differences, even if that means that we do not always agree?

An intervention in the interpersonal work phase may be:

> I wonder if this is a form of reaction that you recognize from other challenging interpersonal situations in your lives? We have here the opportunity to become better acquainted with both ourselves and others. A number of you, however, seem to be sitting this uncomfortably out.

This may be sufficient, or can be supplemented with: "Steve (Doris, Sue...), what do *you* think prevents group members relating more directly with the others in the group?" The hypothesis is again that the members are shying away from the group challenges of the stage, these being to open up, confront others and work with their own and others' dysfunctional relational patterns. The therapist can also address the group as a whole:

The group seems very sad, almost depressed. I also hear self-reproach – but as you may have experienced, the road from this point to blaming others is often short. Many of you have problems criticizing or setting boundaries for others. We also just heard that Sue was unable to refuse a request for overtime, even when she was ill. Something similar is happening here now!

The therapist can share through this his hypotheses with the group.

In the separation phase, a guided facilitation may be: "We don't have much time left, and I wonder if the group resignation that is being conveyed does in fact contain an ocean of emotions, which it might be worthwhile spending time on and trying to differentiate".

Interpretations

The essence of interpretation is to make patients aware of what is unconscious. It is also to make them aware that they should develop their insight into how manifest behavior, such as emotions and thoughts, is influenced by more latent factors such as desires, conflicts and defenses. Interpretation has traditionally been regarded as the most important intervention in psychoanalysis. It was described at length in one of Freud's main works, *The Interpretation of Dreams* (Freud, 1953). Psychoanalysis also claims that symptoms, parapraxes (Freud, 1960), rigid and stereotypical behaviors and irrational, dysfunctional relationship patterns (like dreams) also often reflect intra-psychic, partly unconscious conflicts and/or coexisting rigid or inadequately developed personality traits. Freud also found this insight gave the person greater opportunities for change, through adopting new, more appropriate strategies for interaction with others. Patients should therefore be helped to understand more themselves: their driving forces, desires, feelings, ambitions and goals and the possible conflicts between them. This book, however, places great emphasis on Kernberg's object relations theory, which integrates elements of drive theory, ego-psychology, self-psychology and interpersonal theory. Freud and the first analysts are believed to have been more authoritarian and direct in their interpretations. However, they also understood at an early stage that it is *emotionally experienced* insight that leads to change. Freud's advice was therefore to work "from the surface", that is with phenomena which are closer to the pre-conscious.

Foulkes partly broke with the "tradition of interpretation" when delegating much of the responsibility for the exploratory, uncovering function to the group and introducing the concept of "translation" in the work with transference. He also, however, kept the concept of interpretation and considered that the therapist retained "overall" therapeutic responsibility if the group was not able to carry out this work (Hutchinson, 2009). The view of interpretation within psychoanalysis has changed, however, as theories evolved and as aspects such as the patients' relational needs were included. Greater emphasis is now placed on how intra-psychic relationships characterize the personality and manifest in interpersonal relationships, which led to a growing understanding of transference as an intersubjective phenomenon. This also emphasizes the importance of analyzing the patient's emotionally charged experiences in the here-and-now situation rather than seeing them in a psychogenetic perspective. Today's analysts are therefore more exploratory, less authoritarian and more frequently invite patients to dialogue. We have probably, for these reasons, moved closer toward Foulkes's translation term. I therefore believe that there can, in practice, easily be a smooth transition between that described as guided facilitation and interpretation. Interpretations should be presented through language that is more well-articulated than that used for facilitation and modeling interventions. It should also be implicitly or explicitly stated that an interpretation is just one of a number of ways of understanding the material, and that the interpretation represents the view of the therapist. This also recognizes that interpretations are not based on an inalienable "truth" that is only available to someone with sufficient knowledge and experience, but may be colored by countertransference and by the therapist's personality.

An interpretation can be directed toward an individual, to the interaction between individuals, to a subgroup or to the group as a whole.

The following examples provide suggestions of how to interpret at the subgroup and group level, which can be combined with interpretations at the individual level, at different stages of therapy. I base this on common situations that in my experience can present the therapist with challenges.

Clinical example: "empty chairs"

The session begins and two of the chairs are empty. The therapist has not been informed of any absences and does not know why they are absent. Nor do the other group members. Therapists normally wait to see how the group reacts to this. The therapist should, however, comment on this lack of response from the group relatively early. This can, for example, lead to statements of feeling abandoned, of annoyance, guilt or relief at the absence. Some patients may identify with those absent and envy them being somewhere else having fun. These patients project their ambivalence about being in the group onto the absentees. The therapist can, later in the session and through an interpretation, try to link the group's reactions to reactions that are common at that stage of the group, and possibly to the individual's treatment focus.

In the differentiation phase

> There seems to be a lot of emotion around the empty chairs. Some are annoyed with and feel let down by Steve and Anne not being here. Others feel they have scared them away. We don't know what has happened. But we can hear some envying them because they think they are having fun elsewhere. Some responses express guilt-ridden or relieved feelings, which are in line with the patterns you are working to change in therapy. Both Elsie and Kenneth talked

in the last session about things that were difficult and a little shameful. Two members not showing up next time can quite easily feel more painful and lead to fantasies and feelings of being neglected.

This interpretation gives some support to those attending the meeting.

In the working phase:

> We may need to look at what happened in the group last time to understand why Steve and Anne are absent. Steve talked about many things he was ashamed of, and Anne was not happy with some of the reactions she received to her telling about how she had been unfaithful to her husband. Do you remember how you reacted to what they presented?

This interpretation places greater "responsibility" for the two being absent on those present. The therapist draws on each patient's response to Steve and Anne in the last session, and links these to Steve and Anne's absence if it seems reasonable to do so. Responses are also frequently linked to traits from their individual treatment foci.

In the termination phase:

> We do not have much time left and some members have talked about how difficult it is to separate and to manage without the group. It is not surprising that the reactions are so strong. We react differently and allow the situation to reach us to greater and lesser degrees. Some prefer to remain in the group until the end and work with the feelings and reactions that emerge, while others try to evade their feelings of sadness and loss.

When should one interpret on the individual level?

A follow-up study (Malan et al., 1976) has shown that many group-level interpretations can be perceived as being impersonal and meaningless. This study also showed that use of such interventions alone can result in poor outcomes in group treatment. This work therefore provides empirical grounds for limiting group interpretations and for addressing patients in a group more individually. The therapist can base interventions on expressions of transference such as resistance, desires/impulses/affects and content, and address the patient's fearful expectations of what others' responses to their statements will be. Interpretations can also address intra-psychic phenomena, such as discrepancies between self-images or other conflicts. The therapist can also interpret relational aspects of interactions.

It sometimes becomes clear that the dysfunctional communication (distortion, projection, suspiciousness) of one patient triggers the reactions of others, and that this can lead to conflict. It is, however, usually appropriate, even so, to include other patients or the therapist in the interpretation, despite this only relating to one group member.

The therapist should preferably interpret in the here-and-now situation, but can sometimes draw lines of connection to relationships outside the group and in the past, if these are relatively clear. Interactions in the group should, however, be prioritized. It may be beneficial that the therapist portions out comments over time when, after emphasizing the group or subgroup level of an interpretation, they present comments to one or more group members. Too many words from the therapist at once can easily overwhelm or dull the rest of the group members. It is also important to provide space so that other members can contribute.

The following provide opportunities for individual interpretations:

- It may be necessary to work with individual patients who are particularly resistant and are stunting the development of the group. Patients may, for example, also have different abilities to see psychological connections, and may develop this and other faculties at different rates, so requiring different levels of individual work to progress.
- To demonstrate something that the group has been through, but that a patient did not grasp. The patient showing an interest in understanding this is a benefit.
- If the therapist thinks an insight may help a patient, that it relates to the patient's treatment focus and that the patient is close to grasping the significance of it.
- If one patient in the group is attacked and the therapist needs to protect them.
- In the termination phase when the therapist wants patients to individually "take back their projections" as much as possible and reconcile with each other, so that the group can end in a positive way.

When should one not interpret individually?

- If the therapist is more focused on winning an argument (acting out countertransference), than making sure the patient's needs are met
- If the therapist is more focused on seeing interesting connections, than on these connections being central to the patient's problems
- If the group is working well with the therapist on the sideline
- If a number of patients are involved in a critical situation, and an interpretation can be interpreted as deeming a specific patient "responsible" for the incident
- If individual interpretations have been proven to be useless

That the aspects that the therapist refers to are relatively visible or can be demonstrated, and that the therapist draws lines to aspects that are emotionally charged or experience-near are prerequisites for interpretation. Interpretation may otherwise become more of a facilitating intervention. The difference between guided facilitation and an interpretation directed at a subgroup or the group as a whole may, in short-term groups in particular, be somewhat unclear and can be understood in line with Foulkes's concept of translation (Foulkes & Anthony, 1984). The therapist's contributions, along with the other members' communication and free associations, lead from the manifest expression to a new understanding of more latent, underlying conditions in the dynamic matrix. Many therapists are not concerned about whether they are interpreting or translating. I, however, believe that interpretation may be more important in FGAP, which has a more structured framework and in which individual progression through the process must be quicker than in long-term therapies. I also think that the intervention called interpretation should link the group's (subgroup's) behavior and affective state with the phase-specific challenges and themes facing the group. Interpretation should therefore be reserved for groups that have developed a certain degree of cohesion, and are in the differentiation, interpersonal work or termination phase.

Modeling

Everything the therapist says in a group is often granted extra importance. Therapists, through their attitudes, behavior and interventions, model the behaviors they want the rest of the group to emulate, and the treatment culture they want to develop, that patients can be a part of and grow through. Therapists also want patients to "internalize" the therapist and therapeutic functioning, so that they can continue treatment on their own after group therapy ends. This includes the supportive and controlling function (superego) of the therapist and the group, which can be useful for both neurotics (strict superego) and patients with more personality pathology (defective, rudimentary or punitive superego). The therapist frequently needs to model how the statements and behaviors that many patients find difficult to express or to disclose, should be received and contained. This includes the desire for closeness or dependence on others, irritation or anger toward others and direct communication in incidents that involve the patient's and others' negative feelings, such as envy or shame. Many of the things the therapist does that reveal how he or she thinks, reflects or comments in a psychodynamic group are examples of the behaviors patients should copy.

Clinical examples

A simple example of modeling is a therapist who is open and direct in their communication with patients, and who dares to give feedback and point out aspects the individual patient may not immediately like:

- "Good that you can express your annoyance – so showing that what happened meant something to you".
- "Wondering what lies beneath this squabbling in the group right now? Could it be me that you are dissatisfied with?"
- "It seems that many in the group are bored. Boredom is a gray shadow that often covers stronger underlying emotions. I wonder what the underlying threats in the group are".

Staying with the focus

Staying with the focus covers all statements from the therapist that are made to bring patients who have drifted away from their treatment focus back to it, or to turn a global, impressionistic and seemingly vague interest in a topic into a personal, relevant and emotionally charged private problem complex. The therapist can, in both cases, first confirm the value of what the patient has communicated, and then ask whether they see a connection between what they said and their treatment focus. The therapist can also, through this, activate the group's help to specify the patient's problems, and even contribute to a solution. A similar comment can also be directed to the whole group if the conversation is largely about matters outside of the group.

Switching to the here-and-now

The therapist will, when shifting to the here-and-now, try to turn the patients' attention and interest from stories of present and past events outside of the therapy room, to current and potentially important events that are taking place in the here-and-now interaction in the group.

The movie that a patient watched on TV the night before and which he gives a long and detailed description of, may have relevance to his treatment focus. The therapist should, however, limit the duration of the story by a friendly comment that shows he appreciates the story. At the same time he must ask himself, the patient and the group what it means in light of the patient's own history, and what the sadness and the tears that boiled up in the patient when he told of the heroine in the film being carried out from a burning house, really relates to. Further exploration of this may require the use of both open and managed facilitation, structuring and possibly interpretation, the therapist, through this, modeling an explorative and inquiring attitude. The tears could, for example, be related to the patient often feeling abandoned because his mother failed to protect him from his father's fury and physical abuse when he was a child. In the film, through identification with the heroine, he is not only helped, but also meets someone who is willing to risk their life to help him, which strikes him deeply!

A similar chain of interventions may also be required when the therapist asks the patient and the group to link the past and the present outside the group to the here-and-now situation in the group. This therapist recognizes that the story is important and asks: "How do you think these events have affected you, and how do you think they affect how you may appear in this group?" or, "These events have really been central to your life. I think it's very important that you tell us when similar feelings of being let down, sad, or of despair show up here so we can work more directly with them".

The above examples are complex and borrow aspects from intervention such as maintaining structure, facilitation and modeling. This, furthermore, reminds us of the complexity of the therapist's tasks – therapists need to be "jacks of all trades".

It can be difficult to be a therapist, but therapists do not always have to be "perfect", in order to help their clients. I will therefore conclude this chapter with a story from my own training analysis to counter some of the "idealism" I may have emphasized as important and central in therapist interventions. After complaining for most of a session about a throbbing headache and appealing several times to the therapist to advise me on how to get rid of it, he laconically said: "Have you considered decapitation?" I immediately burst out laughing. But I also, for the first time in the session, saw myself from the outside and what I was doing. Some might argue that the laughter represented a defense against castration anxiety. I think, however, it was an expression of the surprise and pleasure of having a therapist who had a dark sense of humor and who perhaps trusted me enough to take the chance with this comment. However, it may not have been that simple for me after all, as I returned to his rather aggressive comment a few sessions later, labeling it "his acting out of his countertransference", to which I heard him chuckle softly in agreement.

My point is that no therapist is perfectly emotionally attuned to their patients *all* the time. But most patients will generally forgive and tolerate occasional "slips" from a therapist who appears genuine and who is, as a rule, emotionally and cognitively present and seems to be conscientiously engaged in the therapeutic work. In this case I also think it helped that I saw the futility of my plea for a "quick psychological fix" for my throbbing head.

Part III

Clinical quality assurance – Research – Supervision

Chapter 8

Clinical quality assurance – evaluation of therapy outcomes and process

Practicing therapists and mental health institutions have traditionally been able to decide themselves whether or not to use standardized questionnaires or structured interviews to monitor the effectiveness of the therapy they provide. This now seems to be changing in Norway. Health authorities are now issuing guidelines. These guidelines require, for example, patients with specific diagnoses to be guaranteed treatment within a reasonable period of time (waiting list guarantee), that all patients receive an individual treatment strategy, that all levels of health services collaborate when appropriate in the treatment of a patient and that treatment outcomes are monitored during and after therapy (Directorate of Health, 2019).

Therapists and mental health institutions can see standardized measures for monitoring the course and outcomes of therapy as a great deal of work that consumes resources that should be used on other essential tasks. Using standardized measures can, however, in the long run become an integrated part of clinical practice, and, I believe, benefit patients and those who provide health services. Questionnaires and structured interviews have been widely used within mental health care institutions in the last decade, and have contributed to new and useful knowledge. There are, however, still some therapists, especially in private practice, who maintain that psychometrics are artificial and can easily negatively affect the connection between the therapist and patient. My experience from many years of using measures as an integrated part of private psychotherapy practice is that standardized questionnaires provide important information that can strengthen the relationship with patients and improve treatment outcomes. Many patients also see the use of measures as a sign that their disorder and problems are being taken seriously. I have found that the concerns of therapists, including my own, of the consequences of monitoring treatment process or outcomes may be motivated by the therapist's worries about what measurements might show. Systematic research has shown that some therapists have a distorted image of their professional qualities, based on how their patients fare in therapy. Research also indicates that there are a few therapists who nearly always have patients that remain unchanged or deteriorate (i.e. Walfish et al., 2012). These findings should be taken seriously both by those therapists who are opposed to using psychometrics and by administrators who want to introduce comprehensive evaluation programs into

DOI: 10.4324/9781003216377-11

treatment institutions. I will therefore, in this chapter, present arguments for using such measures, and hope that this can be helpful to those who have doubts about using standardized measures in their practice.

It is important to distinguish between evaluation before the patient enters treatment and evaluation after a contract has been established. The initial evaluation is carried out to determine whether and what type of treatment a patient needs. Evaluation after a contract uses measures to monitor if and to what extent the treatment is effective. The collection of measures used prior to therapy should include questionnaires that cover patient aspects targeted in therapy, i.e. they should be relevant to the characteristics of the group of patients receiving treatment (for example, symptoms, interpersonal problems, psychosocial functioning).

It is also important to distinguish between *quality assurance* and *research*. Requirements for the selection of patients, control group, use of treatment manual, check of therapist's competence and adherence to the manual are stricter in research than in quality assurance. A researcher can also sometimes draw causal conclusions about the relationship between treatment and outcome. The objective of quality assurance is, however, to primarily increase the objectivity (reliability and validity) of follow-up and post-therapy evaluations, this traditionally being carried out using interviews alone.

Focused Group Analytical Psychotherapy (FGAP) is based on and has been developed from research and extensive clinical experience. Patients selected for FGAP are carefully assessed and are determined from this to be likely to benefit from the treatment. Why should they, based on this, then be followed up systematically during and after therapy?

Why evaluate?

We do not know enough about whether and why patients change

We know that group psychotherapy is effective for a variety of mental disorders, and that it is as effective as individual therapy (Burlingame et al., 2016a). However, we still do not know enough about the characteristics of patient samples that promote the success of a specific therapy, and we do not know enough about the ingredients that make a specific therapy effective (change mechanisms), despite a great deal of research having been carried out in this area (Burlingame et al., 2013;Burlingame & Strauss, 2021). Quality assurance can not provide definitive answers to such questions. It can, however, awake an exploratory, inquiring attitude in both patients and therapists, and therefore contribute to the formulation of hypotheses about causal relationships.

Therapists have blind spots

The skills in the practicing of psychotherapy and the therapist's grasp of the theoretical basis for understanding a person (background, personality, resources and psychopathology) and the framework of the therapy are important prerequisites for carrying out an effective therapy. Knowledge and experience also helps when it comes to evaluation of treatment results, but is not by itself sufficient for the therapists being able to objectively and reliably evaluate the outcomes of their own therapies. We all have a tendency to "see what we want to see", and most therapists also have "blind spots" that affect their assessments (bias), something that has been experienced by most therapists who have compared outcome results based on their own interview data alone and results from the additional use of standardized measures. Therapists' subjective perceptions do often, however, result in narratives of treatment courses and outcomes which are richer and more nuanced than those offered by the dry numbers from psychometric scales. This speaks for a combined use of quantitative and qualitative approaches in the evaluation of change through psychotherapy.

Evaluations can increase the impact of therapy

Many patients see the use of measures as a sign that the therapist takes treatment seriously. Using measures can also make communication between patient and therapist more direct and varied, and strengthen the therapeutic alliance. Measures in initial assessments can also activate key thoughts and feelings in patients, stimulating a change process which can start there and then, so contributing to a flying start to therapy. I have also found that patients usually find self-report measures interesting if the problems they are struggling with are covered in the questionnaires, this also confirming to them that they are not the only ones suffering. See the therapeutic factor "Universality, Chapter 6.

Use of questionnaires can help patients and therapists clarify the treatment goals described in Chapter 4, IIP-C (interpersonal problems) with a subsequent discussion of the results helping an agreement on treatment focus to be reached.

The systematic monitoring of patients contributes to therapist learning and professional development, which again benefits current and future patients (Horneland et al., 2012). Measures can also give the therapist a greater understanding of the diversity of therapeutic change, such as some symptoms disappearing while interpersonal problems persist, or vice versa.

A final important point can be that self-report measures allow therapists to provide an "objective" report of patient status or change, and to therefore compare the progress of one patient in a group with other group members, and with other groups of patients or norms of non-clinical groups in the population.

An important benefit of clinical quality assurance is that studies are conducted in a situation that represents the clinician's everyday life. This contrasts with formal research, in which patients are often carefully selected, thus potentially making the results less relevant to the patients therapists see in their day-to-day clinical work (lower external validity).

Experiences and findings indicate that systematic monitoring is both desirable and necessary in the day-to-day clinical setting. This understanding has led to a strong increase in the use of standardized measure instruments in mental health, in both institutions and in private practices (Ruud, 2015).

Are there any disadvantages of using measures?

Questionnaires can sometimes, but rarely, be experienced as "threatening" and arouse an anxiety about exposure. This can increase a patient's defenses, and can create tension between the patient and therapist. Questions on the questionnaire that are perceived as being not directly relevant to the patient's condition increase the risk of increased defenses and tension. This can lead to a more intellectual discussions in a group where monitoring results are presented to the group. Questionnaires can also move the focus from the therapist–patient relationship to the role of the therapist as "researcher". The therapist can also receive "distorted" information if patients manipulate scores (questions answered in a haphazard or stereotypical way) or act out by failing to complete or return questionnaires.

Use of questionnaires in psychodynamic psychotherapy

All of the above examples are reflections of a rich dynamic material that can and should be explored in the group. Anxiety to exposure is, however, not limited to questionnaires. It is also activated immediately prior to a patient disclosing something personal or shameful in their lives to the group. Intellectualization (dry theoretical discussions) or distancing from a topic or between group members can also be the result of patients projecting parts of themselves onto other group members, or the therapist presenting unempathetic or premature interpretations, irrespective of whether these are right or wrong. Failure to complete or return questionnaires is often uncovered when the therapist evaluates the results, and can be the subject of exploration and clarification in the group. This failure is often motivated by negative feelings toward the therapist or the treatment, which is a valuable theme to explore in the group context.

It is important that therapists consider how using a test battery affects their relationships with the group members and the group, and continuously reflect on the dynamics associated with the use of questionnaires. Therapists should ideally feel at ease using questionnaires with their patients, but at the same time keep in mind the positive and potentially negative aspects of this use. Above I have tried to indicate that the "mysticism" often associated with the use of psychometrics during therapy is fed by this process becoming a "vehicle" for transference and/or may be rooted in the therapist's countertransference. It might therefore be fruitful for the therapist to keep in mind that the main purpose of using measures is that they, combined with clinical scrutiny, provide a more valid picture of the patient's status or process than clinical scrutiny alone.

I will now briefly describe some principles of how to select measures or questionnaires. I then provide examples of instruments that can be used to monitor a patient in FGAP in regular clinical practice (see overview below). I will also give some tips on how to present questionnaires to patients, and how to interpret the findings.

Principles for selecting outcome measures in psychotherapy

- Multiple goals. Change takes place in therapy in *different areas*. Including a number of types of outcome measures can therefore be beneficial. This can produce a wide spread of results, some areas showing improvement and some areas showing no change or deterioration. A combination of measures can therefore give a more correct picture of the change achieved.
- Outcome measures should ideally be obtained from a number of *different sources*. From the patient (subjective) and therapist (more objective), but also from someone who knows the patient well in their day-to-day life, or an independent observer. Subjective descriptions should be supplemented with objective measures based on behavioral (operationalized) criteria.
- A combination of *individualized* (idiographic) and *standardized* (nomothetic) instruments is desirable. Individually tailored assessments can capture that which is unique to each individual. Standardized goals can often provide important normative data, and opportunities to compare a patient with a non-clinical sample or compare patients with each other.
- It may be useful to evaluate the patient's ability to function within a number of areas: interpersonal functioning, in the family and among friends, general social functioning, at leisure and in working life.
- There should be a balance between time available and the scope of measures used. Instruments that take too much time will probably not be used in a busy clinical setting.

What to evaluate?

Methods for planning and monitoring process and outcome of FGAP

1. Diagnostic interviews before and after therapy, more or less structured: MINI (Sheehan et al., 2002); SCID-5-PF (American Psychiatric Association, 2013).
2. Outcome measures used in pre-therapy, post-therapy and follow-up.
    a. Main (target) problems (Battle et al., 1966) (scored on Likert scale, 6 steps).
    b. The Clinical Global Impression Scale: CGIS (Busner & Targum, 2007).
    c. Symptoms: SCL-90-R (Derogatis, 1977).
    d. Interpersonal problems: IIP-C (Alden et al., 1990).
    e. CORE-OM (see https://www.coresystemtrust.org.uk/).
    f. OQ-45 (Lambert, 2012).
    g. Self-esteem and maybe other personality variables, depending on the patients being treated.

3. Registration of group process and group relationships.
   a. Therapeutic alliance: WAI (Tracey & Kokotevic, 1989).
   b. Group cohesion: (Lese & Mac-Nair-Semands, 2000).
   c. Group climate: GCQ (MacKenzie, 1983).
   d. Group Questionnaire OQ-GQ (Krogel, 2009; Krogel et al., 2013)[1] (see also Chapter 9).

I recommended in Chapter 4 that the assessment of a new patient should begin with a clinical interview combined with a psychodynamic attunement to the here-and-now situation. The interviewer can then, if needed, carry out more structured diagnostic interviews such as the Mini International Neuropsychiatric Interview for symptom disorders and SCID-5 PD for personality disorder (MINI; Sheehan et al., 2002; SCID-5-PF).

Choice of outcome measures

Patients usually seek help for troublesome symptoms, problematic interpersonal relationships or poor social functioning. I therefore find it beneficial to use a symptom measure (SCL-90-R; Derogatis, 1977), a measure for interpersonal problems (IIP-C; Alden et al., 1990) and a measure for psychosocial functioning (Global Assessment of Functioning, GAF; DSM-5; American Psychiatric Association, 2013) when measuring change during and after therapy. The measures of symptoms and interpersonal problems are also available as shorter versions that require less time. Note that it can be difficult to achieve a satisfactory inter-rater reliability with GAF, unless raters have received adequate training. An alternative to GAF could be selecting measures hosting questionnaire items covering all three areas (symptoms, interpersonal problems and psychosocial functioning), such as OQ-45 (Outcome Questionnaire-45; Lambert et al., 1996; Lambert, 2012) or CORE-OM (The Core Outcome Measure; Barkham et al., 1998; Evans et al., 2000; Gray & Mellor-Clark, 2007). CORE-OM has also been translated into a number of languages, including Norwegian (Skre et al., 2013) and can be downloaded free of charge from www.coreims.co.uk.

Measures of symptomatic distress (SCL-90-R) and graphs of interpersonal problems (IIP-C, Alden et al., 1990) often provide clues to the most important aspects that need to be changed during treatment, and aspects from these measures and graphs can therefore often be included in the treatment focus.

Simpler outcome measures can also be used. An example is the selection by the therapist of a few key "target problems" that are included in the treatment focus, and scoring them globally on a Likert scale from 1 to 6 (Battle et al., 1966). Another alternative is to score the patient's "global" change during therapy, and degree of satisfaction with the therapy, on two Likert scales each from 1 to 8 (The Clinical Global Impression Scale; CGIS; Busner & Targum, 2007; Forkmann et al., 2011). Change and satisfaction are only scored after therapy (and at follow-up).

Choice of process measures

The measures that most commonly have been used to capture the processes in the group are measures of group climate (Group Climate Questionnaire; GCQ, MacKenzie, 1983), measures of group cohesion (for example, Piper et al., 1983; The Therapeutic Factors Inventory, Subscale Cohesiveness; TFI-Coh, Lese & MacNair-Semands, 2000) and measures of therapeutic alliance (for example Working Alliance Inventory; WAI, Tracey & Kokotevic, 1989). Studies have found a positive correlation between "engagement" (one of the three GCQ subscales) and cohesion and treatment outcome. Too many overlapping measures have, however, been used, this making unambiguous interpretation of the results difficult (Hornsey et al., 2007). Burlingame et al. (2011) have reviewed the most frequently used cohesion measures and discussed problems moving forward in this research. Burlingame's research group has, for many years, also worked on the development of a multidimensional cohesion measure, which resulted in the Group Questionnaire (GQ; Krogel et al., 2013; Burlingame et al., 2016b; Burlingame et al., 2018; see also www.oqmeasures.com). This questionnaire consists of three structural elements (patient–therapist, patient–patient and patient–group) and three qualitative factors (positive bonding, positive work and negative reactions). GQ seems to be a promising measure for studying the associations between aspects of group relationships and outcome. Below I suggest how it can be used at intervals to monitor the development of group relationships in FGAP. In Chapter 9 it is described in more detail how it is used, especially in non-psychodynamic group therapies, during the whole group course.

Procedures for data collection

How to present a questionnaire to a patient?

Patients should be given an explanation of the rationale behind using questionnaires and of how the information will be processed and used. This is important, as the quality of the information provided to patients often affects patient compliance and the quality of self-reports. This information should ideally be provided to patients during contract work, and immediately before the patient starts in a group. The therapist should explain how the measures can be helpful to the patient, and give therapists a sounder basis for their work.

Time-points and procedures for data collection

Before, during and after therapy

Individual interviews and outcome measures have traditionally been used before and after therapy. I would recommend that the group process (GQ: group relationships) is assessed three times during the course of FGAP, e.g. after the 3rd, 10th and 18th group sessions (early, midway and late in therapy). I also recommend that the outcome measures are completed half-way in therapy, in addition to pre-post-therapy, as the regression line of three data points provides a more valid expression of a process over time than pre- and post-ratings alone.

Follow-up (6 months, 1, 3 and/or 5 years after therapy)

A follow-up study must be carried out if we are to find out whether patients are unchanged, deteriorate or continue to improve (delayed change) after therapy. Time and money restrictions often mean follow-up studies are not carried out, which reduces the value of the evaluation process. Follow-up studies ideally should include personal interviews and questionnaires. Limiting the study to sending patients questionnaires to complete and return (the questionnaire used at the start and end of therapy) is cheaper but still useful. Asking patients to provide detailed information on important life events and additional treatment after the end of the FGAP course and other relevant factors that can explain their present health status increases the likelihood of a valid interpretation of the results.

Discussion of the results with patients

The results from the systematic monitoring of patient progress and the quality of group relationships during FGAP can be used in different ways. Generally, I think that this information primarily should be a reservoir for the therapist to administer, to use as seems fit within each treatment course. I would certainly discuss the results with patients in the group if wanted- or bring issues up in the group myself, e.g. if it turned out to be a big discrepancy between what the patients communicates directly in the group and through their measures.

The developers of the "patient-focused research", have in their later studies started to measure outcome and process at every session, each time giving feedback to the therapists (see Chapter 9) (Lambert et al., 2018; Burlingame et al., 2018; Griner et al., 2018). The therapist can thus discuss the results with each patient between sessions or share the results with all patients in the group.

My experience is that this high frequency and using therapy sessions to share routine data score information is unnecessary. If a group is working well, then I think discussing questionnaire results with each patient face to face individually after the treatment has ended, and in a follow-up and "historical review" of the treatment, is sufficient.

I have earlier in this chapter described and discussed how the FGAP therapist psychodynamically handles reverberations from the use of questionnaires in a psychotherapy group. Patients commenting on the use of questionnaires provide the opportunity to reflect on individual reactions to the use of these in the group. The therapist occasionally can also bring issues such as measures not submitted on time, incomplete questionnaires or questionnaires rated in a stereotypical way back to the group. I also inform the group of patients who fail to notify the group of serious deteriorations in their status or who seem to be about to drop out of the group, where I have not understood this from my perception of events in the group but learned this suddenly from questionnaires. The use of GQ therefore provides the therapist who has not picked up on a member being about to leave, with the opportunity to address the problem, and possibly prevent the patient acting out and leaving the group without notice.

I would like to add that in a process-oriented, interactive group therapy such as FGAP, in which communication, relationships and transferences are constantly in focus, the therapist will usually perceive that a member is considering leaving.

Interpretation and discussion of results

Treatment outcome is assessed by comparing outcome measure scores from before, during and after treatment. It can also be assessed in the follow-up where this data has been collected. Three or more data points produce more valid results than just pre- and post-therapy measurements, because regression lines are not as strongly affected by a patient having one deviant value, for example, at the time of termination. The scores usually show individual patterns – improvements in some areas, and no change or deterioration in other areas. It is important to note the size, direction, consistency and patterns of change across different outcome measures, to obtain a complete picture of how patients change over time. Improvement in a number of outcome variables is better than in just one. This is particularly true where improvements are in therapy focus areas, which the patient and therapist had decided would be worked on in FGAP. Changes reported by both the therapist and patient are more significant than changes reported by only one. A change is even more robust where confirmed by a third party, such as a relative.

Some patients do remain unchanged, or even appear to deteriorate after therapy. This can, however, not be taken as proof of ineffective or harmful treatment. Some patients may have rated items low at the start due to denial or a wish to appear more socially acceptable than they are (or fear not to be). Another explanation may be that the measure does not have the same level of sensitivity to change for all patients. Changes in mood or symptoms may also occur gradually or in "steps". A bad period during therapy does not mean that the therapy has failed. Standardized measures should therefore be used in addition to clinical interviews. It is therefore essential to establish and maintain a relationship with the patient and to also obtain central, more nuanced information. Questionnaires can not replace the observation of the participant by the therapist during therapy, in which the therapist's attention is directed to both the individual patient and the group as a whole. The therapist as "participant observer" and provider of professional assistance can easily be biased toward the view that "everybody gets (much) better". The therapist's clinical assessments during and at the end of therapy are therefore still of the utmost importance. A widespread practice in the termination phase of most psychodynamic therapies is to evaluate the results of therapy and discuss the present status of the problems the patient sought help for with each patient (see Chapter 6). A major advantage of a closed group is that the group members remain together as a group throughout the therapy. The feedback each patient receives will therefore be richer and more nuanced, and the chance of balancing potentially exaggerated or distorted subjective aspects of both patient and therapist assessments will be greater.

I would like to conclude this chapter by emphasizing that a combination of interviews and use of psychometrics can give a richer and truer picture of change during and after psychotherapy. Group psychotherapy (including FGAP) are effective treatments, as has been substantiated in Chapter 9. Reports of negative results in psychotherapy are not, however, often published (Hannan et al., 2005). Clinical studies have estimated that between 5 and 10% of patients in large samples deteriorated (Lambert, 2013b). Therapists should therefore reflect on whether patients who deteriorate have distinctive features such as special diagnoses or personality traits which make them more refractory to change. Therapists should, of course, also reflect on their own potential contributions to lack of improvement, some studies showing that many therapist qualities can affect patients negatively (Barkham et al., 2017; Safran et al., 2005). Patients do not, however, necessarily get worse because of a therapy or a therapist. Some patients who deteriorate may be suffering from disorders that are developing in a negative direction and might have become even worse if they had not taken part in therapy.

Note

1 The measure and scoring form can be ordered from OQ-Measures, PO Box 521047, Salt Lake City, UT 84152, USA, or www.oqmeasures.com

Chapter 9

Empirical research on group psychotherapy

Research on group psychotherapy

The history of group psychotherapy has been described as being complex, confabulatory, conflictual and conglomerate (Anthony, 1971). One reason why this history has been described in this way is that group psychotherapy emanates from many sources, and that contributors have come from many different disciplines and research areas. Parts of theory can be traced back to areas as diverse as personality theory and systems theory, contributions to the way group therapy is defined, evaluated and conceptualized coming from psychoanalytic, group dynamic, existential and behavior-focused theories. The theory and practice of today integrates material from multiple disciplines, including from psychiatry, psychology, sociology, pedagogy, social work and organizational theory.

The field that we researchers and clinicians encounter in our work is one that is made up of interactions between patients, therapists, subgroups and the group as a whole. Some form of interaction is always taking place, irrespective of whether we are processing or measuring it. Attention may, at one point in time, be directed toward one member's problems, while interest in the next moment gathers on an interaction between the therapist and another member. Each group member has inputs that affect the group as a whole, there are also combinations of inputs from members also leading the group in new directions. Inputs – are they additive, cumulative, potentiating, inhibitory or something else? The group is also in motion, developing and forming through entangled parts that then dissolve, the group moving on. The group and the process can never go back to where it was.

A great deal of research has been conducted into psychotherapy, both individual psychotherapy and group psychotherapy. Systematic research into psychodynamic group psychotherapy is, however, still sparse. This is evident in what is popularly called the "bible" of psychotherapy research: Bergin and Garfield's *Handbook of Psychotherapy and Behavior Change* (Lambert, 2013a). Group therapy research, which has its own chapter in this book (Burlingame et al., 2013; Burlingame & Strauss, 2021), presents a number of review articles of controlled individual studies, the authors of these concluding that group psychotherapy is effective both as a primary and adjunctive therapy for a variety of

DOI: 10.4324/9781003216377-12

mental disorders. A review also indicates that group therapy is just as effective as individual psychotherapy (McRoberts et al., 1998). A large number of studies carried out in recent decades examine the effect of cognitive behavioral therapy (CBT). Psychodynamic group therapy, has, however, been less well explored. Searches for outcome studies in larger databases show that there are a number of good quality studies that show that analytic/group analytic groups are effective for a variety of mental disorders (Lorentzen, 2006; Blackmore et al., 2012). These studies are, however, mainly based on studies of long-term therapies. I would therefore like to take this opportunity to look more closely at some of the research that I have participated in (including the research group I led), that compared the effect of short- and long-term group therapy. This research was partly motivated by a desire to contribute to an increase in evidence of the potential effectiveness of psychodynamic therapy, and partly by a desire to fight the resistance to research among psychodynamically oriented therapists, which I found to be threatening to the survival of the art and craft. Studies of the effect of short and long-term group analytic psychotherapy have also given me, and hopefully others in the field, a new perspective on some established clinical "truths". The research, the resulting publications and the intense and valuable cooperation that lies behind these have given me the rationale – and not least the inspiration – for writing this book.

I would like to emphasize two aspects of the lack of empirical evidence in psychodynamic short and long-term group therapy. Firstly, that there is a wealth of research on individual psychotherapy that is also valid for group psychotherapy. For example, the importance of personality factors to individual growth and change. Secondly, research results on group therapy that are based on other theoretical backgrounds, may also be valid in psychodynamic group therapy. This includes aspects such as the importance of leadership, group structure, therapeutic alliance and group cohesion. Some of the results from these areas of research will therefore also be cited here.

It is impossible to do this research field full justice within the framework of a book chapter. I will therefore select the findings that I consider to be particularly important, and that meet my three goals for the following presentation. These goals are that findings show the breadth and complexity of this research field and can be used to draw some general lines in the development of group research over time and finally are of significance to group psychotherapy in general and focused time-limited group analytic psychotherapy in particular.

Why is research on groups so difficult?

Figure 9.1 provides an overview of the variables that may contribute to the improvement of patients participating in group psychotherapy (reworked from Burlingame et al., 2013).

The model is based on research that has shown that group psychotherapy does, by and large, contribute to the improvement of the majority of patients, of their symptoms, interpersonal problems, psychosocial functioning and self-esteem.

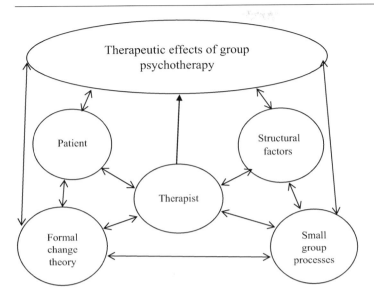

Figure 9.1 Factors contributing to change in group psychotherapy.

The factors that contribute to this improvement arise from five potential sources: formal change theory, small group processes, structural factors, and patient and therapist characteristics. *Formal change theory* encompasses the change mechanisms that are believed to be effective in different theoretical approaches. These approaches include psychodynamic therapy, interpersonal therapy, cognitive behavioral therapy and existentially oriented therapies. These mechanisms are often the same in individual and group therapy. For example insight into underlying conflicts is found to be important to change in psychodynamic therapy (Johansson et al., 2010). The second factor is *small group processes*. These are made up of group mechanisms that are empirically associated with positive outcomes, and the important role phenomena such as group relationships, the alliance between the individual patient and the therapist, and interactions and mutual feedback from participants play in these mechanisms. The therapeutic factors described in Chapter 6 can be included in this. *Patient characteristics* are often factors that are related to the patient's mental health problems. These include diagnosis, severity, type of symptoms, functional impairment, demographic variables, personality type and traits. Psychodynamic therapy often places an emphasis on personality variables such as the patient's ability to mentalize behavior (to understand psychological connections), maturity of defense mechanisms and moral standards (superego functioning). *Structural factors* include the number and frequency of sessions, duration of the therapy, group size and setting. *Therapist characteristics* include the therapist's interventions, but also the therapist's personality, cultural background, training and life experiences.

The many different types and degrees of interaction possible between the different factors shows how complex the research field for a group of six to eight patients and one to two therapists can be.

I will run through some of the research on these factors. But I would first like to present Lambert's simplified estimate of factors that may explain change through psychotherapy (Lambert, 1992). He claims that 40% of the improvement in patients in psychotherapy is due to conditions outside the therapy, such as spontaneous improvement or social support. He also claims that 30% is due to factors that are common to most therapies, such as contract, therapeutic alliance and support from the therapist and other patients, while only 15% is due to the methods and techniques that are specific to that therapy. Finally, he believes that 15% of improvement is due to the patient's optimism and positive expectations of the therapy. Some of his estimates have been replicated by other researchers such as Cuijpers et al. (2012).

Group structure

Aspects of this theme have been discussed earlier in this book, and the significance of the time factor is elaborated later in this chapter under "Our practice-based clinical research". I will therefore limit myself here to mentioning some studies on "patient preparation", a key FGAP structuring factor. Openness about what patients can expect to meet in the group, and instructions on how to behave in different situations have been, in a number of early studies, associated with better treatment outcome (Friedlander & Kaul, 1983; Kaul & Bednar, 1986; LaTorre, 1977; Shapiro & Morris, 1978). Bednar and Kaul (1994) reviewed five studies that included control groups, randomization of patients, equal participants and multiple outcome variables, and found that patients who had been prepared did better than controls (France & Dugo, 1985; Budman et al., 1984; Steuer et al., 1984; O'Farrell et al., 1985; Muller & Scott, 1984).

Patient variables

I will here use our research into group analytic psychotherapy as examples of studies that map patient variables to predict outcomes in group analytic psychotherapies of different durations. These studies demonstrate that length of education, absence of personality disorder, low severity of symptomatic distress, low chronicity, positive expectations and personality traits such as good mentalizing ability, higher ego-strength, high quality of object relations and less interpersonal problems predict better outcomes in short-term therapies, but are less important in long-term therapies (Lorentzen & Høglend, 2004, 2005, 2008; Fjeldstad et al., 2016).

Therapist variables

The therapist's behavior in the group is an important resource in building a group analytic treatment culture. Most professionals were concerned, in the 1970s, with the *nonspecific and personal aspects* of leadership (genuineness, empathy, support and self-disclosure). The therapist's interventions became, however, increasingly more important, evaluations of leadership style to a great extent being based on the degree of the therapist's "directiveness". Dies (1994), after reviewing a number of studies of the associations between leadership and outcomes, demonstrated that active structuring was particularly important in short-term group therapy. The studies he reviewed, however, provided little information on which components of factors such as content, timing or focus were important. Studies of socio-demographic conditions in the therapist have yielded few findings (Beutler et al., 1994). Henry et al. (1990) found that dogmatic and controlling therapists had poorer patient outcomes in short-term psychodynamic therapy. Another study found that therapist characteristics such as openness and flexibility were unrelated to outcome (Zimpfer & Waltman, 1982), while a third study found those aspects to be positively related to subsequent psychotherapy process and outcome (Weinstock-Savoy, 1986). This may indicate that these dimensions interact with other variables such as the type of therapy being offered, or another unknown factor. A meta-analysis of high-quality studies of the effect of the therapists' professional education (Berman & Norton, 1985; Weisz et al., 1987; Crits-Christoph et al., 1991) showed that experienced therapists achieved slightly better results. The studies were conducted in the context of individual therapy. It is, however, reasonable to believe that education is equally important in group therapists, as group interventions are often considered more difficult and more complicated to master than individual therapy. There has been an increase over the last decade in studies of the importance of the therapist's personality, clinical experience and education upon therapy outcome (Wampold & Imel, 2015; Orlinsky et al., 2015). An interesting Norwegian study of participants of small self-experience groups in a group analysis education program found that lower levels of attachment anxiety among therapists and candidates (individually and on average) led, over a year, to a greater improvement in the interpersonal problems of candidates. The degree of avoidance was not related to outcome (Leitemo et al., 2019). There are currently few such studies. Bergin and Garfield's *Handbook of Psychotherapy and Behavior Change* (Lambert, 2013a) introduced a separate chapter on the importance of psychotherapist education/experience (Hill & Knox, 2013), which has been continued in the latest edition (Knox & Hill, 2021). Research within this field is therefore expected to expand in the future.

Use of co-therapists

Co-therapy (two or more therapists) is widely used, but has been less studied systematically. A common argument from clinical practice is that the use of multiple therapists increases the ability to model effective interpersonal interactions. Other arguments are that "four eyes are better than two", that more burdensome groups may be easier to run if two therapists share the challenges of leadership, and that group sessions also do not have to be cancelled if one therapist is absent due to illness or other reasons. McNary and Dies (1993) discovered, however, that co-therapists rarely interacted with each other during sessions. Their study also showed that patients often did not distinguish between co-therapists. Patients in groups for the treatment of borderline patients, however, seem to more often perceive the co-therapists as different, idealizing for example one and devaluing the other. Co-therapists may therefore judge patients differently based on different countertransference reactions. The therapists' recognition of this can provide important information on the patients' inner world, which again can be useful in the therapeutic work (Greene et al., 1985, 1986; Lorentzen, 2009).

Therapeutic factors

Therapeutic factors is a central area of group process research (Yalom, 1995; Bloch & Crouch, 1985). Some of the more recent research in this area has been covered in Chapter 6 (The Group Process), therapeutic factors being important in clinical work and in FGAP. I will therefore provide here some historical background of this research.

It is well documented that group psychotherapy is an effective treatment for a variety of mental disorders (Burlingame et al., 2013). There is, however, relatively little knowledge of the *mechanisms* (causes) behind change in group psychotherapy, and in individual psychotherapy, despite group psychotherapy being widely used as a treatment in mental health care for a long time. Two British psychiatrists studying the state of the art decided, decades ago, to try to distinguish between conditions of change, therapeutic factors (mechanisms behind change) and therapeutic techniques (Bloch & Crouch, 1985; Bloch et al., 1981). They found that very few researchers had been interested in this topic before Corsini and Rosenberg's (1955) large study of 300 clinical publications on *group therapy outcomes*. Corsini and Rosenberg selected 67 articles that contained 220 claims on *"therapeutic elements"* and categorized them into ten therapeutic factors: acceptance, altruism, universality, intellectualization, reality testing, transference, interaction, spectator therapy, ventilation of emotions and a "mixed factor". They then divided these factors into three subgroups: intellectual (cognitive), emotional and action-oriented factors. This study was seen as being the first important step in bringing order and classification to the group therapy stage. Four methods were, in particular, used in later studies: (1) Patients were asked what they had experienced as being helpful in the therapy. (2) Therapists were asked what they thought was effective. (3) Independent evaluators observed the therapies and tried to associate elements of the process with good or poor results. (4) The responses were statistically processed by calculating the strength of associations between process variables and therapy effect, or by factor analyses (Hill, 1975; Berzon et al., 1963; Yalom, 1975; Bloch et al., 1979).

The importance of factors such as catharsis, insight, interpersonal learning and altruism has been demonstrated in group theory and practice over many years.

These factors consist of both interpersonal and intrapsychic mechanisms. The exploration of the actual effect on group members is, however, still at an early stage (Bednar & Kaul, 1994). More recent research has also been conducted in this area (Joyce et al., 2011).

Outcome research on group psychotherapy

The practice of group therapy started over a hundred years ago, and has resulted in a rich descriptive literature that includes anecdotal reports and descriptions of single groups. Interest also increased in investigating the results of the treatment for a wider range of patients, as the number of studies grew. Early reviews such as Burchard et al. (1948) and Thomas (1943) summarized studies that showed a positive, negative or no effect (box-score method). The results were divergent, and control groups were often chosen based on convenience. Review articles from the 1960s were based on studies that contained more information and were methodologically better (Rickard, 1962; Pattison, 1965: Stotsky & Zolik, 1965). Many studies were carried out on groups of prisoners or inmates, the control groups therefore differing from those studied. *The effects* (outcomes) of group psychotherapy was still the most important topic of research in the 1970s, review articles in this period including studies with more stringent method requirements. Seven review articles showed that group therapy not only consistently outperformed control groups, but also yielded results that are as good as individual therapy or alternative psychological treatments (Bednar & Kaul, 1978; Emrick, 1975; Lieberman, 1976; Luborsky et al., 1975; Meltzoff & Kornreich, 1970; Grunebaum, 1975; Parloff & Dies, 1977). The exceptions to this were conditions that included thought disorders or phobias (Bednar & Lawlis, 1971). Several researchers, including Kanas (1986), have later shown that patients with schizophrenia can be helped by groups. The results were more encouraging than previous studies, probably due to the inclusion of more outpatients in the reviews and the use of improved research methodology.

Smith and Glass (1977) introduced meta-analysis, a new method for measuring change in therapy. They, using a standardized measure called *effect size* (ES), were able to take the average of several outcome measures in one study, and so allow the changes to be compared or combined with results from other studies.

Five meta-analyses from the 1980s compared the effect of group therapy and individual therapy, and confirmed that there were no differences in the outcomes of the two (Miller & Berman, 1983; Robinson et al., 1990; Smith et al., 1980; Tillitski, 1990). A similar meta-analysis showed a small, non-significant difference in favor of individual therapy (Shapiro & Shapiro, 1982). Two similar studies reported not only that individual therapy was significantly better, but also that the placebo control had the same effect as group therapy (Dush et al., 1983; Nietzel et al., 1987). Upon closer scrutiny, however, it emerged that the groups in these studies were cognitive behavioral therapy groups that used the group format to run individually oriented, pre-established treatment programs. No attempts were made to use the specific therapeutic qualities of groups such as group cohesion, interpersonal learning, or reliving the family group (Yalom, 1995; Bloch & Crouch, 1985). Fuhriman and Burlingame (1994) describe these therapies as "individual therapy in the presence of others".

It also became more common in the 1980s to look for theoretical and empirical mechanisms of change. Research criteria and designs improved further, and studies were increasingly conducted on specific treatment models and homogeneous patient samples. Several types of group therapy were also gradually developed, and an interest in the effect of specific brands such as gestalt therapy, interpersonal therapy, system-oriented therapy and cognitive behavioral therapy increasingly was at the center of research.

Comparative outcome studies of group and individual psychotherapy have largely shown similar results for therapies based on different theoretical backgrounds. This has been termed "the dodo bird verdict", a term taken from Alice in Wonderland (Carroll, 2012): "Everyone has won and everyone should have a prize!" The term and connotation was introduced by Rosenzweig (1936) and was used by Luborsky and co-workers (1975) to describe different psychotherapeutic approaches that appear to achieve the same results.

I also see the result of McRoberts and co-workers' (1998) meta-analysis that group therapy is as effective as individual psychotherapy, as a kind of "dodo bird verdict". McRoberts only included studies (23) in which differences between the effect of individual and group therapy were examined within the same project. This was an attempt to reduce the effect of confounding (underlying, unknown) factors that might explain differences. The authors, however, found no differences in outcomes. The study showed great heterogeneity in both clinical diagnosis and type of therapies. Most studies were also based on cognitive behavioral therapy that used the group form for didactic or time-saving purposes, without focusing on interaction and specific group processes. The therapies lasted an average 16 sessions. A recent review article that placed even greater emphasis on scientific rigor in design showed similar results (Burlingame et al., 2016a).

One reason for the "dodo bird verdict" may be that nonspecific therapeutic factors are effective in all forms of psychotherapy. Another may be that our research methodology is not sensitive enough to detect important differences between the active ingredients of the group process. Many psychotherapy researchers believe the presence of these factors varies with type of psychotherapy. This should therefore result in different degrees of change, if measurement techniques with adequate sensitivity and specificity are used.

Research into group therapy outcomes has, since the beginning of the 1990s, concentrated on the study of specific patient populations undergoing a specific theoretically founded therapy form, particularly cognitive behavioral therapy (CBT). Structural features of group therapy have also been studied (Burlingame & Jensen, 2017). Strong criticism has been expressed in psychodynamic circles that researchers have relied too much on descriptive, categorical classification of mental disorders rather than emphasizing the evaluation of the level of personality organization and functionality (Shedler & Westen, 2004; Lingiardi & McWilliams, 2017). A lot of research has also focused on hunting for moderators and mediators. A moderator is a factor that contributes to whether a particular therapy goes well or not. For example, the more personality pathology a patient has, the less improvement is achieved in time-limited therapy (Fjeldstad et al., 2017). A mediator is an expression of a mechanism that has a causal relationship with outcomes. For example, this could be that the more insight a patient gains of their internal conflicts, the fewer symptoms they have. The assumption is that an increase in insight precedes a change in symptoms (Johansson et al., 2010).

Psychodynamic short-term groups

Little had been done prior to the early 1980s to develop models for time-limited psychodynamic *group* therapy for outpatients. This contrasts psychodynamic *individual* therapy, several clinicians developing short-term models early on (Alexander & French, 1946; Balint et al., 1972; Mann, 1973; Malan, 1976; Sifneos, 1979). These authors agreed on the importance of using time efficiently, of trying to separate out a core conflict, and of using confrontation and interpretations of unconscious material related to this conflict in the treatment. They also supported patient autonomy and self-esteem by encouraging patients to take responsibility for the treatment, and to believe that they would be able to cope (Marmor, 1979). They all selected patients for treatment based on a set of criteria, such as emphasizing the need for sufficient ego-strength to benefit from the therapy. Patients with psychoses, severe substance abuse, organically based or severe personality pathology were considered unsuitable for short-term individual psychotherapy (Marmor, 1979; Sifneos, 1979).

Time-limited psychodynamic groups were initially used in crisis intervention (Donovan et al., 1979), problem solving (Waxer, 1977) and to work with patients with specific problems such as chronic physical illness. The method was also used later more purposefully in the treatment and research on patients with specific diagnoses, such as pathological grief (Piper et al., 2011; Piper et al., 2007), fatigue syndrome (Sandahl et al., 2011) and eating disorders (Tasca et al., 2006). Time-limited psychodynamic group therapy has also been used in the treatment research of patients with mixed diagnoses (see, for example, Lorentzen et al., 2013). All of these studies used control groups, and show that patients change during therapy in the problem areas the treatment is particularly focused on, or on specific outcome measures such as symptoms, interpersonal problems or psychosocial functioning. Time-limited psychodynamic group therapy has been widely used in clinical practice. There are, however, still relatively few methodologically sound studies and thus limited research evidence of their use. I would, however, like to refer to a naturalistic study by Jensen et al. (2010) in which 236 neurotic outpatients suffering from depression, anxiety and personality disorders (39%) were treated in a psychodynamic group therapy lasting 39 sessions. The authors found that (for symptoms) the changes had an effect size of 0.7 (moderate to large) for patients overall, which increased to about 1.0 (large) when patients with low baseline values were excluded. Forty-three percent of the patients, however, remained unchanged or deteriorated.

Our practice-based clinical research (background for FGAP)

I will describe below some of the research behind the development of Focused Group Analytic Psychotherapy that I have been involved in. The research was based on standard clinical practice, to increase the external validity of the results. The patient sample and diagnoses are therefore heterogeneous. The research focused on the outcomes of psychodynamic group psychotherapy, the significance of treatment length upon outcome, and the relationship between aspects of group process and outcome, and was carried out on two different patient samples. The first project was implemented in my own specialist practice (Lorentzen et al., 2002), the second involved patients from three different district psychiatric centers and patients from groups treated by three private practitioners (Lorentzen et al., 2013).

The effectiveness of long-term group analysis – a naturalistic study

In the late 1980s I started a study of patients treated in three slow-open groups in my private practice. I systematically gathered information from 69 patients over many years. The patients were assessed through evaluation interviews with me before and after therapy, and also through separate follow-up interviews with me and with a psychiatrist who had not been involved in the treatment, one year after the end of therapy. The therapist assessed the patients' psychosocial functioning (Global Assessment of Functioning, GAF), and the patients rated themselves on symptoms and the degree/type of their interpersonal problems. The aim was to investigate the effectiveness of the therapy, predictors of outcomes and the associations between therapeutic alliance, group cohesion and outcome. The patients suffered from different types of anxiety disorders and depressive disorders, 68% being diagnosed with personality disorders. A little over half were women and the mean age was 36 years. The patients spent on average 32.5 months (range six months to eight years) in therapy, only two patients leaving prematurely (before six months). Results: The effect size of change from pre-therapy to follow-up was large, patients also continuing to change during the follow-up year. At follow-up, 61% to 86% of patients were clinically significantly improved or recovered on symptomatic distress, interpersonal problems and psychosocial functioning. The main conclusion was that group analysis was an effective treatment for outpatients with mixed diagnoses. However, we also demonstrated positive associations between process elements and outcome (Lorentzen et al., 2002; Lorentzen & Høglend, 2004; Lorentzen et al., 2004).

The study was carried out in a long-term therapy where the patients themselves had a significant influence on the length of the treatment. Predictor analysis demonstrated that treatment duration of up to two and a half years was a positive predictor of outcome, while patients who received longer treatment in a group did not change further. Based on the hypothesis that several of the patients could have benefitted from a shorter therapy, we investigated whether the interaction between treatment length and patient characteristics could predict outcome. We found that longer therapy seemed to be desirable for patients with a higher degree of depression, a greater level of symptomatic distress, a higher degree of interpersonal sensitivity, a severe personality disorder (Cluster A or B) and patients characterized with "less assertive", more "exploitable" or more "intrusive" traits on the IIP-Circumplex of Interpersonal Problems (Alden et al., 1990; Lorentzen & Høglend, 2008).

These results stimulated our interest in examining the significance of treatment duration more independently of what patients wanted, in a new randomized study with a more stringent research methodology.

Short-term and long-term group analytic therapy – who needs what?

Patients were randomized in the next clinical trial into short-term or long-term manualized group psychotherapy of 20 or 80 weekly sessions of 90 minutes, treatment length being therefore around six or 24 months respectively. The 167 patients were all treated in the outpatient clinics of three district psychiatric centers (DPS) and in three independent private practices. The study included all patients in a total of 18 groups (nine short-term and nine long-term) run by nine therapists, each therapist running one short-term and one long-term group. The patients were interviewed before the therapy started, and three years later by a professional who was not involved in the treatment. The interviewers also rated the patients on psychosocial functioning (GAF; American Psychiatric Association, 2000) at three points in time (before and after therapy, and at three years after baseline). The patients also rated a number of self-report measures repeatedly over time, and were followed-up for seven years after the first evaluation (SCL-90-R, IIP-C). The results are summarized below.

We analyzed the results both for what we have called "the typical patient" (averaged across the whole sample), for patients *with* and *without* personality disorders, and compared the results of the two group formats. We used linear mixed models for longitudinal data analysis (LMM; Fitzmaurice et al., 2004). Therapy effects are expressed in effect sizes, which indicate *the difference in change between patients treated in the two therapy formats*.

The typical patient

The "typical" patient showed significantly greater improvement in the short-term therapy than in the long-term therapy in the first six months (until the end of the short-term therapy). Patients in the long-term sample only caught up about one year later, toward the end of the long-term therapy (Lorentzen et al., 2013).

Patients in the long-term sample continued, however, to improve after the end of therapy and for the next four years (from the end of therapy to follow-up, seven years after baseline). This is called *delayed effect*. The patients in short-term therapy *maintained* the improvement achieved during therapy for seven years after baseline. The effect sizes (differences in change between the two therapies) over the last four years, measured by symptomatic distress and level of interpersonal problems, respectively, were small and moderate, in favor of long-term therapy. These results are quite unique, both because of the long follow-up period, and because the results spring from a study in which the outcomes of short and long-term therapy are compared within the same project (Lorentzen et al., 2015a).

Patients with and without a personality disorder

Patients *with* personality disorders showed, not surprisingly, a larger improvement in the long-term than in the short-term groups. This difference was significant for all outcome measures up to the three-year follow-up. An interesting finding was that patients *without* personality disorder did as well in short-term as in long-term therapy from 0 to 36 months (change modeled linearly between the two time-points). The improvement, however, *started earlier* in the short-term group (as shown by plots of the raw data), patients showing significantly greater improvement in the short-term group at the point in time at which the group terminated. Patients received no additional benefit from long-term therapy. This is an important argument for maintaining that patients with less personality pathology often will receive sufficient help from short-term therapy (Lorentzen et al., 2015b).

We also carried out a seven-year follow-up and again compared the change for patients with and without personality disorder. The results confirmed our hypothesis that patients *with* a personality disorder improved at the group-level significantly more in long-term than in short-term therapy. The effect sizes were moderate. Patients *without* personality disorders, however, responded equally well in the two treatments over the last six and a half years and ended up with the same final value. This confirmed our previous findings, both about change occurring more quickly in short-term therapy, and that these patients did not appear to improve further after six months (Fjeldstad et al., 2016).

Change of interpersonal problems (IIP-C sub-scales)

I describe in detail in Chapter 4 how the Interpersonal Circumplex (IIP-C) provides a picture of how the individual patient experiences dealing with other people. This is expressed within eight interpersonal domains (sub-scales). Fjeldstad and co-workers (2016) found that patients *with a personality disorder* in long-term therapy showed a significantly higher change than in short-term therapy on the sub-scales of *socially avoidant, non-assertive, exploitable* and *overly nurturant*. This also continued for as long as seven years after starting therapy.

There were, however, no significant differences between the groups for the sub-scales of domineering, vindictive or reserved. Fjeldstad and co-workers had by then already demonstrated that short-term therapy had, after six months, led to a significantly higher change in *the typical patient* on the *reserved* and *socially avoidant* sub-scales than long-term therapy had. This difference had, however, disappeared after three years. There was a significant (and equal) change in the areas of *reserved, socially avoidant, submissive, exploitable* and *overly nurturant* for patients in both therapies. The high initial change in sub-scales again suggests that short-term therapy *is more activating* than long-term therapy, and that some of the effect persists for several years after the therapy is terminated (Fjeldstad et al., 2017).

Change in self-concept

We also compared differences in changes of self-concept between the two treatments, using the Structural Analysis of Social Behavior (SASB; Benjamin, 1988). This is a self-report measure that expresses two dimensions of self-image: *affiliation* (self-love versus self-attack) and *autonomy* (self-emancipation versus self-control).

It was found that patients in long-term therapy changed significantly on both variables, while patients in short-term therapy changed only on autonomy. The difference in change in self-love, which is a weighted variable, was explained by the fact that patients in long-term therapy showed a far greater improvement in the sub-scales *self-blame, self-attack* and *self-neglect*. Patients with more negative attitudes toward themselves can be expected to receive greater benefit from long-term than from short-term therapy. Patients achieve increased autonomy in, however, both groups (Lorentzen et al., 2015c).

Process research

There is agreement in group circles that many types of groups are effective for a wide range of mental disorders. Several questions, however, remain. Are all forms of group therapy effective? What type of patient benefits from a particular type of therapy? Are there specific, definable elements in the group process that lead to change? Are the main sources of improvement nonspecific in most types of therapies, such as being accepted and included in the group, and others showing warmth, concern and care? For an in-depth discussion of some of these topics see, for example, Wampold and Imel's book *The Great Psychotherapy Debate* (2015).

Group relationships, cohesion and alliance

Therapeutic elements in the group's ecosystem represent an important field of research. Attempts have been made to measure and analyze interactions in groups and between individuals, the therapist and the group as a whole, the Structural

Analysis of Social Behavior (SASB; Benjamin, 1988) being one such system. Research into the group's developmental phases (MacKenzie, 1997) also describes challenges and transactions in the group process. The idea is that group members change with the group as it transitions through different stages or phases. Each stage places different and new demands on the therapist, and exposes the participants in the group to different development tasks that must be handled in an appropriate way if the group is to progress.

Relatively few had until recently studied the association between therapeutic alliance and outcome in group psychotherapy (Marziali et al., 1997; Budman et al., 1989; Lorentzen, Sexton, & Høglend, 2004; Joyce et al., 2007; Lorentzen et al., 2012). Therapeutic alliance is significantly associated with outcomes in several of these studies. Comparing results may, however, be difficult due to the use of different alliance measures. A new meta-analysis of 29 studies including 3628 patients, indicates that the weighted average correlation between alliance and treatment outcome is significant r = .17 (p < .001) (Allredge, Burlingame, Yang & Rosendahl, 2021).

The most important process factor in group psychotherapy, and the one that has been most studied, is cohesion.

Cohesion and outcome in FGAP

We, in the research project described earlier (Lorentzen et al., 2013), also wanted to study how cohesion was associated with treatment outcome and to study how patient characteristics measured before the start of therapy, such as symptoms, interpersonal problems and the presence of personality disorder, were associated with cohesion. The results showed that cohesion in short-term therapy, in terms of symptoms and interpersonal problems at the termination of therapy, was significantly and positively associated with outcomes but not at follow-up two and a half years later. There was no significant association in the long-term therapy between cohesion and outcome either at six months or one year after termination. This may indicate that cohesion is a more important factor in short-term than in long-term therapy. A higher initial level of interpersonal problems had a negative effect on cohesion, but only in the short-term therapy. This may be due to a higher demand for interactional work early in short-term therapy, problematic relationship patterns therefore being more strongly activated than in long-term therapy (Lorentzen et al., 2018).

The development of group climate in short-term and long-term therapy

In this study we compared the development of group climate in short-term and long-term therapy (early, mid and late phase) for the patient sample used in the previous study (Lorentzen et al., 2013). The Group Climate Questionnaire (MacKenzie, 1981) consists of 12 items and provides scores on three sub-scales:

engagement (cohesion), avoidance and conflict. Engagement correlates highly with many cohesion measures. Patients' scores of engagement were, however, found to increase linearly throughout the short-term therapy, but dipped in the mid-phase in long-term therapy, rising again in the late phase. This may reflect that there is a consistently higher level of activity in short-term therapy, that group members also work more in the here-and-now mode and try to maintain a greater enthusiasm throughout the therapy. A low-high-low pattern was, however, found for both "avoidance" and "conflict" for both therapies. Both dimensions increased in the mid-phase, decreasing most in the end phase of long-term therapy (Bakali et al., 2013).

Research challenges in the cohesion–outcome relationship

The importance of cohesion has been extensively addressed in a relatively new meta-analysis of the associations between cohesion and outcome. The paper, which includes 55 studies and more than 6,000 patients, shows a statistically significant correlation of moderate effect size between cohesion and improvement (Burlingame et al., 2018). The authors found six moderator variables that all predicted the effect size variance found. These variables were type of outcome measures (interpersonal problems, symptoms, depression), therapist interventions aimed at increasing group cohesion, theoretical orientation, group type, emphasis on group interaction and dose (number of group sessions). Most of these elements are also seen to be relevant to FGAP, and attempts have therefore been made to integrate them into this therapy. Clinical implications of the study include that group therapists are routinely recommended to evaluate the development of cohesion, and to actively intervene to improve and develop cohesion in its numerous manifestations during therapy. The Group Questionnaire (Krogel, 2009) described below can be a helpful tool.

Group Questionnaire (OQ-GQ Norwegian)

Cohesion has become synonymous with the therapeutic relationships in a group. The field has, as mentioned earlier, suffered from uncertainties due to the diversity of measuring instruments and definitions of group relationships (Burlingame et al., 2002). Cohesion, from the patient's point of view, consists of three structural components: the patient–patient relationship, the patient–group relationship and the patient–therapist relationship. These three components are also included in the therapist's view, plus the therapist–group relationship and if there is a co-therapist, the therapist–therapist relationship.

Johnson et al. (2005) sought to achieve a conceptual clarification of the conundrum of competing cohesion measures. They therefore carried out a factor analysis of the items in the four most commonly used cohesion measures – Group Climate Questionnaire, cohesion, therapeutic alliance and empathy. This resulted in *three qualitative factors* that encompassed two affective aspects (*positive emotional bonds* and *negative relationships*) and one work-based facet of group relationships (*positive work*). These three qualitative factors were then intersected with the three structural patient factors mentioned above, to capture the diversity of the group relationships. The factors have been partially validated in follow-up studies (Bormann & Strauss, 2007; Bakali et al., 2009). A user-friendly cohesion measure, the Group Questionnaire, was arrived at by reducing the number of underlying items (GQ; Krogel, 2009; Krogel et al., 2013).

The Group Questionnaire (GQ) has 30 items and is based on self-report. The items are rated by the group members on a Likert scale ranging from 1 (totally disagree) to 7 (strongly agree) and provides a score for each of the three sub-scales relative to the other patients, the therapists and the group as a whole. Examples of questions under "positive relationships" are "The group therapists were kind and warm to me" and "I felt I could trust the group therapists". Examples of "positive work" include "The group therapists and I agree on what is important to work with" and "The other group members and I agree on what I need to do in treatment". Examples of "negative relationships" are "The group members were distant and withdrawn in relation to each other" and "There were sparks and irritation among the group members". GQ is also available in Norwegian as "Questionnaire on the group" (Outcome Questionnaire-Group Questionnaire-Norwegian, translated by Lorentzen et al., 2016). This measure has been used and validated on a sample of 369 patients with personality disorders (PD) in Norway, and the study concluded that GQ with three latent factors and eight subfacets can be recommended for future research and clinical practice in patient populations with PD (Pedersen, et al., 2021).

There are still only a limited number of studies on the use of GQ in clinical practice. I therefore conclude this section by referring to two controlled studies that found that continuous feedback to therapists on patients' experiences of group relationships resulted in significantly better treatment outcomes and fewer premature terminations (Burlingame et al., 2018; Gleave et al., 2017).

Chapter 10

Supervision in Focused Group Analytic Psychotherapy (FGAP)

Supervision in psychotherapy is based on the master–apprentice model and a more experienced and knowledgeable professional assisting a less experienced colleague in the execution of their professional duties. In this chapter I will present some of the rationale and theory of supervision, illustrating this with two models of supervision and with clinical examples. I will primarily focus on supervision in FGAP. Some of the material presented also applies to supervision in other psychodynamic group psychotherapies.

The profession of "psychotherapist" is not one in its own right in Norway, and requires postgraduate training. Individual psychotherapy has mainly been provided by psychiatrists and psychologists who have received some training in theory and practice, including supervision, during their basic education. A new trend was, however, begun in the 1980s by the Norwegian Psychiatric Association opening a training program in dynamic group psychotherapy for other members of the mental health profession such as social workers and psychiatric nurses, but also for priests who work closely with mental health services. Systematic and more advanced training in different types of psychotherapy is, however, provided by different private institutes, which usually operate independently of universities and colleges. A weakness of the latter is that it can create and maintain irrational competition around which psychotherapeutic approach is best, and hinder the steady accumulation and integration of a common core of knowledge within each field. Another side effect could be a bias toward the critical evaluation of ongoing teaching. Kernberg (1986, 2012) has argued that psychoanalytic training institutes should develop closer links with universities, to ensure that both the theoretical curriculum and practical activities are based on research, to prevent orthodoxy. I think that the institutes that teach other psychotherapeutic approaches and modes also would benefit from a closer association with academia.

What is supervision?

Purpose/definition

Supervision is a collaboration between colleagues, candidates and supervisor, each of whom may be from different professions. All, however, have experience

DOI: 10.4324/9781003216377-13

as psychotherapists. One of the participants in supervision is, however, usually more experienced than the others. All are usually licensed to work with patients (independently or via being employed in an institution), and are ethically and legally responsible for their treatment.

The primary goal of supervision is to shed light on the therapeutic situation and to, through this, enhance the candidate's skills, in this case within FGAP. Supervision should contribute to the candidate's learning of psychotherapy *practice*, and to the development of their *practical skills* as therapists. Supervision should primarily increase the candidate's craftsmanship in clinical work, which involves the integration of practice and theoretical knowledge, theory being primarily learnt in another context.

Supervision may also have a secondary control function, and be carried out to safeguard professional knowledge standards, ethical guidelines and relevant legislation. Most supervisors, however, emphasize the practical aspect and the candidate's independent responsibility for their treatment. This view may, however, sometimes be too simplistic. Ethical (and legal) dilemmas are implicit parts of supervision. Candidates may, for example, first encounter new good or bad aspects of themselves through the process of supervision. This can, however, activate new and unexpected ethical challenges, which sometimes are more visible to the supervisor than the candidate. The sum of previous training, life experience and personal makeup usually also counts in deciding whether the therapist (candidate) struggling with "weighing and weighting" responses that involve different value choices, and finding solutions to this that are constructive for an individual patient and/or a group, is in need of advice from a more experienced colleague.

Differentiating supervision from other types of learning

The supervisor functions as a teacher. There are, however, different views on how much theory should be included in supervision. Some supervisors maintain that too much theory interferes with the candidate's intuitive resonance with a group, and that long theoretical inputs should be avoided. A good rule of thumb, however, is to take the candidate's experiences of themselves in the clinical situation as a point of departure in further discussions with the supervisor and/or in the supervision group. The timing, emotionality and relevance of what the candidate experiences as problematic are important cues of how material should be addressed and handled in supervision.

Supervision does, however, usually take place within a theoretical framework of a specific therapy model that the candidate is to learn. The supervisor should, therefore, also feel free to take the time to discuss specific interactions or, when the opportunity arises, to use clinical material to illustrate and elucidate key psychodynamic concepts. This must, however, be balanced with the candidate's previous training and degree of experience. The content and form of the supervision should also be regularly evaluated after the parties have cooperated for a while.

Distinguishing between supervision and personal psychotherapy is another boundary issue in supervision. Supervision is primarily a didactic method, in which the supervisor should confine supervision to how candidates consciously perceive themselves in interactions with patients. The question of whether uncovering techniques (inputs) should be applied arises when a candidate appears to be entangled in countertransference reactions, which impede therapy progress. It is important, in such situations, to explore whether these reactions reflect a candidate's lack of knowledge, bad habits, "blind spots" or "hang-ups", and whether these can be corrected during supervision. These situations may also be due to issues that should be worked with further in personal therapy. Repetitive, stereotypical dysfunctional reactions should always be taken seriously and explored in supervision, and the supervisor may recommend the candidate to work further with these issues in his/her personal therapy, although the problems may have firstly materialized and become visible during the supervisory work.

Why do candidates need supervision?

The main reason for supervision is that we all, in our encounters with others, meet aspects of ourselves that may impede our understanding of the other or block development of the relationship (for example countertransference). These reactions can be "induced" by patients and their use of, for example, less mature defense mechanisms such as projective identification, devaluation and primitive idealization. One supervision task is, however, to help the therapist (candidate) contain the impact of interpersonal transactions and communications, and to explore and understand their own repetitive, idiosyncratic reactions that block empathic flow in their encounters and dialogues with patients. The persons involved may regularly be unaware of the reasons why this is happening, such incidents popularly being referred to as individual "hang-ups" or "blind spots". This is the main rationale for including both supervision and personal therapy in training programs for psychotherapy, primarily in programs with a psychodynamic orientation. The main task of supervision is to explore such incidents, to map them, to try to understand what is happening and possibly explain why they are occurring. Such problems can usually be teased out during supervision if they are based on a candidate's misunderstanding, bad habits, lack of life experience, theoretical knowledge or reflect aspects or traits that they know have created problems also in other types of relationship. More rigid countertransference problems may, however, represent the candidate's more ingrained defensive operations, that are embedded in personality traits or other habitual defensive maneuvers, and which protect vulnerabilities, and therefore require more time in personal therapy to work through.

It is implicit, from the nature of supervision, that the ventilation of different ways of understanding the implications of interpersonal transactions can easily be perceived as critical commentary on what the therapist has said or done in the therapy session. Candidates may, however, handle feedback in different ways.

Most welcome it in a safe supervisory situation, and appreciate an expansion of their perspective through alternative ways of understanding phenomena. Others, despite seeking supervision, may have a more perfectionist attitude or may be more vulnerable to criticism, and therefore may be focused on saying or doing the right thing to patients and supervisors. Some candidates, for the same reason, become restrained when asked by a supervisor about something that needs to be explored. Preparations for such incidents are tentatively made during the interviews prior to contract making. See below, under "Establishing the supervisory situation".

Føyn (1995) and Schwarzenbach (1995) have shared a number of interesting experiences of receiving supervision in two different group analytic training programs, one in Norway and one in Switzerland. Many candidates feel anxious and vulnerable, particularly early in the supervisory process. It is therefore important that the supervisor tries to develop a culture which promotes a diversity (pluralism) of understanding, to curb the polarization that can easily take place and of one way of dealing with a problem being seen to be "just right", while another is "just wrong". Some comments or interventions are, of course, better than others. However, "many roads lead to Rome". One study has demonstrated that therapists who are less confident and who need more time in a dialogue to find words and phrases, may generate more trust than a therapist who appears to know it all (Nissen-Lie, 2019).

The discussion often runs more smoothly if candidates, during preliminary interviews with their supervisor, disclose their irrational sides when asked about potential "strengths and weaknesses" in their work with patients. It can also in some instances be important that a supervisor gives specific advice on personal therapy to the candidate, if they request this during supervision.

Growing interest in psychodynamic time-limited group psychotherapy

There has in recent years been a growing interest in use of short-term psychodynamic group therapy in private practice, district psychiatric centers (DPS) and in some hospitals. I think this is partly due to more professionals having completed systematic training in group therapy, and partly because group psychotherapy allows more patients to be treated without a significant increase in resource use. A new public health policy has been introduced which guarantees that patients who meet certain criteria for specific diagnoses receive treatment of a certain standard within a specific time. The need for more cost-effective treatment has therefore also grown after the introduction of this policy.

Training in psychodynamic group psychotherapy, including supervision

The Institute for Group Analysis and Group Psychotherapy's (IGA) training program, which has run continuously since 1984, is essential if the quality of psychodynamic group psychotherapy within public mental health services in Norway is to be maintained. The IGA training is a multi-level program of up to five years, and therefore allows specific modules covering therapy approaches for different groups of patients to be combined into a systematic education. The training program integrates theory with self-experience in small and large groups, and supervision of candidates' clinical work.[1] An option was recently introduced in a two-year group analytic psychotherapy module, to run a psychodynamic short-term group. This is, to the best of my knowledge, the first systematic training program in psychodynamic short-term group therapy in Norway, its inception being partly spurred by cooperation between this author and the IGA training committee in the running of courses in time-limited psychotherapy.

The Institute is a major provider of therapists to a number of mental health care areas in the country, groups having been part of Norway's mental health service for more than 50 years (Lorentzen et al., 2015c). Interest in more systematic training in psychodynamic time-limited therapy is, however, relatively new. This has possibly been motivated by competition with other time-limited treatments, such as cognitive behavioral therapy (CBT). I, however, like to think that interest in the use of psychodynamic time-limited group therapy has increased as a result of research that demonstrates that short-term therapies can be effective for patients with a range of mental disorders.

Who needs supervision in FGAP?

Many public mental health services offer supervision in group psychotherapy to employees. Supervisors may be a member of the institution's staff or an external hired-in supervisor, professionals in independent, specialist practices financing and arranging their own supervision.

I presented an overview of the different types of group therapy available in the public mental health care system in Norway in the first chapter of the book, which is provided at district psychiatric centers (DPS) and in hospitals (Lorentzen & Ruud, 2014). This study showed that about a quarter of groups were psychodynamic. However, only half of the therapists leading these groups had completed systematic therapist training. This and the recent availability of systematic training programs in short-term psychodynamic group psychotherapy mean that there is likely to be a great need for the training of supervisors in short-term group therapy. I therefore hope that this chapter will be useful in promoting this, and can contribute to more courses being held to ensure the standard in the field is maintained.

More experienced practitioners of group psychotherapy may also need FGAP supervision. This is particularly true of practitioners whose primary experience is within long-term psychotherapy. However, I consider it essential that beginners in this field receive supervision that is specifically aimed at FGAP. A more systematic training program in the supervision of time-limited therapy may also be needed to acquire good FGAP competence.

I will now describe how supervision is established and carried out, the type of help candidates need, and how supervisors intervene. I will then discuss, as a conclusion to this chapter, some examples of common problems that candidates experience during FGAP.

Establishing the supervisory situation

It is usually the person who is looking for assistance who contacts and enters into an agreement with a supervisor, after an initial interview.

Contract between supervisor and candidate

The parties should, before supervision begins, discuss the scope of the supervision, how many therapies the candidate wants assistance with, the areas to be covered (evaluation and selection of patients or the complete therapy), and how the clinical material should be presented. It should also be explicitly agreed that the parties will evaluate the supervisory relationship at regular intervals. Practical aspects such as time, place, duration and frequency of sessions, and also financial terms if the candidates themselves arepaying for this, must also be agreed upon.

Contracts, whether written or oral, general or more detailed will vary, with the amount of in-depth information candidates and supervisors want to receive on each other also, for example, varying. I think it is, however, reasonable to expect the supervisor to provide information on their professional background, previous training and experience. This can be formulated in a general way, but could also address the area of supervision. This information can be provided before or after the supervisor interviews.

I always start interviews with new candidates with their professional background and previous training. Do they have experience in psychotherapy, and if so, what type and how much? Do they have experience in or knowledge of FGAP? I ask them about whether they have thoughts about their own choice of profession and career, and also ask them about which areas they usually feel they succeed in with patients, and what they find challenging or difficult. What type of patients they prefer to work with, and the characteristics of those patients they find it difficult to establish a rapport with. What aspects of themselves they see as being a resource and what personal limitations they experience in their work with patients. Then I usually ask about their personal background, where they come from and about their family of origin. Have they established a family? Do they have a partner? Do they have children?

I try to, in this interview, notice and "get a feel of" the candidate's cognitive style, emotionality, faculty of language and ability to reflect on psychological, relational issues. Do they seem interested in their own inner world and that of others? Do they have or show interest in assumptions or hypotheses about motives that may explain their own and/or another person's manifest behavior? I also try to get an impression of whether the candidate seems to be open and inquisitive in general and in the supervision, or if they seem to be "self-sufficient" and to know it all.

The supervisor should, by the end of the interview, have a good overview of the candidate's theoretical knowledge and practical experience in the method, and in psychotherapy in general. The supervisor should also have some idea of the candidate's personal qualifications, including potential strengths and weaknesses as a therapist. However, I think that even though this relationship is between colleagues, the supervisor early on tries to formulate a pedagogical "diagnosis", a hypothesis of the candidate's qualifications and potential obstacles in developing skills in FGAP. The hypothesis would, of course, have to be revised as the relationship develops and the parties become better acquainted.

How does the supervision take place?

Models of supervision

I will now outline two common models of supervision in group psychotherapy. Figure 10.1 provides an overview of the supervision of a candidate who runs a group in an institution. The supervisor is therefore paid by the institution. Figure 10.2 demonstrates another and perhaps the most frequently used supervision model, in which a number of candidates receive supervision in a group.

Figure 10.1 shows a typical individual supervisory situation of one supervisor and one candidate. A third party, the clinical-administrative management, is responsible for the employment and wages of the supervisor, and is included to provide a complete picture (Ekstein & Wallerstein, 1972). The administration usually does not have a day-to-day influence on the practical execution of

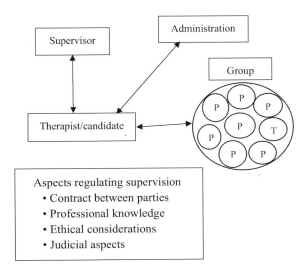

Figure 10.1 Model of individual supervision in group psychotherapy. Actors: therapist (T) (candidate), the supervisor, the administration of the institution in which the therapist is employed and a group of seven patients (P).

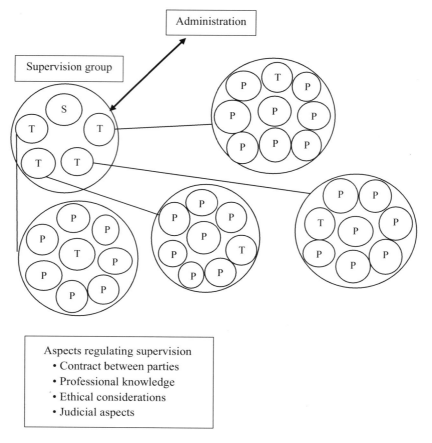

Figure 10.2 Model of group supervision in group psychotherapy. Actors: four therapists (T) (candidates) and one supervisor (S). The therapists practice at independent specialist practices.

supervision, but may affect boundary issues such as by requiring that guidelines of which patients should receive supervision are adopted, and by determining the type of group activities the institution provides. Other "actors" in the arena are the one or more groups included in the supervision, and the patients in these groups. The figure also briefly indicates factors that influence the supervisory situation, such as professional/theoretical qualities, laws and ethical guidelines.

Figure 10.2 shows a model in which the number of participants has been increased to five and consists of a supervisor and four candidates. The field becomes more complex as the number of people, candidates, patients and groups involved increases. This leads to a greater number of and variation in the feedback provided to the person presenting the clinical material. A new group element at the same time emerges. This is the potential impact of the dialogue (or discourse) between the other candidates in the supervisory group on the person who presents clinical material to the group. This factor often needs to be controlled or regulated for an optimal supervision process. The forces that define the supervisory activity are the same as in the previous model.

Advantages and disadvantages of individual and group supervision

Time must be shared in group supervision to give all candidates the opportunity to describe the patients and interactional sequences of their groups. Each candidate will therefore receive less time than in individual supervision. Candidates will have more time in individual supervision to go into greater depth of the clinical material. Group supervision, however, provides the opportunity to become acquainted with a broader spectrum of patients and a larger diversity of groups, and can therefore provide group members with a richer experience. Responses from people with different personalities and who have a different focus on the emotional, cognitive and attitudinal aspects of the clinical material also enrich the experience. This diversity is also useful to supervisors, who are exposed to new ideas and to corrections to their own perceptions and interventions.

What happens in the supervision session?

The supervision should be adapted to the circumstances that motivated the request for supervision. This includes the adaption of supervisor responses to the individual candidate or the supervisory culture that supervisors try to develop in candidate groups. Attention must also be paid to the candidates' background, including their profession, general clinical experience and theoretical knowledge of and practice in FGAP. Supervision can therefore cover a wide range of topics, from evaluation and preparation of individual patients prior to therapy, to assistance in the selection of patients and composition of groups, examination of how candidates instruct their patients to introduce themselves to fellow group members in the opening phase, follow-up of groups through subsequent phases to the final evaluation of treatment results, separation and the mourning of the termination phase. The main focus in supervision should, however, always be the candidates' perceptions and experiences of the different aspects of therapy, and on how this understanding is transformed into actions.

The primary purpose of supervision is to shed light on the therapeutic situation, and to assist candidates in their improvement of their therapeutic skills. The "therapeutic situation" is, however, a broad concept. I will therefore elaborate further on this in the following section.

Supervisory sessions can be briefly described as starting, for both supervision models, with a candidate's presentation of narratives from their therapeutic work. This can be information on individual patients, such as background, history of their disorders, psychodynamic hypotheses or information from one or more treatment sessions. Sometimes this is in a summary form, and sometimes in detail. The information can be presented verbally, as transcripts from therapy sessions or from audio or video recordings of sessions. The use of video recordings has become more widespread, the advantage of this being that the material is richer, through qualities of the speakers' voices, mimicry and other visual expressions of body language being presented. It is important to again emphasize, however, that supervision is primarily focused on the candidates' experiences, and on the assessment of the information they provide on their patients or groups. Planned presentations are often accompanied by a written version that can be used by the supervisor and other candidates. Spontaneous accounts of the candidate's experiences can also at times be helpful, particularly where the candidate feels the therapy has "stalled". The meticulous process of listening to audiotapes and producing a detailed transcript of the transactions and the progress of the group can increase the opportunity to pick up new aspects of the process, including own contributions.

How and when does a supervisor intervene?

The most valuable asset of the supervisor is their knowledge of the theoretical framework of the therapy, and their practical skills and experience in applying it. Supervisors may, as bystanders and observers of the group and individual patients, often have a greater freedom to reflect on the presented material than the candidates, who are entangled in emotional interactions.

The FGAP framework is the backdrop for the implementation of supervision, this framework being described in detail throughout much of this book. The candidates, individual patients and the group are located and interact within this framework. In the foreground, candidates present their experiences and feelings, both good and bad. The supervisor, the other candidates and sometimes the presenter of the clinical material, against this backdrop, catch glimpses of what I previously called the candidate's "pedagogical diagnosis": qualities the candidates often need to change, improve and develop.

FGAP supervisors listen to the candidate's presentation with "free-floating" attention. They must, however, at the same time keep their knowledge of the framework, which may be internalized and intuitively available, at the forefront of their consciousness. The supervisor and the supervisory process will also be subject to time constraints, a culture of exploration and learning needing to be developed, and the individual candidate's development as a therapist needing to be followed and stimulated in the time available. This means that supervisors can at times become more controlling and directive in the candidate's relationship to patient treatment focus, the emergence of signs of process phases and the group remaining primarily in a here-and-now mode. The relationships in the supervision group also represent an additional challenge to the supervisor. The starting point of this is a collegial relationship with defined goals and content. However, irrational elements can along the way often be understood to resonate with what is happening in the therapy groups (parallel processes), or as an expression of the supervisor's transference or countertransferences to one or more candidates, or vice versa.

The supervision should therefore first, after the presentation of clinical material, address the specific problems the candidate is struggling with, before the supervisor and possibly the group turns to topics that the candidates themselves may not experience as being particularly important or problematic. It can often be useful to think through and rate the issues in terms of how sensitive the clinical material is expected to be for the person presenting it. The first two points in the list below probably represent aspects that affect the candidate the most, while the next two can be seen as more "neutral":

- Incidents in which candidates experience that they struggle in their relationships with the group and individual patients. The explorations of the emotionally charged experiences can contribute to a candidate's increased understanding and development.
- What supervisors and colleagues perceive and believe about the candidate's and the group's problems, based on that disclosed in verbal and emotional interactions, possibly also in audio or video recordings.
- Observations of the group's level of functioning, interactions between group members and ultimately the patients' compliance with the group's framework.
- Different theoretical aspects.

The first two points are central aspects of working with the candidates' countertransference reactions or more idiographic responses. These are based on the candidates' potentially anti-therapeutic attitudes, or more or less ingrained personality traits. If the last is the case, the supervision may soon fail unless the features and patterns in question are to some degree recognized and found troublesome by the candidates themselves, and are something they want to change.

The exploration of interactions with the individual patient and the group provide the supervision with the greatest opportunities to develop the candidates' therapeutic skills.

Most supervisors will, after the clinical material has been presented, ask the candidates what they feel are the most important aspects that need to be discussed, and what they want feedback or help with. This will increase the opportunity of finding or reaching the candidates "at home", and to catch the essence of what they are engaged in and struggle with, both in practice and emotionally. Feedback may then be perceived to be more acceptable and easily digested, and be closer to or in line with the person's understanding. It may also be possible to build a more secure platform during the exploration of the most disturbing feelings, this gradually enabling the presenting candidate and the rest of the group to move on to other important and, for the presenter, less acknowledged areas.

The supervisors will, in both forms of supervision, be role models for the candidates through their stance and comments on the clinical material. They should therefore be relatively active in leading, particularly early in the supervisory process. The opportunities for learning in individual supervision consist of the supervisors' inputs and the candidates' capacity to reflect on themselves in their interactions with their group. Supervisors must therefore balance the level of their activity with the time allotted for the candidate's reflections. These should, furthermore, be activated and expanded throughout the supervision. The supervisor seeks, in group supervision, to develop a "supervision culture" in the same way as an "analytical culture" is developed in a therapy group. This means that the supervisor's modeling function becomes particularly important. It is, however, important that all candidates have enough room to make their comments, and are given the opportunity to individually enter into a dialogue with the person presenting the material. A unique aspect of group supervision is the dialogue and process that occurs between colleagues in the supervision group. All in the group have more or less different views of what really is going on in the therapy. If the course of such discussions becomes uncontrolled, then the process can easily become confusing or at worst detrimental to the person presenting material. It may therefore be necessary, in such cases, for the supervisor to actively suggest how the group members should weigh and weight the form and content of their feedback.

I will conclude this section by outlining a model of group supervision which handles "blind spots" in a way that is different from that sketched above. One candidate presents clinical material, while the others are explicitly asked to associate freely around and discuss this material without the intention of giving specific advice to the candidate who submitted the material (Norman & Salomonsson, 2005). The presenters listen to but do not participate in the group's discussion, and are free to make use of and pursue any ideas and suggestions that they find to be relevant to the material presented. The therapist's integrity and personal reflections can therefore be more protected.

I below briefly outline a procedure and schedule for a session of one and a half hours.

The presenter has prepared printed details of the clinical material, for example from a group session, which they distribute to all in the group. A similar model of group analytics supervision is described by Einar Johnsen (2003).

- The candidate presents the material, the participants following the narrative on their written draft (around 25 minutes).
- The presenter is then asked what part of the interactions they struggle the most with and would like to discuss. The group and the supervisor are, however, also free to ask for additional information on any topic (five to ten minutes).
- The group then freely discusses (for about 25 minutes) what has been presented, from their own point of departure. The presenter is, in this section, only allowed to listen and is not to comment. The supervisor is free to make comments at any time.
- Finally, the whole group enters the discussion. This could be concluded by the presenting candidate saying something about what they found useful in the group discussion.

Frequency and duration of sessions

Individual and group supervision sessions can be held weekly or less frequently, and have a session length that meets the candidate's wishes or the objectives of the supervision. The candidate's personal needs and experiential background are therefore taken into consideration. Whether supervision is something the therapist wants to take part in, to improve their professional skills or whether this is a requirement stipulated by clinical management or the organizer of a systematic training program (the number of supervision sessions for certification being set) will also influence session frequency and duration.

Examples of supervisory problems (FGAP)

There has until recently been no systematic training in time-limited psychodynamic group psychotherapy in Norway. The literature on time-limited psychodynamic group psychotherapy supervision is also relatively sparse. There are, however, some publications on supervision in long-term group analytic psychotherapy, in group analytic training programs (Behr, 1995; Karterud, 2003; Berg & Island, 2011). *Matrix: The Nordic Journal for Psychotherapy* has also published three theme numbers on supervision.[2] The literature on supervision in FGAP is even sparser, the therapy being quite new. Some of those I have supervised in FGAP have completed shorter or longer training in long-term psychodynamic psychotherapy at IGA, but not all. They have also completed a theoretical training in psychodynamic theory and group psychotherapy, but to varying degrees. I will, therefore, because of this diversity, limit myself to mentioning some types of problems candidates have experienced, and not describe detailed therapy sequences.

Problems with selection and evaluation of patients: patients who can benefit from focused group analytic psychotherapy can be found in day care and outpatient units at public community mental health centers (DPS), and private psychologist or psychiatrist practices. The FGAP supervisions I have conducted have partly focused on how to select patients that have the recommended level of personality organization (PO) – normal, neurotic or higher-level borderline PO. Some candidates have needed help with aspects of the evaluation. Evaluations are relatively comprehensive and require some knowledge of the psychodynamic evaluation of personality traits and structure. Others have wanted help with psychodynamic case formulation, which concludes with a psychodynamic hypothesis. The treatment focus is, after this, formulated by the therapist and the patient together, based on this hypothesis and the patient's self-reports on interpersonal problems.

Problems in the process: these problems can be diverse. They often, however, revolve around how the therapist should intervene and what to address. The first issue is often how to keep the therapeutic work in or return it to the "here-and-now mode", how to help patients remain within the treatment focus, and how to address elements of transference and resistance. Difficulties in recognizing transference and in spotting boundary incidents are examples of problems associated with knowing what to address, correct recognition and spotting allowing the therapist and others to explore and comment on this. One example could be knowing how to comment when a group member uses their iPad in a group session, or when the group plans to start a web group after the group ends. Some candidates have difficulties identifying the features of the four process stages, and are therefore less well equipped to monitor patients' progress through therapy. A further problem could be what factors should be evaluated before deciding to take a deteriorated patient out of the group.

Too much use of long-term psychodynamic therapy techniques (attitudes): some therapists show too much restraint or too little, or alternatively intervene too much with individual patients or the group as a whole. Other therapists may give long, unproductive pauses too much room or alternatively work too much with material from the there-and-then (outside the group) or with psychogenetic material (from the past).

Lack of confidence in one's own leadership: one candidate was criticized for passivity. He, however, replied that he was afraid of "prodding" patients too much and of reminding them of their therapy focus, pointing out their transferences and important parts of their treatment focus at the first meeting for those who did not present this. This candidate also had difficulties reflecting upon whether this could be a countertransference reaction on his part, or whether he thought the patients were in fact more vulnerable than he initially thought when selecting them for the group. Another candidate had a pervasive tendency of automatically (and stereotypically) asking the patient why she did this or that, instead of committing through a more direct comment on what he thought of the patient's repetitive, stereotypical, but emotionally charged outputs. Direct comments might have stimulated the patient to "think twice" or made it possible for her to observe herself from the outside.

The problems described above may be partly due to lack of experience and lack of FGAP method knowledge, and partly due to the candidates' previous experience being mainly within long-term therapies. Some of the problems are due to countertransference, these sometimes being reactions elicited by patient inputs. Most are, however, due to the candidates' attitudes or personality traits.

I will conclude this chapter by describing countertransference reactions that affect a candidate's ability to intervene.

Countertransference reactions. Clinical example

One of the candidates reported, in a supervisory session, that she recently in one of her groups canceled a group session at short notice, because she had decided to attend a conference. Several patients complained at the next session, two weeks later, of having had some trouble since the last session. Two had visited their parents after the last session, both ending up in a serious argument with their mothers about trifles. Both had also felt poorly understood and were disappointed that their mothers had not pulled back when they realized how upset their daughters were. The candidate reported in the supervision that she had suggested to the patients that they might have been too demanding with their mothers, who seemed hurt by the arguments, which the two patients confirmed.

The supervisor noticed that the candidate had handled her patients' reports of the incidents in quite a matter of fact way, working "outside the group" (in the there-and-then). The supervisor also noticed that the candidate seemed to be a little annoyed with her patients' sulking complaints about their mothers (countertransference?). The supervisor therefore suggested to the candidate that she had felt criticized by her patients' complaints, a feeling that made her defend their mothers and prevented her from bringing the incident into the here-and-now. The candidate could have brought this into the here-and-now mode by suggesting that her patients felt let down at her cancellation of a session at such short notice. The candidate hesitated, wondering why her patients should be angry with her? The supervisor then suggested that the patients (in the transference) had developed an emotional attachment to her and/or the group, and felt ignored or neglected when she prioritized other activities, so responding to the cancellation with disappointment and anger.

The candidate agreed to present this interpretation to the group at the start of the next session. When she did, one patient who had quarreled with her mother immediately responded by saying that she had felt very annoyed with the therapist when she, late in the last session, suddenly told them that she had to cancel the next session. The other patient who quarreled with her mother had not felt any anger, but remembered that he thought that he disliked the gray, sad-looking and dirty hallway outside the therapist's office as he left the session room.

An important element of this story is that the candidate had put off telling the group she had to cancel, because she felt uncomfortable about it as the group had just started to function well. Sharing this information with the group opened it up for a freer, safer discussion about mutual positive and negative expectations of the participants in the group. The candidate had brought the group back into the here-and-now mode, the task then being to bring the exploration as far as possible in the direction of the individual patients' treatment foci. She, at the same time, confronted her patients with pieces of transference, and with displacement onto someone outside of the group. The supervisor had also demonstrated how the countertransference had inhibited the therapist from working within the framework of the therapy.

Notes

1 An overview of the Institute of Group Analysis and Group Psychotherapy training program can be found at https://www.iga.no/utdanningstilbud/
2 Vol. 20(4), 22(4) and 28(4). These can be downloaded free of charge from matrixtidsskrift.no/tidligere utgivelser.

Afterword

This book is the result of a long journey – a journey that spans a wide field and very many experiences over many years.

I have throughout the three-year writing period of this book constantly experienced the truth of Anthony's assertion that the development of theory, practice and research in group therapy can be experienced as a complex, conflict-filled and confabulatory conglomerate (Anthony, 1971). I have, however, as a clinician and researcher, in this book asked the questions that I have found to be relevant in the treatment of a more closely described sample of patients seeking help. I also have attempted to gather and integrate knowledge from existing theory, and from my own and others' research and practical experience, so that some of this knowledge can be disseminated back to the clinical field from which practical experience and research findings come.

This book is based on the most important research in the field and on recognized clinical knowledge. I have, however, weighed different findings against each other, and included those I consider to be most valid. My conclusions are therefore based on the questions I ask, the methods I use and the experiences I have chosen to inform them. I have, however, tried to make the text systematic and critical, and to share some of the reflections that have guided this process. Like all other research, my findings are subject to a certain degree of uncertainty.

I hope many find the treatment method I describe in this book interesting and useful, and can apply it in their own work. This will allow some of my conclusions to be further tested/verified in clinical practice and further research, and the subject to continue to evolve.

Appendix

Appendix I

Demonstration group

This appendix provides more information on the eight patients that were found to be suitable for Focused Group Analytic Psychotherapy (FGAP), and were briefly introduced in Chapter 5. The appendix presents biographical data, reasons for referral, background data on developmental and medical histories, clinical diagnoses, a psychodynamic case formulation and treatment focus. Patient scores on some of the central personality structures (identity, object relations, defense mechanisms, affect tolerance and control, moral values and narcissism) are also given, the first five collectively indicating the patient's level of personality organization (STIPO-R, clinical edition). Space limitations mean that only four of the patients are described at length. Mary's psychodynamic case formulation and Steve's and Mary's treatment foci were used as clinical examples in Chapter 4. These are included again in the appendix to make it easier for the reader to get hold of a comprehensive overview of the clinical material, which is meant to illustrate the theory presented in this book.

Patient I: Mary

Mary is a 39-year-old married teacher with two boys aged six and seven.

Reasons for referral: Mary has suffered a number of depressive episodes, the first being after the birth of her second child. These episodes have caused short periods of absence from work. She attributes the depressions to her having to bear too much of the responsibility for the home and children, as her husband weekly commutes and is away during the working week. She asked her GP to refer her to a specialist, to find a solution to her problems.

Psychodynamic case formulation

Symptoms: moodiness, frequent depressions, irritability, somatizations and a shaky self-image.

Symptomatic behavior (interpersonal): Mary feels easily controlled. Her husband is somewhat domineering, and she easily feels irritated and angry with him. She mostly ends up after conflicts feeling discouraged and guilty. She now and then appears somewhat rigid and stubborn at work, and may sometimes be a little too strict with pupils. She can, at home, frequently lose control and shake her boys roughly when she feels they quarrel too much. She has control of her negative emotions most of the time at school.

Avoidance: she keeps some distance from others both at home and at work, to control her irritation and anger. She tries to avoid conflicts by withdrawing, but often gets headaches and neck/shoulder pain.

Precipitating factors (stressors): she feels she has sole responsibility for the home and children. She also sometimes thinks that her job is too demanding, both the teaching side and the discipline side and setting limits for undisciplined students. She has also recently lost contact with the previous principal when he retired and misses him. He trusted her and let her work on her own, delegated tasks to her and was supportive and warm. Her new principal is, however, more demanding and authoritarian. Two parents also criticized her some time before the last referral at a school parent/teacher open meeting, for being unreasonable and too strict with their children.

Predisposing factors (vulnerability): Mary is the second oldest of five siblings and grew up on a small farm. The family's finances were poor during her childhood, but they never lacked food or clothing. Mary's mother has always been anxious and resembled Mary's grandmother, who had once been hospitalized for a "nervous breakdown". There was some abuse of alcohol in her father's family, and one of his brothers hanged himself as a youth. They never talked about this at home. Her father was short-tempered and often exploded over trifles when she was a child. He also had long periods in which he was sulky and silent. He never missed an opportunity to criticize Mary, and seldom praised her. All the children had to work on the farm, and there was little time for play and fun. Her mother took it for granted that the children participated in the day-to-day activities of the farm, as she had done in her childhood. An older brother was her father's favorite and was invited to accompany him everywhere. Everything her brother did was good, according to the father. The mother left all important decisions in the home to the father, and usually abided by what he decided.

Mary was almost surprised when her father allowed her to attend high school when she was 16 years old, which meant moving out of the family home and to a nearby town. After leaving home, she changed from being "kind and obedient" to becoming more rebellious. She was in opposition to teachers, often threw herself into discussions with peers and became assertive and a know-it-all. She also easily felt wronged, angry or humiliated if she didn't have the last word. Occasionally she would stay away from school on the day after such events to "lick her wounds". She had a couple of good friends at school who were also "in disarray", but eventually began to spend time with a group of slightly older adolescents who partied. She was uncritical of her use of alcohol, indulged in unprotected sex with random contacts, and visited her family less and less often. Finally, she passed her exams with moderate grades, but could have done better if she had not been so engrossed in her group of friends and at odds with her teachers.

Mary, shortly after high school graduation, moved to Oslo and worked for a few years as an assistant in a nursing home. She made some new friends at work and in a social club, calmed down and gradually adopted a more stable life. She eventually returned to school, re-took and improved some of her subject grades and decided to study to become a teacher. The period in which she studied was relatively stable, she enjoyed the curriculum and was happy with the company of her small network of friends. She also engaged in a short love relationship, but did not seriously connect with anyone until she met Hans, a fellow student, about six months before her final exams. She became pregnant after three months, and wanted to get married, but felt "badly treated" and "used" when he hesitated. The pregnancy ended in a miscarriage, but they did finally marry in a hurry. Both also passed their final exams. The marriage has had its ups and downs, and a good deal of bickering. She has tended to fluctuate between being critical and unhappy and feeling easily offended, wronged and ill-treated. Her husband has been more patient and accommodating, but has also tried to control her. Having children has mainly been positive for the marriage, although disputes over how the children are brought up have been frequent. They both share an interest in the outdoor life, films and music, and can sometimes enjoy going for a walk or to the cinema or a concert together.

Personality: Mary was timid, submissive and afraid of authority as a child. She never protested, even when she had to do things that she did not like doing. She was obedient and conscientious until she, in puberty, became more rebellious and critical of others. She became more self-assertive, got involved in discussions and easily reacted with anger if she did not get her way. She was somewhat self-righteous and showed disrespect for other people's views, something that annoyed many. These traits persisted into adulthood, when she learned to suppress both the need to dominate and win disputes, and to protect herself from being hurt by creating distance from the people around her. She is in touch with her irritation and angry feelings. There is, however, frequently "friction" between her and others, despite her efforts to control these feelings. She has largely managed to control herself, but also has a tendency to signal dislike by avoiding contact, through sulkiness and use of irony. She has experienced more and more bodily "aches" over the years, probably with a psychological background.

Psychodynamic hypothesis: Information on the characteristics of her caregivers and her relational competence nurtures the hypothesis that Mary's inner world of self and object representations is characterized by a lack of early positive affirmation, and of anxiety from having been the target of unpredictable outbursts of aggression. This manifests itself in unstable self-esteem, vulnerability in relationships and in relatively high needs for affirmation, support and care. These are only met to a limited extent, because she distances herself from others. Her inner representations are also colored by her mother's self-effacing attitude. At puberty, she tried to become less needy by becoming more self-sufficient and independent. Early father identifications and insecurity as a person, however, led her to become more rebellious and aggressive, others therefore avoiding her. Some of her anger is also directed toward herself, this leading to somatization, poor self-esteem (self-hate) and depression. She has relatively large conflicts around domination and submission and feels easily controlled, which makes her feel worthless. She has a strong expectation of being rejected if she clearly expresses who she is, and she uses distance to protect herself from this. This expectation of rejection is, however, partly irrational and is governed more by her inner world than by the reality of the people around her. The mechanisms behind her problems are mainly psychological, although information about her father's problems, and the suicide and alcohol abuse of family members could support a hypothesis that there is a genetic disposition to bipolar disorder (mainly depression) in the family.

IIP-C

She, in her profile of interpersonal problems (IIP-C), describes herself to be to some extent more socially elusive, nonassertive, exploitable and self-sacrificing than others. She also, to some extent, feels more intrusive, but less domineering.

Treatment focus

Mary and the therapist, after exploring and discussing all the data, decided that the focus of her therapy should be on recognizing and problematizing her tendency to avoid and distance herself from others. It was also emphasized that she, despite her IIP-C profile showing that she perceives herself to be low on "domineering" and high on "avoidance", was at times somewhat controlling and rigorous toward her pupils, her children and her husband. She should therefore, during treatment, try to understand how she uses these behaviors to protect aspects of her inner world, and explore how they affect others' behavior toward her. She was instructed (through being given behavioral tasks) to convey her wishes, feelings and boundaries more directly to the other members of the group. This included her wish to be seen and cared for. She also should acknowledge others when they expressed similar feelings, and regularly ask for feedback from the others on how they perceived her. It was emphasized that these aspects of her personality were probably related to repeatedly becoming depressed and to her somatic pains.

Level of personality organization (PO)

Identity: 2.5 – unstable self-esteem, depends on confirmation from others. Impaired sense of others and of describing others coherently, especially when stressed.

Object relations: 2 – some impairment and conflicts in intimate relationships.

172   Appendix

Defense mechanisms: 2.5 – some increase in the use of projection and splitting, unaware of her tendency to dominate and control others, but mainly uses more mature defense mechanisms.

Aggression: 2.5 – affect tolerance somewhat weakened. Has some impaired affect control under stress and can "shake" her children. Has not, however, intentionally inflicted pain on others. Directs some aggression toward herself, including somatization.

Moral values: 2 – feels guilty about her anger, for being rough with her children. She is sometimes more self-blaming (self-accusations) than feels guilt.

Narcissism: 1.5 – slightly elevated. More than usual concern with confirmation from others.

Diagnosis (descriptive)

Axis 1 – Recurrent depressive disorder. Some somatoform symptoms.
Axis 2 – Some personality pathology, but no PD.

Patient 2: Henry

Henry is a 36-year-old married, Lutheran preacher, with a girl and a boy of four and six.

Reasons for referral: Henry has in recent weeks experienced sleep problems and problems with waking early. He has also started to doubt whether he is suited to being a priest, and whether his faith is "strong enough". He feels remorse for many things including "not taking good enough care of" a group of confirmation candidates and is reluctant to go to church because he feels people "are angry with him". He also feels that people increasingly see through him. He thinks that he is a poor Christian and perhaps not as kind and helpful as he likes to appear.

Psychodynamic case formulation

Symptoms: has felt very tired both at work and at home for many weeks, partly due to the lack of sleep. Has become increasingly depressed, sits around staring into space, unable to do anything. Full of self-blame and guilt because he can not function at work. There have, however, been no complaints.

Symptomatic behavior (interpersonal): usually very positive (a "yes person") but takes on too much that quickly overwhelms him. People then get annoyed because he does not get things done. He is afraid of disappointing others and of them become angry with him or disliking him. He has some problems making decisions, and usually questions colleagues and superiors a great deal about problems at work. He consults his wife about these problems, but sometimes finds her a bit domineering and controlling.

Avoidance: he has poor contact with his aggressive feelings and can sometimes become annoyed, but suppresses these feelings. He is afraid to express disagreement, and of the anger of others, so shying away from conflicts. He has difficulties delegating tasks and usually does things himself.

Precipitating factors (stressors): Henry's boss is somewhat domineering and strict, Henry feeling that he has recently increased his workload and demands on him. His wife, who also has a demanding job, has complained a lot that "he is so willing to help everybody else" despite there being so many things that need to be done at home.

Predisposing factors (vulnerability): Henry was born and raised in a coastal town and has a sister who is three years older. His mother stayed at home with him and his sister when they were small and his father, who was a trained photographer, ran a successful studio/shop. The family's finances were good. His mother was an assertive woman who not only ran the home, but was also critical of the way her father ran his business. She was also very critical of the in-laws, especially her mother-in-law. Her father spent a lot of time at work and therefore became a somewhat distant figure in the children's lives. He was a quiet man and appeared to be quite compliant to his wife's demands. This is probably why everyone was very surprised when he suddenly moved out of the home when Henry was six years old. His parents divorced shortly after this, his father quickly remarrying. Henry and his sister both missed him. They were also angry with him. Henry, however, felt guilty and fantasized a lot about what he had done wrong to make his father leave. Contact with their father was sporadic for the first three years. However, they did not get on well with his new wife and the visits ended when his father had a son with his new wife, partly because she was jealous of his children from the previous marriage.

Henry's mother, after a long period of depression, then remarried and the children became quite strongly attached to their stepfather, which was a positive development for Henry. They had a little girl a couple of years later, Henry not showing any signs of jealousy, and enjoyed taking care of her. He sat and cuddled her a lot when she was small and played a lot with her when she was older.

Henry did well at school and enjoyed playing chess with his stepfather. After a somewhat lonely childhood, he made some friends at school, especially as he approached puberty and not least when he joined the scouts and a Christian society at school. His interest in religion and Christianity was awoken by the influence of his friends and in particular a scout leader he became attached to. He started theological training right after high school and graduated with honors from the 6.5 year course.

He was shy around girls and met his first girlfriend Dorothy, who is now his wife, through his sister when he was 22. They fell in love immediately and married two years later, a couple of years before completing their studies. She was a social worker and supported him financially for the rest of his studies. He describes her as an assertive woman who knows what she wants. She is also caring, practical and good at getting things done.

After his ordination, he worked as a parish priest in a mainstream church, where he took a share of the responsibility for ordinary ecclesiastical duties both there and in surrounding churches.

Personality: he is gentle, kind and helpful, but shy. He finds it difficult to say no when someone asks him to do something. He has always been insecure about himself and depended on his older sister and mother, also later on his stepfather, when making decisions in everyday life. He is emotionally controlled and never expresses anger or criticism of others. He dislikes being alone and is vulnerable to separation. He is also faithful and conventional, and is known for delivering somewhat dogmatic, boring sermons.

Mental health: he easily took to tears as a child and disliked being alone. He, however, developed well, adapted well in pre-puberty and enjoyed school and his scouts activities. However he became quite depressed immediately before his final high school exams, was reluctant to get out of bed and doubted his abilities to take the exams. He got back on track after consulting a GP and a course of antidepressant medication, and completed school with good results. He had a new depressive episode one year before marring Dorothy who, during a quarrel, expressed doubts about whether they were suited for each other. This depression was also brief, the couple attending a few sessions with a student health service psychiatrist.

Psychodynamic hypothesis (resultant, mechanisms): Henry's object representations are characterized by a distant and partially absent father and by his mother's dominance and tendency to invade him (define what he felt, meant and needed). He felt abandoned and partly guilty when his father left. His mother's depression made it hard for her to comfort him, and there was a low tolerance of his grief and anger about his father. Henry did not, therefore, properly mourn the loss of his father. His self-representations are characterized by a lack of mirroring, an uncertain sense of identity, an unstable self-esteem regulation and an impaired tolerance for conflict and aggression. His stepfather, who he became strongly attached to, became his alternative male role figure. He still, however, showed an early vulnerability to abandonment and being pushed aside. He mastered his neediness and longing for closeness in his relationship with his little sister, by being overly helpful to her and identifying with her parents' needs (altruism/reaction formation). His altruistic attitude was further reinforced when he became a patrol officer in the scouts, assisting and training younger scouts. His desire to help and be helped may also be linked to his career choice, a relationship with God including being loved as one is, and providing the opportunity to help, comfort and preach to others.

Henry has two central conflicts. He wants to be autonomous, to assert himself, to express his own opinions and to implement what he thinks is right. He is, however, also afraid of being abandoned and insecure about his own worth. He is therefore vulnerable to "not being liked or loved" if he becomes too independent. This may also explain his low tolerance of aggression, which he unconsciously fantasizes can destroy the other. He therefore directs his aggression toward himself (depression, self-reproach) and strives to live up to what he believes are others' expectations. This causes him to easily neglect his needs, including private life responsibilities such as his home and family.

IIP-C

Henry experiences himself as more overly nurturant, exploitable, nonassertive and socially avoidant, and less domineering and intrusive than others.

Treatment focus

Henry needs to get more in touch with his aggression. He has therefore been given behavioral tasks in which he is to address things, events or what is said in the group that he does not like. Henry's dislikes and criticism should be formulated in an appropriate, socially acceptable way. He should also set boundaries to a greater extent and say no to some demands made by others inside and outside the group. He should take some time every session to talk about himself, preferably his wishes and longings, but also his criticism of others, which the therapist should support him in. He will hopefully find that others, both inside and outside the group "endure" his becoming more assertive, without abandoning him. He may also get in touch with his healthy needs and should disclose them in the group and to his family and friends.

Level of personality organization (PO)

Identity: 2 – self-critical, neglects himself, eager to serve others. Self-esteem depends to some extent on the mirroring of others.

Object relations: 2.5 – impairment and conflict in intimate sexual relationship with his wife.

Defense mechanisms: 2 – fairly mature, altruism, sublimation, suppression and reaction formation, but also some projection (of anger).

Aggression: 2.5 – low affect tolerance, especially aggression. Suppresses anger and directs it partially toward himself (feels inadequate, that he has done something wrong or not enough for others). He also projects and expects others to be angry or dissatisfied with him.

Moral values (superego functioning): 2.5 – strict image of God, strict superego, poorly integrated with confirmatory object representations.

Narcissism: 2 – depends a little too much on the confirmation of others.

Diagnosis (descriptive)

Axis 1 – Recurrent depression. Current condition: depressive episode, moderate.
Axis 2 – Dependent PD, several avoidant PD traits.

Patient 3: Emily

Emily is 28 years old, has been cohabiting with a man for one year, and has no children. She has a bachelor's degree in financial management.

Reason for referral: Emily has been referred for anxiety problems. Her anxiety is related to her going out of her home, going to the shops or traveling by train or bus. She usually manages to limit her anxiety, but sometimes suffers panic attacks with palpitations and difficulties in breathing. She tried medication prescribed by her GP, but stopped due to nausea, and asked to be referred to a specialist.

Psychodynamic case formulation

Symptoms: her anxiety has been increasing in the last year, this being related to visiting stores or being in larger assemblies of people. She occasionally has a panic attack with somatic symptoms, but usually manages to calm down and avoid a full-blown attack. She had similar symptoms in puberty and three years ago after a break-up with a partner. She then received a few sessions of cognitive behavioral therapy and managed better. She has, however, had a number of relapses over the past year. She also has obsessional thoughts that her cohabitant boyfriend wants to leave her, and that he is lying to her when he says he loves her.

Symptomatic behavior (interpersonal): Emily quickly gets angry when she feels that she is being treated unfairly. She is usually outspoken about this, which easily leads to conflicts with others. The atmosphere then deteriorates, and she ends up feeling shame and anxiety about losing control of her feelings. She usually feels that she has the right to speak up. She can, however, once in a while feel that she has treated others unfairly. A typical example is her experience that "many colleagues at work do not do their job", which means she has to take on a heavier workload. She has also, increasingly, had problems with her partner, who she feels does not confirm her enough. She has felt less sexually attracted to him, even though things worked well at the beginning of the relationship. She does not fully trust him and is a little controlling. She, at the same time, fears that he will leave the relationship if it gets too difficult.

Avoidance: it is difficult for her to express warm and close feelings, both to her cohabitant and to friends. It is easier to criticize than to praise. It is also difficult to ask for the concern and care of her partner and she constantly worries that he will leave as the last one did.

Precipitating factors (stressors): Emily has a demanding job within banking. There are frequent deadlines and a shortage of staff due to a high level of sick leave. This "forces" her to work more and harder. She is also obliged to pay regular visits to a cousin with severe mental problems, to make sure she is well and follows up her treatment.

Predisposing factors (vulnerability): Emily comes from a small village. She has a sister three years older than her and a brother who is three years younger. Her father is a plumber, and her mother works in a care profession. They lived in a large house and had good finances in her childhood. Her mother has said that her brother's birth strongly affected Emily. She became incontinent and cried a lot for a period of time. Emily also alternated between clinging to and "showing no interest in" her mother. Her father had an unpredictable temper that overshadowed the atmosphere in the family when they were children. This anger was directed in particular at her older sister, who took much of the blame. Her sister was also more oppositional than the other children. Emily was, however, careful with the things that could irritate her father. She was very fond of him, especially when he took the family on walks in the forest. It was, however, difficult to bring friends home because she became embarrassed if her father became angry when others were present. Her mother was shy and timid, but more caring than her father. Emily, however, felt that her mother had failed her children by trivializing her father's behavior. Her mother cared for a sick nephew and old people in their neighborhood. Emily felt jealousy whenever her mother helped someone else, and felt she was swept aside and neglected. Her mother was also particularly focused on justice, Emily once having to apologize to a boy she had bullied at school. She remembers this as being very humiliating. Both girls were afraid of their father when they were younger. Emily at puberty, however, became more critical and oppositional and could also express anger toward both parents.

Emily did well at school and in sports and dance. Her parents rarely, however, followed up on her activities. She was good looking and from early on was surrounded by boys. She had a few romances, none being too important to her. Her interest in sports was greatest when she lived with her parents, but later as a student she preferred to spend time with the group of girl friends she lived with. She has lived with a boyfriend for the last year, a freelance architect who is self employed, and described as being somewhat elusive and "into his own business".

Her father left when Emily was 15 years old, allegedly under pressure from her mother. Emily felt this was a relief, but did experience shortly after this her first onset of panic attacks, which felt as if she was about to die. The mother and the children remained in the house, and the father moved out. He continued to see them every second weekend in his new home.

Emily's relationship with her father has changed a lot as she grew older. They can now share a more meaningful dialogue, joke and have fun. She is, even so, always a little guarded, and still carries a grudge against him for the things that happened in childhood. She has a good relationship with both her mother and her siblings. The family has, despite former conflicts and divorce, managed to maintain contact over the years, the family still celebrating Christmas together.

Psychodynamic hypothesis (resultant, mechanisms): object representations are partly characterized by anger and dominance (from the father) and distance and a strict sense of justice (from the mother), while self-representations are characterized by neglect with regard to positive mirroring and care. Her several good friendships as an adult, however, also indicate that she must have experienced some early intimacy/closeness. Emily still feels a bit like a victim and "will not become as timid as mother was in her relationship to father". It is better to "hit back" and "demand respect" when others deceive you or behave unjustly. She has developed an unforgiving attitude to those at work "who don't do their job or who skive". She also often sees people in black or white: some are OK, while others are completely reprehensible. She tries to suppress longings and latent anger, or "transform" these feelings into restless activity through exercise and working hard. Her anger often seems to be activated when underlying longings for closeness and care are not met, an activation that may again be associated with her panic attacks. Emily's early "loss of her mother" when her brother was born, may have contributed to a vulnerability to feeling abandoned, which she compensates for with activity and a forced autonomy. Emily seems to have an impaired ability for intimacy and empathy, as demonstrated by her feelings for ex-boyfriends and her current cohabitant partner. Her ambivalence toward her partner and obsessions about him wanting to leave her can, via projection, manifest as a fear of being abandoned. Her "demand" to be confirmed and denial of a need for reciprocity in a close relationship constitute narcissistic features that should be activated and explored further in therapy.

IIP-C

Emily perceives herself to be more vindictive, domineering and intrusive than others, but at the same time perceives herself as being more nonassertive and slightly more exploitable, overly nurturant and cold (reserved).

Treatment focus

Emily, during the evaluation and through the therapist's exploratory questions, "let go of" her previous idea that her anxiety is only due to her fear of a panic attack. The therapist's hypothesis of a relationship between panic attacks and suppressed anger, which is activated when she does not get the care and support she wishes (or sometimes demands), seems to have given her something to think about. She also seems to accept the idea that suppression of her feelings of void and pain may cause her to feel less empathy in close relationships. The focus in her therapy is therefore to explore whether she could be using her high levels of activity to keep painful feelings away. She should also explore whether her frequent harsh remarks, sarcasm and critical outbursts come when she feels angry, and possibly start to work on finding other more acceptable ways of conveying her anger and the boundaries she sets for herself. She was also encouraged to explore the reciprocity in her relationship with her cohabitant partner, and her ability and desire for closeness/intimacy. She has been instructed to "practice empathy" by commenting and showing empathy for other patients directly when they disclose something they think is painful, and to communicate directly with the group when she feels hurt, preferably in a socially acceptable way.

Level of personality organization (PO)

Identity: 2.5 – somewhat weakened ego-identity and a shaky self-esteem. Has an impaired ability to give a coherent picture of herself and others.

Object relations: 2.5 – deficits or conflicts in her closest relationship.
Defense mechanisms: 3 – some are quite mature (suppression, reaction formation), but also has a moderate tendency to use projection and black-and-white thinking.
Aggression: 3 – has more contact with angry than with loving and tender feelings. She sometimes thinks she gets too angry.
Moral values: 2.5 – she has a strict, punitive superego, can be critical and judgmental, but more toward others than herself.
Narcissism: 2 – slightly increased, needs confirmation from others. She also has a tendency toward self-righteousness. Part of her feels a little better than others, and that she deserves more attention and care.

Diagnosis (descriptive)

Axis 1 – Panic disorder with mild agoraphobia.
Axis 2 – Mixed PD, with a few paranoid, dependent and obsessional traits.

Patient 4: Doris

Doris is a 41-year-old married, auxiliary nurse. She has a ten-year-old son.
  Reason for referral: Doris has been referred by her GP because she has, over the years, had a number of periods of sickness absence due to repeated episodes of depression and a constant feeling of fatigue. She was absent from work for nearly three months immediately before this referral. She spent some of this time in bed, but managed to return to work after anti-depressive medication (Cipralex). She is often frustrated with herself and her reactions and "would like to do something about it".

Psychodynamic case formulation

  Symptoms: repeated episodes of depression. In difficult times, she can want to die, but would rather only be "gone for a while" and then come back when "things are okay" again. She often feels very tired, and gets headaches when too stressed. She feels incompetent in many contexts.
  Symptomatic behavior/avoidance (interpersonal): Doris was often, in the past, angry with her son and could sometimes pull his hair, hit him or pull his ears. She would then feel guilty and could bang her head against a wall. She frequently feels annoyed and angry when something does not go her way or people demand too much from her. She has great difficulties expressing this in a proper way. This applies both to the elderly people she works with in the nursing home, and also with her colleagues and her husband, who she thinks is too demanding and critical.
  Precipitating factors (stressors): Doris and her husband have had marital problems for a number of years, and the intimacy and closeness she once felt in the

marriage is gone. Sex has become a "duty", which gives her little or no pleasure. Her husband has a different ethnic background, and a number of differences in cultural backgrounds including in gender roles have increasingly caused friction (conflicts) in their marriage.

Predisposing factors (vulnerability): Doris is number four of five siblings. She was raised in a small town in western Norway, where her father worked in a factory. Her mother was a housewife when the children were school age, but later started working in a grocery store close to their home. Doris's grandmother and an aunt have both had problems with anxiety and depression. There is, however, no history of mental health problems in her father's family. Doris was separated from her family, including her mother, when she was seven to eight months old, and lived with an aunt for six weeks while her mother underwent extensive back surgery. Doris "did not recognize her mother" when the family was reunited, and responded by rejecting her for a while. She, however, remembers a lot of warmth and care from her parents and among the children during childhood.

Doris was bullied as a child because she was overweight, even by those who allegedly were her friends. She therefore did not like school much and did poorly in many subjects. She sang in a Christian girl choir during much of her school years, eventually finding several good friends there. The same happened when she started high school, where she felt better and her school performance improved for a while. The results of her final exams were, however, middling.

Doris moved to Bergen after finishing school, to train as an auxiliary nurse. She also got her first job in Bergen at a large somatic hospital. She enjoyed the job, but always felt a little inferior because of her low status at the hospital. She therefore, after a few years, tried to retake some school subjects to improve her results and to become a nurse. She was not, however, able to be sufficiently disciplined and to get through the course reading. She eventually, and despite a hectic working life, developed a small social network and was a member of the local church choir. A sister and a brother that she has a good relationship with have been living in the city in recent years. They help and support each other in a number of ways.

She also had a couple of romantic relationships in her first years in Bergen that lasted for a few months. She did not, however, become seriously attached to any of these men. She met her husband in her late 20s when on holiday in southern Europe and, after several visits back and forth in the following year, he moved to Norway where they married. After a couple of years they had a son, who has developed well. They, however, decided early on not to have more children. He is a few years older than her, works long hours as a marketer in a fish canning company and leaves all care of the son and home to her.

He is a quiet man, but can sometimes get "worked up" during discussions, and may at such times seem a little brusque. They have their own house and satisfactory finances.

Mental health: Doris had problems with anxiety and a depressive episode about 1.5 years after her son was born. She was absent from work for three months, before gradually returning to work. Her son at this time began in a nursery. She did well for a year, before she again became depressed when one of her sisters became suddenly seriously ill and died. She has, in recent years, been absent from work a few days at a time because she has struggled to get up in the morning. She has gradually become more irritable and dissatisfied with her husband, who does not seem to care much for their son. She consulted a psychiatrist who "only gave her medication". She didn't like him because he seemed "reserved and cold". She, after this, had some sessions with a psychologist and returned to work.

Personality: she has an unstable self-image, is somewhat self-critical, but also has periods when she is more satisfied with herself. She often thinks that others are more important and successful than she is, and tries to compensate for this by being kind and helpful. This, however, can easily become "too much". She loves her son and tries to be a good mother. She, however, often feels that she does not do it right and then becomes discouraged and irritable. Other people may perceive her as being a "slightly stressed person" who is always in a hurry, but who nevertheless is kind and dutiful.

Psychodynamic hypothesis (resultant, mechanisms): Doris experienced care and warmth from her parents and siblings in childhood. However, all the family had to help with domestic chores from an early age because of her mother's back problems and other ailments. Doris was also subjected to a separation from mother in her first year, which may have affected her feelings of self-worth. Her parents were loving. There was, however, also some "strictness" in the family based on fundamentalist, ascetic Christian ideals. Many things were perceived as being "sinful". The films they were allowed to watch on TV or at the cinema, who they could be friends with, and not least what was allowed between two persons of the opposite sex being restricted. Her object and self-representations seem to be characterized by a lack of mirroring/confirmation and by her separation trauma. She easily feels that she is small and inferior to others and also that others let her down. She often, therefore, lets others take the lead, for example at work. She also tries to avoid criticism by being kind, caring and docile toward others. This may, through identification with those she "cares for", represent a form of "self-care". An underlying discontent is reflected in irritability and somatizations (pain) when she feels overloaded.

IPC-C

Doris perceives herself as more loving and caring (overly nurturant) than others, but also more exploitable (focused on the needs of others), nonassertive, socially avoidant and cold (reserved) than others.

Treatment focus

Doris needs help to establish a more stable regulation of her self-esteem and a better-integrated identity. Her feelings of being inadequate/inferior are often activated in interpersonal situations. Sometimes parts of these feelings are "rational" because she, out of fear of not being liked, has agreed to take on more work and responsibilities than anyone possibly can be expected to manage. Part of these feelings are, however, "echoes" from poorly integrated self-representations affected by early abandonment or other traumatic events. A third source for feeling inadequate is that sometimes others *do demand* too much of her, for example her husband, who leaves everything at home to her. She should therefore explore and scrutinize interpersonal situations, to learn more about what actually is going on, interpersonally and in herself. She should ask: "Is it me or is it the other?" She should train herself to set boundaries to the demands of others, take more space in the group and stand up and more clearly express her wishes and needs. She should also take her irritability and anger seriously, and convey her feelings to the other group members as they arise, so that the situation can be explored. She should try to do this both at work and in her relationship with her husband.

Level of personality organization (PO)

Identity: 2.5 – she has an unstable self-esteem, and easily feels inferior and that she is not good enough. Her inner images of others, such as her parents and her husband, are slightly weakened and she has difficulties in fully describing them as "real people". She has some problems with being goal-directed at work, especially when feeling overwhelmed.

Object relations: 3 – some friendships and sibling relationship with reciprocity. But lack of intimacy and closeness in marriage, and partly feels she is exploited.

Defense mechanisms: 2.5 – she splits, as she has a tendency to see herself as "unsuccessful", while seeing others as managing well and "knowing best". Has a tendency to deny problems, for example with her husband.

Aggression: 2.5 – much of her aggression is aimed at herself as somatizations, depression and self-criticism.

Moral values (superego functioning): 2 – she is a little strict, but mainly guided by intrinsic values such as doing one's duty, being honest and careful to do the right thing. She has a too strong tendency to feel guilt (or inadequate) if something is wrong.

Narcissism: 2 – she depends on a level of external affirmation and praise. She has an impaired ability to maintain a good image of herself when she is overloaded.

Diagnosis (descriptive)

Axis 1 – Recurrent depression.
Axis 2 – No diagnosis.

Patient 5: Steve

Steve is a 28-year-old taxi driver. He is unmarried and has no children. He has had some short-term relationships with women, but has not attached to any of them as he has found "something wrong with all of them".

Reason for referral: Steve sometimes feels dissatisfied with life and is overwhelmed by a feeling of emptiness. He has, on a few occasions when he has been drinking, had thoughts of throwing himself in front of a subway train. He easily gets into quarrels with others and has few friends. He took the advice of a GP to seek specialist help and was referred.

Psychodynamic case formulation

Symptoms: Steve has periods of low mood when he feels indifferent and feels there is no joy in life (ahedonia). He sometimes feels he is a little better than others, but also has times when he feels a little inferior. He drinks moderate levels of alcohol, but there is no addiction.

Symptomatic behavior (interpersonal): he argues a lot with colleagues, bosses and sometimes passengers. He can be quite aggressive verbally, and many people think he is too intrusive and too neglective of other people's points of view. He has had many short-term relationships with women and he likes sex, but is not so interested in the closeness of a relationship. He usually breaks up a relationship when too many feelings develop and demands on him increase. He misses a steady partner, but does not really understand how to "find the right one".

Avoidance: he doesn't like too much "small talk" and can be silent for long periods of time. He is "opposed to" too much emotion and therefore shies away from social connections. He also has a strong opinion on immigration and believes that immigrants are to blame for many of society's problems.

Precipitating factors (stressors): he sometimes feels that he misses having a girlfriend, his thoughts about this maybe accentuating his feelings of emptiness. He has recently been criticized by the owner of the taxi he drove about two speeding fines. There have also been a couple of complaints from passengers about him behaving inappropriately. He often feels that little in life, other than exercise, makes sense.

Predisposing factors (vulnerability): Steve was born in Oslo. His mother, who was loving and caring, remained at home with Steve and his sister who is two years younger. His mother became, however, less available to him when his sister was born, and Steve was sent to nursery. His father was a traveling salesman and could be away for up to a week at a time. His father, when at home, usually slept a lot or sat in front of the TV. He did not spend much time with the children, even when Steve sought contact. The parents were a silent couple and there was little warmth and intimacy between them. Steve remembers, however, that they twice had a terrible row, screaming and shouting at each other at the top of their voices. His father on both occasions left the house afterwards and was gone for a number of days.

Steve received more attention when his maternal grandmother moved into the home when he was five, after she became a widow. She was passionate about everything he did, talked to him, read to him and accompanied him to school when he started. He had a tendency at school, from the start, to be alone during breaks, but eventually made a few friends in his class. He received more attention when he was selected for the school handball team. He enjoyed and was skilled at sports, but his performance was average in all other subjects at school. He eventually joined a sports club, which he attended diligently and got several new friends, and also some positive adult contact with the sports leaders.

His father's absences from home gradually became longer, until he was promoted to the position of marketing manager at the head office in Oslo of the company he had for some years been working for. Steve was then 14 years old and his relationship with his father improved. They talked more and occasionally went to the cinema or a football game together. The relationship between the parents, however, deteriorated and when they spoke it was mostly about practical matters. The father also got along poorly with his mother-in-law, and she eventually left and moved into her own apartment a couple of years after his father stopped traveling. Steve supported his grandmother in her conflict with his father, and blamed him for "throwing her out" of the house. The quarrels were fierce for a long time and strongly affected the atmosphere of the home. Steve achieved only poor grades at high school, but was at that time quite popular with the other boys at the sports club. He was also popular with girls, but was quite shy and did not have any girlfriends at school. He had his first girlfriend after joining the military, where he had some random and usually sexual connections with girls he met on the town. Steve enjoyed the military, but was once reprimanded for using obscene language when speaking to an officer.

Steve's father suddenly died of a heart attack when he was in the military, without them reconciling. He attended the funeral but did not mourn the loss.

Steve, after military service, started working for a construction company as a laborer and driver and moved into his own flat. He completed the training for a taxi driver license and worked for a while for a number of different taxi owners, without really enjoying his work. He left the sports club, and started to lift weights in a studio several times a week. He has a few friends, and usually visits his grandmother once a week and has dinner with his mother on Sundays. He has little contact with his sister and her family.

Personality: Steve thinks it is important to be independent, self-sufficient and not need other people. He easily feels awkward if someone gets too close. He has had some short-term relationships with women, but he breaks them off quickly if he thinks there are too many feelings and they are demanding too much of him. He likes to be on his own, even though he misses having a girlfriend. He is focused on his body and being in good shape, he dislikes people who smoke, but usually enjoys drinking when he goes out. He is seemingly a quiet man, but he does not like to be contradicted when engaging in conversation and can easily get into arguments with colleagues, his boss and sometimes passengers. He is, however, by and large, reliable in his job, which he has held on to despite warnings for "rough treatment" of drunk passengers.

Psychodynamic hypothesis (resultant, mechanisms): Steve was a "wanted child" and had a close, warm attachment to his mother until his baby sister came along, who seemed to replace him and leave him with a feeling of losing his mother. His father was distant, both because he was away a lot and because of his somewhat "closed" personality. The arrival of his sister in his separation-individuation phase may have negatively affected his autonomy, while his father's frequent absence from home may have weakened his masculine identity. His somewhat distorted "manliness", being a self-sufficient man of few words, with dislike for dependency and other "soft" feelings and focus on a strong body, may indicate this. His yearning for attention and care was met when his grandmother moved in, his uncertainty about his identity and a shaky self-esteem being compensated by fantasies of being better than others. He tends to idealize or devalue others and often projects responsibility for conflicts on to others. He is easily offended, but maintains a balance through self-sufficiency and social avoidance. He seems to be split between longing for a romantic relationship and his preference for solitude. His fear of being abandoned was strongly activated when his grandmother moved out, something Steve resolved by "starting a war" with his father rather than mourn. His skills in sports and physical fitness increased through training and bolstered his masculine identity. This also contributed to his sense of mastery, his high level of physical activity also pushing away his feelings of neediness, weakness and a sense of inferiority.

IPC-C

Steve scores within the norms in the population on all sub-scales, and therefore perceives himself as having "no interpersonal problems" compared with others. This can also be interpreted as a consequence of having a poor ability to self-reflect or as an attempt to maintain a socially acceptable facade.

Treatment focus

Steve was able to acknowledge, during the evaluation and the discussion of his IIP-C, that he sometimes perceives himself as weak and inferior to others. He at other times, however, felt others "were stupid" and saw himself as belonging to "a higher league". These feelings were frequently activated when he did not have the last word in a discussion or when he did not feel sufficiently appreciated for something he had accomplished. He would then be offended and want revenge. He also accepted, during the evaluation, the therapist's suggestion that his frequent break-ups in relationships were linked to "a fear of being abandoned".

A number of aspects of his problematic attitudes (self-sufficiency, wish for revenge and devaluation of others) were explored, defined and placed at the center of his treatment focus as aspects he should try to change during therapy. It was predicted that the interpersonal conflicts he reported from his life situation would also occur in the group. It was also predicted that he might then be tempted to leave the group. The therapist emphasized that if this happened, then this would be a call for him to remain calm and ask for help to explore in detail what was taking place.

Steve's behavioral tasks were to practice a more "laid back" stance, observe and listen to other members of the group and try to understand how they were thinking and feeling (mentalizing). He was to report when he felt offended, but to remember that we all live in a subjective world that is characterized by differences in backgrounds, development and choices.

Level of personality organization (PO)

Identity: 3 – this is moderately impaired. Limited enjoyment of his work and uncertain about future career and family wishes and plans. His sense of self is also weakened and split. He may at times be a little too complacent, while at other times feels inferior and has difficulties giving a cohesive picture of himself and others.

Object relations: 3 – he has few friends and sometimes feels a bit lonely. Has difficulty connecting with others or committing to relationships.

Defense mechanisms: 2.5 – he has some access to more mature defense mechanisms such as suppression, rationalization and isolation of emotions and thoughts. He, however, frequently uses immature mechanisms and tends to idealize/devaluate others (especially women). He projects the more unwanted part of himself onto others, has a split image of himself and a tendency to think "in black and white".

Aggression: 3 – he has contact with his own anger, but sometimes has problems with control and has on occasions verbally abused colleagues and others. He can also be too rough when physically "helping" inebriated passengers who cause trouble at night, out of his taxi. He has, however, never physically harmed anyone. Some of his self-directed aggression is reflected as suicidal thoughts when he has been drinking.

Moral values: 2.5 – he "takes liberties" if the opportunity arises, such as receiving payments without registering and issuing a receipt, and overpricing. He can sometimes feel guilty if he has been verbally abusive, but is more likely to feel that he has behaved stupidly (shame).

Narcissism: 3 – he has a hint of a sense of "entitlement", that he by and large is right in discussions and therefore is entitled to be heard. He also thinks he deserves admiration for his looks and his well-trained body.

Diagnosis (descriptive)

Axis 1 – No diagnosis.
Axis 2 – Emotionally unstable PD, borderline type.

Patient 6: Anny

Anny is a 43-year-old nurse who is divorced, but has a new partner. She has a 22-year-old daughter.

Reason for referral: Anny was referred because of depression and anxiety, and difficulties working through feelings of guilt after ending her relationship a few years ago with her husband.

Psychodynamic case formulation

   Symptoms: a lot of guilt, shame and anxiety after having left and divorced her husband a few years ago, and then moving in with a new man she fell in love with.

   Symptomatic behavior (interpersonal): she is usually too controlled and eager to live up to the expectations of others at work, in the family and also of her ex-husband until she broke out of the marriage.

   Avoidance: a tendency to isolate from others, keep away from her family of origin, and avoid disagreement and conflict.

   Precipitating factors (stressors): no obvious recent triggering events, except the ending of her marriage and divorce.

   Predisposing factors (vulnerability): Anny was raised as sibling number two out of three. She has a brother who is four years older and a sister who is seven years younger. Her mother stayed at home until Anny was 12. Everything in the home was, as seen from the outside, perfect. Her mother, however, showed little warmth in close relationships and is described as an emotionally distant woman who is "lost in her own thoughts". Her father was a teacher, but also held a position in the central school administration which resulted in him being away from home a couple of times each year. He was always warm and kind, and is described as being a gentle Christian man with a clear view of the difference between right and wrong. Both parents focused on school performance and good behavior. The family's finances were good. Her older brother was always kind and helpful to Anny, but she had to take care of her little sister. Her sister has since puberty tended to suffer from mild depression during adversity, and is currently struggling with her marriage. Her brother is a bit quiet and emotionally confined. Both siblings are college educated, function well at work and have stable jobs.

   Anny did well in school, was well behaved and had several good friends both inside and outside of a Christian youth club she belonged to. She had a "youth rebellion" toward the end of high school and became more "spiteful and rebellious". She started to go to parties, occasionally drank wine and also engaged in some brief sexual episodes. Her parents learned about this and reproached her strongly. After school, she started nurse training and was an excellent student in every way, practically and theoretically. She went straight from graduation to work at a local hospital.

   She married a man her age while studying who was kind, harmonious, social and knowledgeable within his field. They quickly had a daughter, who is now studying medicine. She was never really in love with her husband, but he had all the qualities "one could wish for in a man", except in their sexual life which she characterized as "quite tame". She was unhappy in her marriage, but hid it from others. They appeared to others to be, for many years, a successful couple. She often thought, however, that they were not going to be married forever.

Mental health: when Anny was in her early 30s, she began having sleeping problems in association with shift work, and slowly developed a moderate depressive episode, prompted by marital frictions, lack of sleep and conflicts at work. She was absent from work for two and a half months. Her GP prescribed medication, which seemed to have a good effect. She started on the day shift when she returned to work, which improved her sleeping. Her marriage, however, continued to be unhappy and difficult. She had a further depressive episode four years later, this time more severe and with thoughts of taking her own life. She therefore began a new round of medication. This time she was also referred, with her husband, to family counseling, which she ended after a short period of time as she "did not feel that it really helped". Shortly after this she shocked her family and those around her by leaving her husband after 18 years of marriage. She had fallen in love with a man at work, whom she moved in with after a quick divorce. The last few years have been difficult and turbulent. But her life, overall, has been far better than before the divorce. She feels that everything matches with her new partner, they have many common values, she feels that they can talk about everything and their sexual life is intimate and satisfying.

Personality: Anny is a very conscientious person and eager to live up to other people's expectations, even though they are often at odds with her own wishes. She is a perfectionist and very keen on presenting a pleasant facade, which she thinks has fallen to pieces due to the divorce. Other people's suffering and problems often affect her strongly. She empathizes with and tries to understand everyone and is sensitive and somewhat melancholy, which she thinks gives a richer life, but also more pain. She rarely gets really angry, and when she gets annoyed, she smiles and retreats instead of asserting herself and starting a discussion or an argument.

Psychodynamic hypothesis (resultant, mechanisms): Anny has identified quite a bit with her father's kindness and calm and with her parents' lack of tolerance of protest and self-assertion. There were many strict concealed or more overt rules in the family during her childhood, which were not to be broken. Her needs and opinions were often frowned upon or directly unwelcome, not least her expressions of anger or dissatisfaction. Self-representations associated with her wishes and needs are linked to object representations that represent prohibition, condemnation and rejection. The internal conflicts this entails easily lead to her feeling demanding, dominant or "bad" if she wants something on her own behalf. Anny has also identified with some of her mother's distanced attitude toward her, which partly represented her mother's way of covering up dissatisfaction and criticism. Anny, as a consequence of this, suppresses her feelings of anger and dissatisfaction. She is also afraid of conflicts and aggression that emanate from others.

IIP-C

Anny perceives herself as more domineering, cold (reserved) and intrusive than others, but at the same time perceives herself as more nonassertive and avoidant than others.

Treatment focus

Anny's depressions and eventual "flight" from her marriage must be seen in the light of the intrapsychic conflicts described above. She has, through this break, rebelled against her parents' ideals and injunctions, which are also to a certain extent her own. Exploration of this in the group must be based on the admission that she has made choices that have negatively affected others. The main emphasis should, however, be placed on the fact that the main purpose of changing her life was to do something positive for herself, which turned out be more conflictual than she had expected. The hope is that encouraging her to highlight and share her dilemmas with the group, and through feedback and support from the therapist and other group members, she can work through these conflicts, and reconcile with, sympathize with and eventually accept the choices she has made.

Some of this process began during the evaluation, through the therapist confronting her with her IIP-C scores. These indicate that she perceives herself to be more "intrusive" and "domineering" than others, while her relationship stories were more in line with her perceptions of herself as too "submissive" and too "socially avoidant". The relationship stories also pictured her as more "exploitable" and "overly nurturant". She reacted as if this was new to her, and started straight away to reflect around them. Her behavioral tasks should challenge her to explore the differences between how she sees herself and how she is perceived by others, and through this to achieve a better-integrated, truer image of herself. She was therefore instructed to regularly present her needs and longings in the group, and to practice setting boundaries for herself in the group.

Level of personality organization (PO)

Identity: 2.5 – she has a moderately distorted ego-identity and some impaired self-esteem. Has some difficulties in giving a coherent picture of herself and others.

Object relations: 1.5 – reduced pleasure in the company of others. Mainly focuses on meeting the needs of others. Combines intimacy and sexuality in her current romantic relationship.

Defense mechanisms: 2 – mainly uses mature defenses such as reaction formation, suppression and perfectionism. But also some use of projection and black and white thinking.

Aggression: 2.5 – impaired contact with both angry and loving/tender feelings. She sometimes thinks that she is too angry, which is not apparent in her accounts of close relationships. She directs aggression toward herself, quickly becoming self-punishing and self-blaming.

Moral values: 3 – she has a strict superego, can be critical and judgmental both of herself and others. Usually suppresses negative feelings of others.

Narcissism: 2 – slightly elevated. Lack of mirroring of needs for autonomy. Her kind, docile and obedient sides are, at the same time, too strongly confirmed. Part of her feels a little better than others.

Diagnosis (descriptive)

Axis 1 – Depressive episode, moderate.
Axis 2 – Avoidant PD.

Patient 7: Elsie

Elsie is a 36-year-old secretary who is divorced, but lives with a new partner. She has a son of 11 from her marriage who lives with them.

Reason for referral: Elsie was referred to a psychiatrist after experiencing, on several occasions in the last couple of years, diffuse anxiety when with others. She feels easily criticized and avoids places where there are many people, such as parties, shopping malls and restaurants.

Psychodynamic case formulation

Symptoms: she has felt a little anxiety in social situations since the age of 16, the degree varying over the years. She had a depressive episode a few years ago with low mood and feelings of guilt after an episode at work where she was unfairly criticized by a colleague. She was treated by a GP, medicated for three weeks and then returned to work.

Symptomatic behavior (interpersonal): she feels that "inside herself" there is an anxious girl who is afraid of others criticizing or looking down on her. She believes that others do not see that she is struggling as she tries to be open, direct and social. She suspects that she sometimes becomes too domineering and intrusive in social situations, as she tries to ignore and hide her anxiety.

Avoidance: she often tries to avoid social situations, for example parties. She does, however, play the trombone in a band. This situation is, however, different because everyone is looking at the conductor and the attention is on the music.

Precipitating factors (stressors): no direct cause for her to seek help now, except that her anxiety has increased.

Predisposing factors (vulnerability): Elsie grew up with two younger siblings, a brother and a sister. The parents were happy together and there was a warm atmosphere in the home. They had their own house and the family's finances were satisfactory. There were, however, some conflicts and quarrels between her parents when Elsie entered puberty. She had a great time at primary school and was "friends with everyone". After high school, she took a combined mercantile/financial management education and got a job with a branch of a major oil company. She had a couple of brief romantic relationships when at school, and married a childhood friend when she was in her early 20s. They had a son. Both were a little insecure and restless, but at first felt strongly that they needed each other. It soon became clear that they had few interests in common, except for the son whom they both loved. They spent less and less time together, both missing the closeness and intimacy of the other and gradually slid apart, despite trying couples therapy on two occasions. The divorce process itself, which began after five years of marriage, and the following years have been troublesome. She has few close friends, except one woman in the band. But she does have a number of buddies, both at work and in the band. She has also received support from her younger sister and her partner, who moved into her home one year before her referral.

Her son has lived with her since the divorce, but has a satisfactory and regular contact with his father.

Mental health: the anxiety first hit her at the beginning of high school after a boyfriend broke up with her. Another possible stressor was an event in class in which a teacher made fun of her when she stuttered a little and pronounced a foreign word incorrectly when reading aloud to the class. Everyone laughed and she felt very ashamed and blushed. The anxiety has varied in strength. She, however, believes that it has frequently made it impossible for her to participate in social events, and that it maybe also once prevented her from embarking on further education at a university.

Personality: the patient has a split view of herself. On the one hand, she sees herself as honest and fair, and she believes that she is able to hide her anxiety, and manages to communicate directly, socialize and make contact with others. On the other hand, she feels that she is just displaying a facade, and that she is not sure whether she likes other people or herself and often worries about what others think of her. She can sometimes feel that she is false and that people will see through her one day.

Psychodynamic hypothesis (resultant, mechanisms): Elsie believes that she was raised in a harmonious home with good relationships between everyone. However, she seems to have a tendency to idealize both her parents' marriage and the relationships between her and her siblings and the parents. Some of the stories she told indicate that she has only been supported and confirmed when kind, gentle and obedient. They, however, also show that her parents' tolerance for negative emotions such as sadness, anger and spite was very low, such behavior being met with condemnation and rejection. She has identified with these attitudes of her parents, which has probably contributed to her impaired ability to regulate self-esteem, and also to her fear of criticism and rejection from others if she discloses negative emotions. These conflicts could lie behind her counter-phobic tendency to sometimes dominate and somewhat frantically engage with others, this alternating with a more anxious, restrained and elusive attitude.

IIP-C

Elsie perceives herself as more avoiding and nonassertive than others, but at the same time scores herself as more domineering and intrusive, but less exploitable, than others.

Treatment focus

Elsie, during the evaluation, was confronted with her contradictory IIP-C scores. These indicate that she perceives herself *both* as domineering and intrusive *and* as submissive and avoidant in contact with others. She, following this, disclosed that this is conflict for her. She can feel that she both wants to show off, entertain and be appreciated and admired, while at other times fearing being criticized and ridiculed. She was encouraged to try to observe her own fluctuating self-esteem by noting how and when it changes when she is in the group. She was also encouraged to report when this happens and what causes it. She should also explore whether this happens when someone in the group is critical of her, or whether the fear of being criticized stems from herself and is something she carries with her. Elsie's images of her parents began to crack when she and the therapist discussed her childhood. She discloses that her sister has some negative memories from childhood that go beyond what Elsie remembers. Elsie is therefore given the home assignment to talk more with her sister about potential differences in childhood memories, and to ask her parents individually how they related to her when she was helpless, despondent or spiteful.

Level of personality organization (PO)

Identity: 2.5 – somewhat impaired. She is successful and focused as a musician, but has failed to advance in her job. She has an impaired regulation of self-esteem (fluctuates) and thinks this may be the reason why she has not been promoted at work. She displays a slightly false facade to others and gives a slightly idealized picture of both parents (sense of others).

Object relations: 2 – slightly impaired. She has few friends, but has a close relationship with a sister and one person in the band. She keeps her distance from others. There was lack of closeness and intimacy in her marriage, but this has improved with her new partner.

Defense mechanisms: 2.5 – she has a tendency to idealize her parents and has a split image of herself (both domineering and submissive). Her sense of herself as a weak, small and anxious girl may be enhanced by her projecting aggressive feelings onto others, and her fearing reprisals. She also uses more mature defenses such as suppression, repression and displacement.

Aggression: 2 – she has an impaired aggression tolerance and is careful to not disclose irritation or anger.

Moral values: 3 – she is quite strict about what she calls her own "negative" aspects. This conflicts with her wish to be "fair and kind" to everyone. She tries to suppress negative emotions. These are, even so, activated by frustrations and demands in her day-to-day life, and may be linked to her phobic and elusive traits.

Narcissism: 2 – slightly elevated. She depends on more than usual confirmation from others to feel good about herself.

Diagnosis (descriptive)

Axis 1 – Social phobia.
Axis 2 – Avoidant PD.

Patient 8: Frank

Frank is a 41-year-old divorced auditor. He has no children.

Reason for referral: Frank feels completely "trapped" in his life. He was diagnosed with and operated for bowel cancer 13 years ago. This shocked him and he began to worry about how his future would be. The operation was successful, and he has had no relapses. He has been told that he is cured, which is hard for him to believe. However, not long after this he was hit by another "shock", his wife suddenly leaving him two years after the operation. He misses her a lot. He gradually lost some direction in life and in recent years has withdrawn from friends and family. Now he wants to see a specialist to help him reconnect with life.

Psychodynamic case formulation

Symptoms: he has a persistent depression, but occasionally has better days between dark days. He is able to work satisfactorily. This often, however, takes all his energy. He sometimes has some diffuse abdominal pain, which scares him and he starts thinking about the possibility of his tumor spreading, that the doctors have not told him the truth about his cancer and that they cannot be trusted.

Symptomatic behavior (interpersonal): he does not really have any difficulties in socializing with others, but does not enjoy socializing anymore. He is a little bitter about his fate as a cancer patient. He feels that he has had bad luck and that everyone else has a better life than him.

Avoidance: he has isolated himself at home and has gradually withdrawn from family, friends and acquaintances. He mostly watches TV and often finds a pretext to refuse suggestions from others that they do something together.

Precipitating factors (stressors): his illness and his wife leaving have strongly affected his sense of self and life. These constitute traumas that he has been unable to work through. He feels that the cancer hangs over him like a sword of Damocles and still finds it difficult to accept that she left.

Predisposing factors (vulnerability): Frank was raised in a small town as the oldest of three siblings. His father died suddenly when Frank was eight years old. His mother was "shattered" for a number of years, and Frank had to early on take responsibility for the younger siblings, whom he had a good relationship with. He was bright at school, played in the school band and was helpful at home. He had several friends, including a romantic relationship with a girl from his class which ended when they finished school. After high school, he trained as an auditor and got a job in a small auditing firm, where he has worked ever since. He kept in touch with two friends from school and eventually met a woman, through a friend, whom he quickly married when he was 26 years old, after a short romance. The first years of their marriage were happy. Things, however, started to change when he began experiencing stomach symptoms, and contracted colon cancer with the possibility of it having spread. The treatment lasted approximately one year, and included surgery, chemotherapy and absence from work. His illness took all the time and attention of both of them. He recovered well physically after the illness, kept in contact with friends and family through it all, and gradually resumed some of his old activities, including work. Mentally, however, he gradually changed, becoming more pessimistic, complaining and introspective. He also began to question whether his wife loved him. He gradually isolated himself, preferring to be at home after work, and did not want his wife to leave the house. His wife found his demands and restrictions unbearable, the result being a divorce after six years of marriage.

Personality: Frank seems to have changed after his illness and divorce, probably because of his protracted depressive condition. He is still conscientious with his work and has managed to work in spite of his mood swings. He has, however, become passive, withdrawn and emotionally distant from others. He is bitter about his destiny and covertly blames and envies others because they have "a better life" than him. He is, on the other hand, unhappy about his passivity in relation to social activities, and feels ready to try to change this.

Frank remembered little of his childhood during the evaluation. He thinks there were some quarrels between his parents and that something "scary" happened at home. His parents were not always kind to the children. The children were, however, able to support each other. Frank was almost desperate about the changes he had undergone as a person in recent years, which he saw as the main reason why he felt lonely, occasionally empty and depressed. He seemed genuinely motivated to try to change. The therapist thought it would therefore be possible to establish a therapeutic alliance, and engage him in treatment.

Psychodynamic hypothesis (resultant, mechanisms): Frank has probably received little confirmation from early in his life and had to "stretch his autonomy" to take responsibility for younger siblings. He has tried, through reaction formation, to become self-sufficient, also due to his father dying and mother "collapsing".

His serious illness and long treatment was a major "trauma" that took all his attention and energy. His wife then left him after he recovered. Both events were severe blows to Frank's identity, which had to be "reorganized". He became depressed, but seemed unable to mourn. His personality seems to have developed in a depressive direction, his sense of self (body-self included) and sense of others being negatively affected. He partly directed his aggression toward himself, to punish himself for what had happened. He also feels that he does not get enough out of life and is envious and angry with others, who he thinks are doing well and do not care for him. His anger is more or less covertly expressed as a bitterness about others not caring about or looking down on him because of what he became. This feeling is probably fed by him projecting parts of his aggression onto others who, because of this, appear more dismissive than they really are.

It seems important to explore the bitterness and the anger, how it made him erect a wall to keep others out and how it undermines the quality of his life.

IIP-C

The profile shows that Frank perceives himself to be more cold (reserved), avoidant and exploitable than others. He considers himself to be fairly nurturant (but less than he was before) and less vindictive, domineering and intrusive than others.

Treatment focus

Frank, during the evaluation, came to clearly see how his withdrawal and isolation from others had made his life poorer, and that he wants to change this. He should explore this change after his cancer in the group, by actively interacting with the other group members. He should ask himself and the other group members how his bitterness, withdrawal and envy affect them. He should also try out the realities of his image of himself and others, by asking at least one fellow patient in each session about their specific problems. This is to give him a more realistic understanding of the lives of others, and of "what they struggle with inside". He may also, through this, get in better touch with the caring, empathetic aspects of himself that he has previously demonstrated, for example by taking care of younger siblings. Outside the group, there is an urgent need to work on restoring relationships with family and friends. He was also encouraged to talk more with a favorite sister, to discuss memories of childhood.

Level of personality organization (PO)

Identity: 2.5 – Frank has been quite goal-orientated in taking responsibility for siblings, in education and work. He had a slightly impaired sense of self (forced autonomy). He needed to reorganize his identity after his recovery from cancer. His sense of others deteriorated after his illness.

Object relations: 3 – he had friends from early on in life, a close relationship with siblings, and a close and intimate relationship with his wife until he withdrew and "pushed her away".

Defense mechanisms: 3 – he uses a mix of defenses. He uses higher levels of altruism, reaction formation, displacement. He also partly idealizes and devalues others and projects his anger onto others. This provides the basis for envy and fear of retaliation.

Aggression: 3 – much aggression aimed at himself, and also at others in the form of bitterness, envy and reproach, making him believe that others dislike him.

Moral values (superego functioning): 2.5 – he is quite strict with himself, blames himself for becoming ill, which is unfounded.

Narcissism: 2.5 – experiences himself as a victim, feels entitled to more concern and care, and is envious of and angry with others.

Diagnosis (descriptive)

Axis 1 – Dysthymia, hypochondria, possibly secondary to depression.
Axis 2 – Mixed personality disorder, traits from Paranoid and Dependent PD.

Appendix 2

Norms for IIP-C

Reference values of IIP-C, based on a non-clinical sample of the Norwegian population As a basis for comparison of the eight patients in the demonstration group, I have chosen a sample from the Norwegian population. It consists of 302 persons who completed a battery of self-report measures, including IIP-C (Alden et al., 1990). One half of the sample were psychology students, and the other half were recruited among employees at large companies, by friends and acquaintances of the same students. Gender: mean age was 33 years (range 18 to 65), gender: women 60% (Monsen et al., 1999). Values given as mean (standard deviation):

Norms

IIP-64, average total 0.97 (0.44)
   IIP sub-scales:

- Domineering: 0.78 (0.55)
- Vindictive: 0.72 (0.54)
- Cold/Reserved: 0.73 (0.59)
- Socially avoidant: 0.95 (0.69)
- Nonassertive: 1.09 (0.70)
- Exploitable: 1.37 (0.66)
- Overly nurturant: 1.16 (0.59)
- Intrusive: 0.93 (0.58)

Appendix 3

STIPO-R – Clinical anchors for personality organization: identity, object relations, defenses, aggression, and moral values across the range of severity[1]
The Structured Interview of Personality Organization-Revised (STIPO-R) anchors are intended to serve as general guidelines for clinicians and researchers assessing personality organization. The following anchors have been adapted to benefit clinical use. For an in-depth evaluation using these anchors for research use, see the full STIPO-R interview and score sheet available at www.borderlinedisorder.com.

For each 1–5 rating, a series of descriptors is provided for each anchor, in which 1 = normal and 5 = most severe pathology. It is expected that some, but not all, descriptors will apply to a particular patient.

The domains are first graded individually by severity level (Caligor et al., 2018) based on all information about the individual patient. After an overall assessment, the patients are weighted against an overview chart of the level of structural PO (normal, neurotic and high, medium and low level of borderline) shown in Table 4.1 in Chapter 4.

[1]Reprinted with permission from *Psychodynamic Therapy for Personality Pathology*, (Copyright 2018). American Psychiatric Association. All rights reserved.

Identity

1. **Consolidated identity** – Sense of self and others is well integrated, with in-depth investment in work/school and recreation.
2. **Consolidated identity, but with some areas of slight deficit** – Sense of self and others* is well integrated for the most part, but with a mild superficiality, instability, or distortion and/or with some difficulty in investment in work/school or recreation.
3. **Mild identity pathology** – Sense of self and/or others is somewhat poorly integrated (evident superficiality or incoherence and instability, at times contradictory and distorted),* with clear impairment in capacity to invest in work/school and/or recreation; or individual invests largely to meet narcissistic needs.
4. **Moderate identity pathology** – Sense of self and others is poorly integrated (significant superficiality or incoherence; markedly unstable, contradictory, and distorted),* with little capacity to invest in work/school or recreation.
5. **Severe identity pathology** – Sense of self and others is extremely superficial, incoherent, and chaotic (grossly contradictory and extremely distorted),* with no significant investment in work/school or recreation.

* Narcissistic pathology is suggested by the presence of a marked discrepancy between (1) instability or superficiality in the individual's sense of others and (2) relative stability or specificity in the individual's sense of self.

Object relations

1. **Attachments are strong**, durable, realistic, nuanced, satisfying and sustained over time; relationships are not seen in terms of need fulfillment; capacity for interdependence and empathy is fully developed; the individual is able to combine sexuality and intimacy.
2. **Attachments are generally strong**, durable, realistic, nuanced and sustained over time, with some conflict or incomplete satisfaction; relationships are not seen in terms of need fulfillment; capacity for interdependence and empathy is fully developed; there is some degree of impairment or conflict in intimate/sexual relationships.
3. **Attachments are present but are superficial**, brittle and marked by conflict and lack of satisfaction; relationships tend to be viewed in terms of need fulfillment; there is some capacity for concern for the other or some degree of empathy; sexual relationships have limited intimacy.
4. **Attachments are few and highly superficial**; relationships are consistently viewed in terms of need fulfillment; there is little capacity for empathy;

despite any demonstrated efforts to seek intimacy, few to no intimate relationships have developed.
5. **No true relationships exist** (may have acquaintances); the individual may be severely isolated, lacking even acquaintances; any relations that exist are based exclusively on need fulfillment; there is no demonstrated capacity for empathy; no capacity for intimacy and/or any attempts at intimacy are evident.

Defenses

1. **Flexible, adaptive coping is used**; no evidence is seen that lower-level (splitting-based) defenses are employed; stress resilience is evident in most areas; a variety of adaptive coping strategies are consistently used.
2. **Adaptive coping strategies are used with less consistency or efficacy**, or in some areas but not others, with general resilience to stress. Some lower-level defenses are endorsed (may be limited to idealization and/or devaluation), but these are clearly not the predominant defensive style of the respondent; limited or no impairment in functioning is seen from use of lower-level defenses.
3. **Lower-level defenses have a mixed pattern of endorsement**; shifts in perception of self and others are present. Some impairment in functioning is seen from use of lower-level defenses.
4. **Lower-level defenses are consistently endorsed**; shifts in perception of self and others are relatively severe and pervasive. Clear evidence of impairment in respondent's life is seen from use of lower-level defenses.
5. **Lower-level defenses are used pervasively across situations**. Severe, radical shifts in perception of self and others are to a degree that grossly interferes with functioning, with multiple examples of instability and distortion.

Aggression

1. **Control of aggression** – any episodes of anger and verbal aggression appear to be appropriate to the situation.
2. **Relatively good control of aggression** – maladaptive expressions of aggression are limited to inhibitions (failure to express aggression), minor self-destructive behaviors or neglect, a controlling interpersonal style, or occasional verbal outbursts.
3. **Moderately poor control of aggression** – maladaptive expressions of aggression include significant self-destructive or higher risk behaviors, self-neglect or noncompliance, and/or frequent tantrums or outbursts of hateful verbal aggression, chronic hostile control of others and/or deriving sadistic pleasure from other's discomfort or misfortune.
4. **Poor control of aggression** – if self-directed, aggression is severe to lethal, but somewhat less pervasive, less chronic (i.e., more episodic), and/or less life-threatening than aggression in item 5. If other-directed, aggression is episodic but frequent, with hateful verbal abuse of others, frequent verbal and physical threats to hurt self or other, and/or physical intimidation that may

involve physically threatening or assaulting the other, with pleasure in hurting and/or hostile control of others.
5. **Little or no control of aggression** – pervasive tendency toward chronic, severe, lethal expressions of aggression is evident. Frequent, vicious, sadistic and hateful verbal abuse and/or physical attack on others and/or self is intended to cause physical harm and pose a serious danger to the safety of others and/or self. Self- and other-directed aggression involves sadistic pleasure in torture and control; self-directed aggression may involve extreme self-mutilation and/or multiple suicide attempts with intent to die.

Moral values

1. **Internal moral compass is autonomous, consistent and flexible**; no evidence is seen of amoral or immoral behavior: the individual demonstrates a mature and appropriate sense of concern and responsibility for potentially hurtful or unethical behavior; there is no exploitation of others for personal gain; the individual experiences guilt appropriately.
2. **Internal moral compass is autonomous and consistent, with rigidity and/or ambiguity involving questionable opportunities for personal gain**; no evidence is seen of frankly amoral or immoral behavior; the individual demonstrates some rigidity (either excessive or some laxity) in sense of concern and responsibility for potentially hurtful or unethical behavior; the individual experiences guilt, but in such a way that ruminative self-recrimination is more prevalent than proactive efforts to make amends.
3. **Some sense of internal moral standards exists, but they are excessively rigid and/or lax**; the individual may demonstrate considerable difficulty using these standards to guide behaviors, which may include some unethical or immoral behavior without confrontation of a victim (e.g., plagiarism, cheating, lying, tax evasion); the individual can be exploitative, with difficulty taking responsibility for behaviors that are hurtful to others; the individual lacks appropriate experience of guilt and concern and/or may experience "guilt" in the form of sadistic self-recrimination without true remorse.
4. **Moral values and internal standards are weak, inconsistent and/or corrupt**; moral orientation is toward not getting caught and may include presence of aggressive antisocial behavior (e.g., robbery, fraud, blackmail); such behavior may involve confrontation of victims, but without assault, and any violence that occurs is generally not premeditated; exploitation of others is ego-syntonic and the individual freely pursues opportunities for personal gain at the expense of others; guilt or remorse is lacking.
5. **No comprehension of the notion of moral values** is evident; the presence of violent, aggressive antisocial behavior (assault, battery, premeditation) or frank psychopathy (no comprehension or notion of moral values) with or without violent behavior is evident; there is no sense of guilt or remorse.

References

Aagaard, S., Bechgaard, B. & Winther, G. (Eds.) (1994). *Gruppeanalytisk Psykoterapi. [Group analytic psychotherapy]*. Copenhagen: Hans Reitzel's Forlag.

Agazarian, Y.M. & Gannt, S.P. (2000). *Autobiography of a theory*. London: Jessica Kingsley.

Alden, L.E., Wiggins, J.S. & Pincus, A.L. (1990). Construction of circumplex scales for the inventory of interpersonal problems. *Journal of Personality Assessment*, 55, 521–536.

Alexander, F. & French, T. (1946). *Psychoanalytic therapy: Principles and applications*. New York: Ronald Press.

Allredge, C.T., Burlingame, G.M., Yang, C., & Rosendahl, J. (2021). Alliance in Group Therapy: A Meta-Analysis. *Group Dynamics: Theory, Research, and Practice*, 25(1), 13–28.

American Psychiatric Association. (2000). *Diagnostic and statistical manual of mental disorders* (4th ed. text rev.). Washington, DC: Author.

American Psychiatric Association. (2013). *Diagnostic and statistical manual of mental disorders* (5th ed.). Washington, DC: American Psychiatric Association.

Anthony, E.J. (1971). The history of group psychotherapy. In H.I. Kaplan & B.J. Sadock (Eds.), *Comprehensive group psychotherapy* (p. 4). Baltimore, MD: Williams & Wilkins.

Askevold, F. (1958). Gruppeterapi i en observasjonsavdeling. [Group therapy in an observation Ward]. *Nordisk Psykiatrisk Medlemsblad*, 12, 213–218.

Astrup, C. (1958). Group therapy in a mental hospital with special regard to schizophrenics. *Acta Psychiatrica Scandinavica*, 33, 1–20.

Bakali, J.V., Baldwin, S.A. & Lorentzen, S. (2009). Modeling group process constructs at three stages in group psychotherapy. *Psychotherapy Research*, 19(3), 332–343.

Bakali, J.V., Wilberg, T., Klungsøyr, O. & Lorentzen, S. (2013). Development of group climate in short- and long-term psychodynamic group psychotherapy. *International Journal of Group Psychotherapy*, 63(3), 367–393.

Balint, M., Ornstein, P. & Balint, E. (1972). *Focal psychotherapy: An example of applied psychoanalysis* (Vol. 22, Mind and medicine monographs). London: J.B. Lippincott.

Barkham, M., Evans, C., Margison, F., McGrath, G., Mellor-Clark, J., Milne, D. & Connell, J. (1998). The rationale for developing and implementing core batteries in service settings and psychotherapy outcome research. *Journal of Mental Health*, 7, 35–47.

Barkham, M., Lutz, W., Lambert, M.J. & Saxon, D. (2017). Therapist effects, effective therapists, and the law of variability. In L.G. Castonguay & C.E. Hill (Eds.), *How and why are some therapists better than others? Understanding therapist effects* (pp. 13–36). Washington, DC: American Psychological Association.

Barkham, M., Lutz, W., & Castonguay, L.G. (2021). *Bergin and Garfield's Handbook of Psychotherapy and Behavior Change.* (7th ed.). Hoboken, NJ: John Wiley.

Barwick, N. & Weegmann, M. (2018). *Group therapy: A group-analytic approach.* London and New York: Routledge.

Bateman, A. & Fonagy, P. (2016). *Mentalization-based treatment for personality disorders. A practical guide.* Oxford: Universities Press.

Battle, C.C., Imber, S.D., Hoehn-Saric, R., Stone, A.R. & Frank, J.D. (1966). Target complaints as criteria of improvement. *American Journal of Psychotherapy, 20,* 184–192.

Bednar, R.L. & Kaul, T.J. (1978). Experimental group research: Current perspectives. In A.E. Bergin & S.L. Garfield (Eds.), *Handbook of psychotherapy and behavior change: An empirical analysis* (2nd ed., pp. 769–815). New York: Wiley.

Bednar, R.L. & Kaul, T.J. (1994). Experimental group research: Can the cannon fire? In A.E. Bergin & S.L. Garfield (Eds.), *Handbook of psychotherapy and behavior change* (4th ed., pp. 631–663). New York: Wiley.

Bednar, R.L. & Lawlis, G. (1971). Empirical research on group therapy. In A.E. Bergin & S.L. Garfield (Eds.), *Handbook of psychotherapy and behavior change: An empirical analysis* (pp. 812–838). New York: Wiley.

Behr, H. (1995). The integration of theory and practice. In M. Sharpe (Ed.), *The third eye: Supervision of analytic groups* (pp. 4–17). London and New York: Routledge.

Behr, H. (2016). *The French Revolution: A tale of terror and hope for our times.* Sussex: Academic Press.

Behr, H. & Hearst, L. (2005). *Group-analytic psychotherapy: A meeting of minds.* London and Philadelphia: Whurr Publishers.

Bender, D.S., Skodol, A.E., First, M.B. & Oldham, J.M. (2018). Module I: Structured clinical interview for the level of personality functioning scale. In M.B. First, A.E. Skodol, D.S. Bender & J.M. Oldham, *Structured clinical interview for the DSM-5 alternative model for personality disorders* (SCID-5-AMPD). Arlington, VA: American Psychiatric Association Publishing.

Benjamin, L.S. (1974). Structured analysis of social behavior. *Psychological Review, 81,* 392–425.

Benjamin, L.S. (1984). Principles of prediction using structural analysis of social behavior. In R. Zucker, J. Aronoff & A. Rabin (Eds.), *Personality and the prediction of behavior* (pp. 121–173). New York: Academic Press.

Benjamin, L.S. (1988). *SASB short form user's manual.* Madison, WI: INTREX Interpersonal Institute.

Berg, E.M. & Island, T.K. (2011). Tillit og skam i veilednings-matrix. [Trust and shame in the supervision matrix]. *Matrix, 28*(4), 295–308.

Berman, J.S. & Norton, N.C. (1985). Does professional training make a therapist more effective? *Psychological Bulletin, 98,* 401–407.

Bertalanaffy, L.v. (1968). *General system theory: Foundations, development, applications.* New York: George Braziller.

Berzon, B., Pious, C. & Farson, R. (1963). The therapeutic event in group psychotherapy: A study of subjective reports by group members. *Journal of Individual Psychology, 19,* 204–212.

Beutler, L.E., Machado, P.P. & Neufeldt, S.A. (1994). Therapist variables. In A.E. Bergin & S.L. Garfield (Eds.), *Handbook of psychotherapy and behavior change* (4th ed., pp. 229–269). New York: Wiley.

Bion, W.R. (1946). The leaderless group project. *Bulletin of the Menninger Clinic, 10*(3), 71–81.

Bion, W.R. (1961). *Experiences in groups and other papers.* London: Tavistock Publications.

Bjerke Ness, S. (2018). Anvendelse av gruppeterapi i Norge. [Use of group therapy in Norway]. In S. Ness Bjerke (Ed.), *Gruppeterapi [Group therapy. The basics of why and how]* (pp. 70–97). Oslo: Gyldendal.

Blackmore, C., Tantam, D., Parry, G. & Chambers, E. (2012). Report on a systematic review of the efficacy and clinical effectiveness of group analysis and analytic / dynamic group psychotherapy. *Group Analysis, 45,* 46–69.

Bloch, S. & Crouch, E. (1985). *Therapeutic factors in group therapy.* Oxford: Oxford University Press.

Bloch, S., Reibstein, J., Crouch, E., Holroyd, P. & Themen, J. et al (1979). A method for the study of therapeutic factors in group psychotherapy. *British Journal of Psychiatry, 134,* 257–263.

Bloch, S., Crouch, E. & Reibstein, J. (1981). Therapeutic factors in group psychotherapy. *Archives of General Psychiatry, 38,* 519–526.

Bond, M. & Perry, J.C. (2004). Long-term changes in defense styles with psychodynamic psychotherapy for depressive, anxiety and personality disorders. *American Journal of Psychiatry, 161,* 1665–1671.

Bordin, E.S. (1979). The generalizability of the psychoanalytic concept of the working alliance. *Psychotherapy: Theory, Research and Practice, 16,* 252–260.

Bormann, B. & Strauss, B. (2007). Group climate, cohesion, alliance, and empathy as components of therapeutic relationships in group psychotherapies - reviewing a multi-level model. *Group Psychotherapy and Group Dynamics, 43*(1), 3–22.

Borthwick, A., Holman, C., Kennard, D., McFetridge, M., Messruther, K. & Wilkes, J. (2001). The relevance of moral treatment to contemporary mental health care. *Journal of Mental Health, 10*(4), 427–439.

Bowlby, J. (1968). *Attachment and loss, Vol. 1: Attachment.* New York: Basic Books.

Bowlby, J. (1973). *Attachment and loss, Vol. 2: Separation, anxiety, and anger.* London: Penguin Press.

Bowlby, J. (1980). *Attachment and loss, Vol. 3: Loss: Sadness and depression.* New York: Basic Books.

Brabrender, V. & Fallon, A. (2009). *Group development in practice.* Washington, DC: American Psychological Association.

Bratfos, O. & Sagedal, E. (1961). Enkel gruppeterapi ved sinnsykehus. [Simple group therapy at the mental hospital]. *Nordisk Medisin, 66,* 1533–1537.

Brown, D. (1994). Self development through subjective interaction. In D. Brown & L. Zinkin (Eds.), *The psyche and the social world* (pp. 80–98). London and New York: Routledge.

Brown, D. & Zinkin, L. (1994). *The psyche and the social world.* London and New York: Routledge.

Buchele, B.J. & Rutan, J.S. (2017). An object relations theory perspective. *International Journal of Group Psychotherapy, 67*(Supp. 1), 36–43.

Budman, S.H., Demby, A., Feldstein, M. & Gold, M. (1984). The effects of time-limited group psychotherapy: A controlled study. *International Journal of Group Psychotherapy, 34,* 587–603.

Budman, S.H., Soldz, S., Demby, A., Feldstein, M., Springer, T. & Davis, M. (1989). Cohesion, alliance, and outcome in group psychotherapy: An empirical examination. *Psychiatry, 52,* 339–350.

Burchard, E., Michaels, J. & Kotkov, B. (1948). Criteria for the evaluation of group therapy. *Psychosomatic Medicine*, *10*, 257–274.

Burlingame, G.M. & Jensen, J.L. (2017). Small group process and outcome research highlights: A 25-year perspective. *International Journal of Group Psychotherapy*, *67*(Suppl. 1), 194–218.

Burlingame, G.M., Fuhriman, A. & Johnson, J. (2002). Cohesion in group psychotherapy. In J. Norcross (Ed.), *Psychotherapy relationships that work* (pp. 71–87). New York: Oxford University Press.

Burlingame, G.M., McClendon, D.T. & Alonso, J. (2011). Cohesion in group therapy. In J.C. Norcross (Ed.), *Psychotherapy relationships that work* (pp. 110–131). New York: Oxford University Press.

Burlingame, G.M., Strauss, B. & Joyce, A.S. (2013). Change mechanisms and effectiveness of small group treatments. In M.J. Lambert (Ed.), *Bergin and Garfield's Handbook of psychotherapy and behavior change* (pp. 640–690). Hoboken, NJ: John Wiley.

Burlingame, G.M., Gleave, R., Beecher, M., Griner, D., Hansen, K. & Jensen, J. (2016). *Administration and scoring manual for the Group Questionnaire-GQ*. Salt Lake City: OQ Measures.

Burlingame, G.M., Seebeck, J.D., Janis, R.A. & Whitcomb, K.E. (2016). Outcome differences between individual and group formats when identical and nonidentical treatments, patients, and doses are compared: A 25-year meta-analytic perspective. *Psychotherapy*, *53*(4), 446–461.

Burlingame, G.M., McClendon, D.T. & Yang, C. (2018). Cohesion in group therapy: A meta-analysis. *Psychotherapy*, *55*(4), 384–398.

Burlingame, G.M., Whitcomb, K.E., Woodland, S.C., Olsen, J.A., Beecher, M. & Gleave, R. (2018). The effects of relationship and progress feedback in group psychotherapy using the Group Questionnaire and Outcome Questionnaire – 45: A randomized clinical trial. *Psychotherapy*, *55*(2), 116–131.

Burlingame, G.M., & Strauss, B. (2021). Efficacy of Small Group Treatments: Foundation for Evidence-Based Practice. In M. Barkham, W. Lutz & L.G. Castonguay (Eds.), *Bergin and Garfield's Handbook of psychotherapy and behavior change* (pp. 583–624). (7th ed.). Hoboken, NJ: John Wiley.

Busner, J. & Targum, S.D. (2007). The clinical global impression scale: Applying a research tool in clinical practice. *Psychiatry (Edgmont)*, *4*(7), 28–37.

Cabaniss, D.L. (2013). *Psychodynamic formulation*. Chichester: John Wiley & Sons.

Caligor, E., Kernberg, O.F., Clarkin, J.F. & Yeoman, F.E. (2018). *Psychodynamic therapy for personality pathology: Treating self and interpersonal functioning*. Washington, DC: American Psychiatric Association.

Carroll, L. (2012). *Alice in wonderland*. Oslo: Ashes.

Carson, R. (1969). *Interaction concepts of personality*. Chicago: Aldine.

Clarkin, J.F., Caligor, E., Stern, B.L. & Kernberg, O. (2016). *The Structured Interview of Personality Organization: STIPO-R*. Retrieved from The Personality Studies Institute, 122 East 42nd Street, Suite 3200, New York, NY, 10168. https://www.borderlinedisorders.com

Coombe, P. (2020). The northfield experiments- a reappraisal 70 years on. *Group Analysis*, *53*(2), 162–176.

CORE-OM. Retrieved from CORE: Clinical Outcomes in Routine Evaluation (and CST). https://www.coresystemtrust.org.uk

Corsini, R. & Rosenberg, B. (1955). Mechanisms of group psychotherapy: Processes and dynamics. *Journal of Abnormal and Social Psychology*, *51*, 406–411.

Crits-Christoph, P., Baranackie, K., Kurcias, J.S., Beck, A.T., Carroll, K., Perry, K.,... Zitrin, C. (1991). Meta-analysis of therapist effects in psychotherapy outcome studies. *Psychotherapy Research*, *1*(2), 81–91.

Cuijpers, P., Driessen, E., Hollon, S.D., van Oppen, P., Barth, J. & Andersson, G. (2012). The efficacy of non-directive supportive psychotherapy for adult depression: A meta-analysis. *Clinical Psychology Review*, *32*(4), 280–291.

Dalal, F. (1998). *Taking the group seriously: Towards a post-Foulksian group analytic theory*. London and Philadelphia: Jessica Kingsley Publishers.

De Maré, P. (1972). *Perspectives in group psychotherapy*. London: Allen and Unwin.

Derogatis, L.R. (1977). *The SCL-90-R: Administration, scoring and procedures. Manual I*. Baltimore, MD: Clinical Psychometric Research Unit, Johns Hopkins University School of Medicine.

Dies, R.R. (1994). Therapist variables in group psychotherapy research. In A. Fuhriman & G.M. Burlingame (Eds.), *Handbook of group psychotherapy: An empirical and clinical synthesis* (pp. 114–154). New York: John Wiley & Sons.

Directorate of Health. *Treatment and follow-up-mental disorders*. Retrieved from. https://www.helsedirektoratet.no/produkter/om-helsedirektoratets-normerende-produkter#pakkeforlop

Donovan, J.M., Bennett, M.J. & McElroy, C.M. (1979). The crisis group: An outcome study. *The American Journal of Psychiatry*, *136*(7), 906–910.

Durkin, H.E. (1982a). Boundaries and boundarying: A systems perspective. In M. Pines & L. Rafaelsen (Eds.), *The individual and the group* (pp. 257–267). Boston, MA: Springer.

Durkin, H.E. (1982b). Change in group psychotherapy. Therapy and practice: A systems perspective. *International Journal of Group Psychotherapy*, *32*(4), 431–439.

Durkin, H.E. (1983). Developmental levels: Their therapeutic implications for analytic group psychotherapy. *Group*, *7*, 3–10.

Dush, D.M., Hirt, M.L. & Schroeder, H. (1983). Self-statement modification with adults: A meta-analysis. *Psychological Bulletin*, *94*, 408–422.

Eells, T.D. (Ed.) (2011). *Handbook of psychotherapy case formulation*. New York: Guilford Press.

Ekstein, R. & Wallerstein, R.S. (1972). *The teaching and learning of psychotherapy*. Oxford: International Universities Press.

Emrick, C. (1975). A review of psychologically oriented treatment of alcoholism. *Journal for the Study of Alcoholism*, *36*, 88–108.

Engel, G.L. (1977). The need for a new medical model: A challenge for biomedicine. *Science*, *196*(4286), 129–136.

Evans, C., Mellor-Clark, J., Margison, F., Barkham, M., McGrath, G., Connell, J. & Audin, K. (2000). Clinical outcomes in routine evaluation: The CORE-OM. *Journal of Mental Health*, *9*, 247–255.

Ezriel, H. (1950). A psycho-analytic approach to group treatment. *British Journal of Medical Psychology*, *23*, 59–74.

Fairbarn, W.R.D. (1952). *Psychoanalytic studies of the personality*. London: Tavistock / Routledge.

Falkum, E. (2008). Den biopsykososiale modellen. Bør den formuleres på nytt i lys av nevrobiologisk og stressmedisinsk forskning? [The biopsychosocial model. Should it be reformulated in the light of neurobiological and stress medical research?]. *Michael*, *5*, 255–263.

Fitzmaurice, G., Laird, N.M. & Ware, J.H. (2004). *Applied longitudinal analysis*. New York, NY: Hoboken.

Fjeldstad, A., Høglend, P.A. & Lorentzen, S. (2016). Presence of personality disorder moderates the long-term effects of short-term and long-term psychodynamic group therapy: A 7-year follow-up of a randomized clinical trial. *Group Dynamics: Theory, Research, and Practice, 20*(4), 294–309.

Fjeldstad, A., Høglend, P.A. & Lorentzen, S. (2017). Patterns of change in interpersonal problems during and after short-term and long-term psychodynamic group therapy: A randomized clinical trial. *Psychotherapy Research, 27*(3–4), 350–361.

Flückiger, C., Wampold, B.E., Del Re, H.C. & Horvath, A.O. (2018). The alliance in adult psychotherapy: A meta-analytic synthesis. *Psychotherapy, 55*(2), 316–340.

Forkmann, T., Scherer, A., Boecker, M., Pawelzik, M., Jostes, R. & Gauggel, S. (2011). The clinical global impression scale and the influence of patient or staff perspective on outcome. *BMC Psychiatry, 11*, 83.

Foulkes, S.H. (1977). *Therapeutic group analysis*. New York: International University Press. First published 1964.

Foulkes, S.H. (1984). *Introduction to group-analytic psychotherapy*. London: Maresfield Reprints. First published 1948.

Foulkes, S.H. (1986). *Group analytic psychotherapy. Method and principles*. London: Maresfield Library. First published 1975.

Foulkes, S.H. & Anthony, E.J. (1984). *Group psychotherapy: The psychoanalytical approach* (2nd ed.). London: Maresfield Reprints. First published 1957.

Foulkes, S.H. & Lewis, E. (1944). Group analysis: Studies in the treatment of groups along psychoanalytic lines. *British Journal of Medical Psychology, 20*, 175–184.

Føyn, P. (1995). Supervisor: Experiences from five years of the block course of group-analytic training in Norway. In M. Sharpe (Ed.), *The third eye: Supervision of analytic groups* (pp. 103–106). London and New York: Routledge.

France, D.L. & Dugo, J. (1985). Pretherapy orientation and preparation for psychotherapy groups. *Psychotherapy, 22*, 256–261.

Freud, A. (1934). *Ego and the mechanisms of defense*. London: Hogarth Press.

Freud, S. (1953). The interpretation of dreams. In J. Strachey (Ed.), *The standard edition of the complete psychological works of Sigmund Freud* (Vol. IV and V). London: Hogarth Press. (Originally published in 1900–01).

Freud, S. (1955). Group psychology and the analysis of the ego. In J. Strachey (Ed.), *The standard edition of the complete psychological works of Sigmund Freud* (Vol. XVIII, pp. 67–143). London: Hogarth Press. (Originally published in 1921).

Freud, S. (1958). Remembering, repeating and working through. In J. Strachey (Ed.), *The standard edition of the complete psychological works of Sigmund Freud* (Vol. XII, pp. 145–156). London: Hogarth Press. (Originally published in 1914).

Freud, S. (1960). The psychopathology of everyday life. In J. Strachey (Ed.), *The standard edition of the complete psychological works of Sigmund Freud* (Vol. VI). London: Hogarth Press. (Originally published in 1901).

Freud, S. (1961). The ego and the Id. In J. Strachey (Ed.), *The standard edition of the complete psychological works of Sigmund Freud* (Vol. XIX, pp. 3–66). London: Hogarth Press. (Originally published in 1923).

Friedlander, M.L. & Kaul, T.J. (1983). Preparing clients for counseling: Effects of role induction on counseling process and outcome. *Journal of College Student Personnel, 24*, 207–214.

Friis, S. (1977). Differensiering av terapeutiske miljøer. [Differentiation of therapeutic milieus]. *Nordisk Psykiatrisk Tidsskrift, 31*, 13–24.

Fuhriman, A. & Burlingame, G.M. (Ed.) (1994). *Handbook of group psychotherapy: An empirical and clinical synthesis* (pp. 114–154). New York: John Wiley & Sons.

Gabbard, G.O. (2004). *Long-term psychodynamic psychotherapy*. Washington, DC: American Psychiatric Publishing.

Garland, C. (Ed.) (2010). *The groups book. Psychoanalytic group therapy: principles and practice*. London: Karnac.

Gleave, R., Burlingame, G.M., Beecher, M., Griner, D., Hansen, K. & Jenkins, S. (2017). Feedback-informed group treatment. Application of the OQ-45 and Group Questionnaire (GQ). In S. Miller, D. Prescott & C. Maeschalck (Eds.), *Feedback-informed treatment in clinical practice: Reaching for excellence* (pp. 141–166). Washington, DC: American Psychological Association.

Gray, P. & Mellor-Clark, J. (2007). *The CORE: A decade of development*. Rugby: CORE IMS, Page Bros.

Greenberg, J.R. & Mitchell, S.A. (1983). *Object relations in psychoanalytic theory*. London: Harvard University Press.

Greene, L.R., Rosenkrantz, J. & Muth, D.Y. (1985). Splitting dynamics, self-representations and boundary phenomena in the group psychotherapy of borderline personality disorders. *Psychiatry, 48*, 234–245.

Greene, L.R., Rosenkrantz, J. & Muth, D.Y. (1986). Borderline defenses and countertransference: Research findings and implications. *Psychiatry, 49*, 253–264.

Griner, D., Beecher, M.E., Brown, L.B., Millet, A.J., Worthen, V., Boardman, R.D.,… Gleave, R.L. (2018). Practice-based evidence can help! Using the Group Questionnaire to enhance clinical practice. *Psychotherapy, 55*(2), 196–202.

Grunebaum, H. (1975). A soft-hearted review of hard-nosed research on groups. *International Journal of Group Psychotherapy, 25*, 185–197.

Gullestad, S. & Killingmo, B. (2019). *The theory and practice of psychoanalytic therapy. Listening for the subtext*. London: Routledge.

Hannan, C., Lambert, M.J., Harmon, C., Nielsen, S.L., Smart, D.W., Shimokawa, K. & Sutton, S.W. (2005). A lab test and algorithms for identifying clients at risk of treatment failure. *Journal of Clinical Psychology, 61*, 155–163.

Harrison, T. & Clarke, D. (1992). Northfield experiments. *The British Journal of Psychiatry, 160*(5), 698–708.

Hartmann, H. (1964). Comments on the psychoanalytic theory of the ego. In H. Hartmann, *Essays on ego psychology: Selected problems in psychoanalytic theory* (pp. 113–141). New York: International Universities Press.

Henry, W.P., Schacht, T.E. & Strupp, H.H. (1990). Patient and therapist introject, interpersonal process, and differential psychotherapy outcome. *Journal of Consulting and Clinical Psychology, 58*(6), 768–774.

Hill, C.E. & Knox, S. (2013). Training and supervision in psychotherapy. In M.J. Lambert (Ed.), *Bergin and Garfield's Handbook of psychotherapy and behavior change* (pp. 775–811). Hoboken, NJ: John Wiley.

Hill, W.F. (1975). Further considerations of therapeutic mechanisms in group therapy. *Small Group Behavior, 6*, 421–429.

Hilsenroth, M.J., Defife, J.A., Blagys, M.D. & Ackerman, S.J. (2006). Effects of training in short-term psychodynamic psychotherapy: Changes in graduate clinician technique. *Psychotherapy Research, 16*(3), 293–205.

Hopper, E. (2003). *The social unconscious*. Selected papers. London and Philadelphia: Jessica Kingsley Publishers.

Horneland, M., Børnes, D.S., Høbye, K., Knutsen, H. & Lorentzen, S. (2012). Can the clinician-researcher gap be bridged? Experiences from a randomized clinical trial in analytic / dynamic group psychotherapy. *Group Analysis, 45,* 84–98.

Hornsey, M., Dwyer, L. & Oei, T. (2007). Beyond cohesiveness: Reconceptualizing the link between group processes and outcomes in group psychotherapy. *Small Group Research, 38,* 567–592.

Horowitz, L.M. (1979). Cognitive structure of interpersonal problems treated in psychotherapy. *Journal of Consulting and Clinical Psychology, 47*(1), 5–15.

Horowitz, L.M. & Vitkus, J. (1986). The interpersonal basis of psychiatric symptoms. *Clinical Psychology Review, 6,* 443–469.

Horowitz, L.M., Rosenberg, S.E., Baer, B.A., Ureno, G. & Villasenor, V.S. (1988). Inventory of interpersonal problems: Psychometric properties and clinical applications. *Journal of Consulting and Clinical Psychology, 56*(6), 885–892.

Horvath, A.O. & Luborsky, L. (1993). The role of the therapeutic alliance in psychotherapy. *Journal of Consulting and Clinical Psychology, 61,* 561–573.

Horvath, A.O., Del Re, A.C., Flückiger, C. & Symonds, D. (2011). Alliance in individual psychotherapy. In J.C. Norcross (Ed.), *Psychotherapy relations that work* (pp. 25–69). Oxford: University Press.

Hutchinson, S. (2009). Foulkesian authority: Another view. Response to lecture by Morris Nitsun. *Group Analysis, 42*(4), 354–360.

Jensen, H.H., Mortensen, E.L. & Lotz, M. (2010). Effectiveness of short-term psychodynamic group therapy in a public outpatient psychotherapy unit. *Nordic Journal of Psychiatry, 64*(2), 106–114.

Johansson, P., Høglend, P., Ulberg, R., Amlo, S., Marble, A., Bøgwald, K.-P.,... Heyerdahl, O. (2010). The mediating role of insight for long-term improvements in psychodynamic therapy. *Journal of Consulting and Clinical Psychology, 78,* 438–448.

Johnsen, E. (2003). Modell for gruppeanalytisk veiledning [Model for group analytic supervision]. *Matrix, 20*(4), 400–407.

Johnson, J.E., Burlingame, G.M., Olsen, J.A. Davies, D.R. & Gleave, R.L. (2005). Group climate, cohesion, alliance, and empathy in group psychotherapy: Multilevel structural equation models. *Journal of Counseling Psychology, 52,* 310–321.

Jones, M. (1971). *Det terapeutiske samfunn. [The therapeutic community].* Oslo: Gyldendal Fakkel.

Joyce, A.S., Piper, W.E. & Ogrodniczuk, J.S. (2007). Therapeutic alliance and cohesion variables as predictors of ouctomes in short-term group psychotherapy. *International Journal of Group Psychotherapy, 57*(3), 269–296.

Joyce, A.S., Tasca, G.A., MacNair-Semands, R. & Ogrodniczuk, J.S. (2011). Factor structure and validity of the therapeutic factors inventory-short form. *Group Dynamics: Theory, Research, and Practice, 15*(3), 201–219.

Jørstad, J. & Karterud, S. (1983). Group psychotherapy in Norway. In H.I. Kaplan & B.J. Sadock (Eds.), *Comprehensive group psychotherapy* (pp. 330–332). Baltimore, MD: Waverly Press.

Kampe, K., Zimmermann, J., Bender, D., Caligor, E., Borowski, A.-L., Ehrenthal, J.C.,... Hörz-Sagstetter, S. (2018). Comparison of the structured DSM-5 clinical interview for the level of personality functioning scale with the structural interview for personality organization. *Journal of Personality Assessment, 100*(6), 642–649.

Kanas, N. (1986). Group psychotherapy with schizophrenics: A review of controlled studies. *International Journal of Group Psychotherapy, 36,* 339–351.

Karterud, S. (1999). *Gruppeanalyse og psykodynamisk gruppepsykoterapi* [Group analysis and psychodynamic group psychotherapy]. Oslo: Pax.

Karterud, S. (2003). Veiledning i gruppeanalytisk utdannelse [Supervision in group analytical training]. *Matrix, 20*(4), 380–387.

Karterud, S. (2015). On structure and leadership in mentalization-based group therapy and group analysis. *Group Analysis, 48*(2), 137–149.

Kassaw, K. & Gabbard, G.O. (2002). Creating a psychodynamic formulation from a clinical evaluation. *American Journal of Psychiatry, 159*(5), 721–726.

Kaul, T.J. & Bednar, R.L. (1986). Experimental group research: Results, questions, and suggestions. In A.E. Bergin & S.L. Garfield (Eds.), *Handbook of psychotherapy and behavior change: An empirical analysis* (3rd ed., pp. 671–714). New York: Wiley.

Kennard, D., Roberts, J. & Winther, D.A. (2000). *A workbook of group-analytic interventions*. London: Jessica Kingsley Publications.

Kernberg, O.F. (1975). *Borderline conditions and pathological nacissism*. New York: Jason Aronson.

Kernberg, O.F. (1980). *Internal world and external reality: Object relations theory applied*. New York and London: Jason Aronson.

Kernberg, O.F. (1984). *Severe personality disorders: Psychotherapeutic strategies*. New Haven and London: Yale University Press.

Kernberg, O.F. (1986). Institutional problems of psychoanalytic education. *Journal of the American Psychoanalytic Association, 34*(4), 799–834.

Kernberg, O.F. (1996). A psychoanalytic theory of personality disorders. In J.F. Clarkin & M.F. Lenzenweger (Ed.), *Major theories of personality disorders*. New York: Guilford Press.

Kernberg, O.F. (2012). Suicide prevention for psychoanalytic institutes and societies. *Journal of the American Psychoanalytic Association, 60*(4), 707–719.

Kernberg, O.F. (2016). What is personality? *Journal of Personality Disorders, 30*(2), 145–156.

Kernberg, O.F., Burstein, E.D., Coyne, L., Applebaum, A., Horwitz, L. & Voth, H. (1972). Psychotherapy and psychoanalysis: Final report of the Menninger Foundation's Psychotherapy Research Project. *Bulletin of the Menninger Clinic, 36*, 1–275.

Kernberg, O.F., Goldstein, E., Carr, A., Hunt, H., Bauer, S. & Blumenthal, R. (1981). Diagnosing borderline personality organization. *Journal of Nervous and Mental Disease, 169*, 225–231.

Kiesler, D.J. (1983). The 1982 interpersonal circle: A taxonomy for complementarity in human transactions. *Psychological Review, 90*, 185–214.

Killingmo, B. (1989). Conflict and deficit: Implications for technique. *International Journal of Psychoanalysis, 70*, 65–79.

Klein, M. (1952). The origins of transference. *International Journal of Psychoanalysis, 33*, 433–438.

Klein, M. (1975). *The writings of Melanie Klein, Vol. I: Love, guilt and repair: And other works 1921–1945*. London: Hogarth Press.

Knox, S. & Hill, C.E. (2021). Training and Supervision in Psychotherapy: What W Know and Where We Need to Go. M. Barkham, W. Lutz, and L.G. Castonguay (Eds.). *Bergin and Garfield's Handbook of Psychotherapy and Behavior Change* (pp. 327–359). (7th ed.). Hoboken, NJ: John Wiley.

Kohut, H. (1968). The psychoanalytic treatment of narcissistic personality disorders: Outline of a systematic approach. *The Psychoanalytic Study of the Child, 23*, 86–113.

Kohut, H. (1971). *The analysis of the self*. New York: International Universities Press.
Kohut, H. (1984). *How does analysis cure?* Chicago, IL: University of Chicago Press.
Krogel, J. (2009). *The Group Questionnaire: A new measure of the group relationship*. Prove: Brigham Young University.
Krogel, J., Burlingame, G., Chapman, C., Renshaw, T., Gleave, R., Beecher, M. & MacNair-Semands, R. (2013). The Group Questionnaire: A clinical and empirically derived measure of group relationships. *Psychotherapy Research, 23*(3), 344–354.
Krogh, T. (1998). Debatten om metodologisk individualism. [The debate on methodological individualism]. *Matrix, 14*(4), 281–302.
Lambert, M.J. (1992). Psychotherapy outcome research: Implications for integrative and eclectic therapists. In J.C. Norcross & M.R. Goldfried (Eds.), *Handbook of psychotherapy integration* (pp. 94–129). New York: Basic Books.
Lambert, M.J. (2012). Helping clinicians to use and learn from research-based systems: The OQ analyst. *Psychotherapy, 49*(2), 109–114.
Lambert, M.J. (2013a). *Bergin and Garfield's Handbook of psychotherapy and behavior change* (6th ed.). Hoboken, NJ: John Wiley.
Lambert, M.J. (2013b). The efficacy and effectiveness of psychotherapy. In M.J. Lambert (Ed.), *Bergin and Garfield's Handbook of psychotherapy and behavior change* (6th ed., pp. 169–218). Hoboken, NJ: John Wiley.
Lambert, M.J., Hansen, N.B., Umphress, V., Lunnen, K., Okiishi, J., Burlingame, G.M.,... Reisinger, C.W. (1996). *Administration and scoring manual for the Outcome Questionnaire (OQ-45.2)*. Wilmington, DE: American Professional Credentialing Services.
Lambert, M.J., Whipple, J.L. & Kleinstäuber, M. (2018). Collecting and delivering progress feedback: A meta-analysis of routine outcome monitoring. *Psychotherapy, 55*(4), 520–537.
Lange-Nielsen, F. & Retterstøl, N. (1959). Gruppebehandling av astmatikere innen en medisinsk avdeling [Group treatment of asthmatic patients within a somatic ward]. *Nordisk Medisin, 61*, 270–282.
Laplanche, J. & Pontalis, J.B. (1988). *The language of psychoanalysis*. London: Karnac Books.
LaTorre, R.A. (1977). Pretherapy role induction procedures. *Canadian Psychological Review, 18*, 308–321.
Leary, T. (1957). *Interpersonal diagnosis of personality: A functional theory and methodology for personality evaluation*. New York: Ronald Press.
Le Bon, G. (1995). *The crowd*. London: Transaction.
Leitemo, K., Vestbø, H.S.B., Bakali, J.V. & Nissen-Lie, H.A. (2019). The role of attachment anxiety and avoidance for reduced interpersonal problems in training group analytic therapy. *Group Dynamics: Theory, Research and Practice, 24*(1), 26–41.
Lese, K.P. & MacNair-Semands, R.R. (2000). The therapeutic factors inventory: Development of a scale. *Group, 24*(4), 303–317.
Leszcz, M. & Malat, J. (2012). The interpersonal model of group psychotherapy. In J.L. Kleinberg (Eds.), *The Wiley-Blackwell Handbook of Group Psychotherapy* (pp. 33–58). Oxford: Wiley-Blackwell.
Lieberman, M. (1976). Change induction in small groups. *Annual Review of Psychology, 27*, 217–250.
Lingiardi, V. & McWilliams, N. (Eds.) (2017). *Psychodynamic diagnostic manual* (2nd ed.). New York and London: The Guilford Press.

Lorentzen, S. (1981). Problems of establishing a therapeutic community ward within a mental hospital. *Journal of Oslo City Hospitals, 31*, 47–49.
Lorentzen, S. (2005). Manualer for kort- og lang-tids gruppeanalytisk behandling *[Manuals for short- and long-term group analytic psychotherapy for psychotic patients with anxiety disorders, affective disorders and/or personality disorders]*. Unpublished. Faculty of Medicine, University of Oslo, Norway.
Lorentzen, S. (2006). Contemporary challenges for research in group analysis. *Group Analysis, 39*(3), 321–340.
Lorentzen, S. (2009). Miljøterapi av borderlinepasienter: Fokus på motoverføringsreaksjoner i staben [Milieu therapy of borderline patients. Focus on countertransference reactions in the staff]. *Matrix, 26*(1), 158–176.
Lorentzen, S. (2014). *Group analytic psychotherapy. Working with affective, anxiety and personality disorders*. London: Routledge.
Lorentzen, S. (2018). Korttids Fokusert Gruppeanalytisk Psykoterapi. Et eksempel på anvendt psykoanalyse [Short-term focused group analytic psychotherapy. An example of applied psychoanalysis]. *Tidsskrift for Norsk Psykologforening, 55*(6), 428–436.
Lorentzen, S. (2020). Short-term focused group-analytic psychotherapy (SFGAP): An integrative approach to change based on research. *Group Analysis, 53*(3), 343–360.
Lorentzen, S. & Høglend, P. (2002). The change process of a patient in long-term group psychotherapy. Measuring and describing the change process. *Group Analysis, 35*(4), 500–524.
Lorentzen, S. & Høglend, P. (2004). Predictors of change during long-term analytic group psychotherapy. *Psychotherapy and Psychosomatics, 73*, 25–35.
Lorentzen, S. & Høglend, P. (2005). Predictors of change during and after long-term analytic group psychotherapy. *Journal of Clinical Psychology, 61*(12), 1541–1553.
Lorentzen, S. & Høglend, P. (2008). Moderators of the effects of treatment length in long-term psychodynamic group psychotherapy. *Psychotherapy & Psychosomatics, 77*, 321–322.
Lorentzen, S. & Ruud, T. (2014). Group therapy in public mental health services: Approaches, patients and group therapists. *Journal of Psychiatric and Mental Health Nursing, 21*(3), 219–225.
Lorentzen, S., Herlofsen, P., Karterud, S. & Ruud, T. (1995). Block training in group analysis. The Norwegian program 1984–1992. *International Journal of Group Psychotherapy, 45*, 73–89.
Lorentzen, S., Bøgwald, K.-P. & Høglend, P. (2002). Change during and after long-term analytic group psychotherapy. *International Journal Group Psychotherapy, 52*, 419–429.
Lorentzen, S., Sexton, H.C. & Høglend, P.A. (2004). Therapeutic alliance, cohesion and outcome in a long-term analytic group. *Nordic Journal of Psychiatry, 58*(1), 33–40.
Lorentzen, S., Bakali, J.V., Hersoug, A.G., Hagtvet, K.A., Ruud, T. & Høglend, P. (2012). Psychodynamic group psychotherapy: Impact of group length and therapist professional characteristics on development of therapeutic alliance. *Clinical Psychology and Psychotherapy, 19*, 420–433.
Lorentzen, S., Ruud, T., Fjeldstad, A. & Høglend, P. (2013). Comparison of short- and long-term dynamic group psychotherapy: Randomized clinical trial. *British Journal of Psychiatry, 203*, 280–287.
Lorentzen, S., Wilberg, T. & Martinsen, E.W. (2015). Group psychotherapy in Norway. *International Journal of Group Psychotherapy, 65*(4), 543–551.

Lorentzen, S., Fjeldstad, A., Ruud, T. & Høglend, P. (2015a). Comparing short- and long-term group therapy: Seven-year follow-up of a randomized clinical trial. *Psychotherapy and Psychosomatics*, *84*(5), 320–321.

Lorentzen, S., Ruud, T., Fjeldstad, A. & Høglend, P. (2015b). Personality disorder moderates outcome in short- and long-term group analytic psychotherapy: A randomized clinical trial. *British Journal of Clinical Psychology*, *54*, 129–146.

Lorentzen, S., Fjeldstad, A., Ruud, T., Marble, A., Ulberg, R. & Høglend, P.A. (2015). The effectiveness of short- and long-term psychodynamic group psychotherapy on self-concept: Three-year follow-up of a randomized clinical trial. *International Journal of Group Psychotherapy*, *65*(4), 543–551.

Lorentzen, S., Marble, A., Kvarstein, E., Wilberg, T. & Pedersen, G. (2016). *Outcome Questionnaire-Norwegian*. Retrieved from OQ measures. https://www.oqmeasures.com

Lorentzen, S., Strauss, B. & Altmann, U. (2018). Process-outcome relationships in short- and long-term psychodynamic group psychotherapy: Results from a randomized clinical trial. *Group Dynamics: Theory, Research, and Practice*, *22*(2), 93–107.

Lorr, M. & McNair, D.M. (1963). An interpersonal behavior circle. *The Journal of Abnormal and Social Psychology*, *6*(1), 68–75.

Luborsky, L., Singer, B. & Luborsky, L. (1975). Comparative studies of psychotherapy. *Archives of General Psychiatry*, *32*, 995–1008.

Lundquist, G., Svedin, C.G., Hansson, K. & Broman, I. (2006). Group therapy for women sexually abused as children. *Journal of Interpersonal Violence*, *21*(12), 1665–1677.

MacKenzie, K.R. (1981). Measurement of group climate. *International Journal of Group Psychotherapy*, *31*, 287–295.

MacKenzie, K.R. (1983). The clinical application of a group climate measure. In R.R. Dies & K.R. MacKenzie (Eds.), *Advances in group psychotherapy: Integrating research and practice* (pp. 159–170). Madison, CT: International Universities Press.

MacKenzie, K.R. (1990). *Introduction to time-limited group psychotherapy*. Washington, DC: American Psychiatric Press.

MacKenzie, K.R. (1997). *Time-managed group psychotherapy. Effective clinical applications*. Washington, DC: American Psychiatric Press.

Main, T.F. (1946). The hospital as a therapeutic institution. *Bulletin of the Menninger Clinic*, *10*, 66–70.

Main, T.F. (1977). The concept of the therapeutic community: Variations and vicissitudes. *Group Analysis*, *10*, 2–17.

Malan, D.H. (1976). *The frontier of brief psychotherapy*. New York and London: Plenum Medical Book Company.

Malan, D.H., Balfour, F.H., Hood, V.G & Shooter, A.M. (1976). Group psychotherapy. A long-term follow-up study. *Archives of General Psychiatry*, *33*, 1303–1315.

Mann, J. (1973). *Time-limited psychotherapy*. Cambridge, MA: Harvard University Press.

Marmor, J. (1979). Short-term dynamic psychotherapy. *American Journal of Psychiatry*, *136*(2), 145–155.

Marziali, E., Munroe-Blum, H. & McCleary, L. (1997). The contribution of group cohesion and group alliance to the outcome of group psychotherapy. *International Journal of Group Psychotherapy*, *47*, 475–497.

May, R. (1994). *The discovery of being*. New York: W.W. Norton & Company.

McDougall, W. (1920). *The group mind*. London: Cambridge University Press.

McNary, S.W. & Dies, R.R. (1993). Co-therapist modeling in group psychotherapy: Fact or fantasy? *Group, 17*, 131–142.

McRoberts, C., Burlingame, G.M. & Hoag, M.J. (1998). Comparative efficacy of individual and group psychotherapy: A meta-analytic perspective. *Group Dynamics: Theory, Research and Practice, 2*, 101–117.

McWilliams, N. (2011). *Psychoanalytic diagnosis: Understanding personality structure in the clinical process*. New York: Guilford Press.

Meltzoff, J. & Kornreich, M. (1970). *Research in psychotherapy*. New York: Atherton Press.

Messer, S.B. (2001). What makes brief psychodynamic therapy time efficient? *Clinical Psychology: Science and Practice, 8*(1), 5–22.

Messer, S.B. & Wolitzky, D.L. (1997). The traditional psychoanalytic approach to case formulation. In T.D. Eells (Ed.), *Handbook of psychotherapy case formulation* (pp. 26–57). New York: The Guilford Press.

Miller, R. & Berman, J. (1983). The efficacy of cognitive behavior therapies: A quantitative review of research evidence. *Psychological Bulletin, 94*, 39–53.

Monsen, J., Kallerud, J.E., Eilertsen, D.E. & von der Lippe, A. (1999). *The database for the Norwegian multisite study of process and outcome in psychotherapy*. Unpublished manuscript. Oslo: University of Oslo, Norway.

Moreno, J.L. (1972). *Psychodrama* (Vol. 1). New York: Beacon House.

Muller, E.J. & Scott, T.B. (1984). A comparison of film and written presentations used for pregroup training experiences. *Journal of Specialists in Group Work, 9*, 122–126.

Nielsen, J. & Sørensen, P. (2013). *Brug Gruppen. Psykodynamisk gruppeterapi [Use the group: psychodynamic group therapy]*. Copenhagen: Hans Reitzel's Publishing House.

Nietzel, M., Russel, R., Hemmings, K. & Gretter, M. (1987). Clinical significance of psychotherapy for unipolar depression: A meta-analytic approach to social comparison. *Journal of Consulting and Clinical Psychology, 55*(2), 156–161.

Nissen-Lie, H.A. (2019). Klinisk tenkning og terapeutens personlige bidrag [Clinical thinking and the therapist's personal contribution]. In E. Stänicke, H. Strømme, S. Kristiansen and L.I. Stänicke (Eds.), *Clinical thinking and psychoanalysis* (pp. 36–59). Oslo: Gyldendal.

Nitsun, M. (1996). *The anti-group: Destructive forces in the group and their creative potential*. London and New York: Routledge.

Nitsun, M. (2015). *Beyond the anti-group. Survival and transformation*. London and New York: Routledge.

Norman, J. & Salomonsson, B. (2005). Weaving thoughts. A method for presenting and commenting on psychoanalytic case material in a peer group. *The International Journal of Psychoanalysis, 86*, 1281–1298.

O'Farrell, T.J., Cutter, H. & Floyd, F.J. (1985). Evaluating behavioral marital therapy for male alcoholics: Effects on marital adjustment and communication from before to after treatment. *Behavior Therapy, 16*, 147–167.

Orlinsky, D.E., Strauss, B., Rønnestad, M.H., Hill, C., Castonguay, L., Willutzki, U.,... Carlsson, J. (2015). A collaborative study of development in psychotherapy trainees. *Psychotherapy Bulletin, 50*, 21–24.

Palvarini, P. (2010). Is the concept of corrective emotional experience still topical? *American Journal of Psychotherapy, 64*(2), 171–194.

Pantone, P.J. (2013). A sea change in psychoanalysis. *Contemporary Psychoanalysis, 49*, 3–7.

Parloff, M.B. & Dies, R. (1977). Group psychotherapy outcome research. *International Journal of Group Psychotherapy, 27*, 281–319.

Pattison, E. (1965). Evaluation studies of group psychotherapy. *International Journal of Group Psychotherapy, 15*, 382–397.

Pedersen, G., Kvarstein, E.H., Wilberg, T., Folmo, E.J., Burlingamem, G.M. & Lorentzen, S. (2021). The Group Questionnaire (GQ) – Psychometric properties among outpatients with personality disorders. Group Dynamics. *Theory, Research, and Practice*. http://dx.doi.org/10.1037/gdn0000176

Perry, J.C. (1990). *Defense Mechanism Rating Scales (DMRS)* (5th ed.). Cambridge: Author.

Perry, J.C. (1993). Defenses and their affects. In N.E. Miller, L. Luborsky, J.P. Barber & J.P. Docherty (Eds.), *Psychodynamic treatment research: A handbook for clinical practice* (pp. 274–306). New York: Basic Books.

Perry, J.C., Lingiardi, V. & Ianni, F. (1999). Psychodynamic research can help us to improve diagnosis and therapy for personality disorders. In J. Derksen, C. Maffei & H. Groen (Eds.), *Treatment of Personality Disorders* (pp. 39–52). Boston, MA: Springer.

Pines, M. (1983a). The contribution of S.H. Foulkes to group therapy. In M. Pines (Ed.), *The evolution of group analysis* (pp. 265–285). London: Routledge & Kegan Paul.

Pines, M. (Ed.) (1983b). *The evolution of group analysis*. London: Routledge & Kegan Paul.

Pines, M. (1994). The group-as-a-whole. In D. Brown & L. Zinkin (Eds.), *The psyche and the social world* (pp. 47–59). London: Routledge.

Piper, W.E., Marrache, M., Lacroix, R., Richardsen, A.M. & Jones, B.D. (1983). Cohesion as a basic bond in groups. *Human Relations, 36*, 93–108.

Piper, W.E., McCallum, M., Joyce, A.S., Rosie, J.S. & Ogrodniczuk, J.S. (2001). Patient personality and time-limited group psychotherapy for complicated grief. *International Journal of Group Psychotherapy, 51*(4), 525–552.

Piper, W.E., Ogrodniczuk, J.S., Joyce, A.S., Weideman, R. & Rosie, J.S. (2007). Group composition and group therapy for complicated grief. *Journal of Consulting and Clinical Psychology, 75*(1), 116–125.

Piper, W.E., Ogrodniczuk, J.S., Joyce, A.S. & Weideman, R. (2011). *Short-term group therapies for complicated grief: Two research-based models*. Collana: American Psychological Association.

Poulsen, S. (2000/01a). Gruppeanalytisk og interpersonel korttidsgruppeterapi. Teori og forskning: Almene principper [Group analytical and interpersonal short-term group therapy. Theory and research: General principles]. *Matrix, 17*(1), 5–25.

Poulsen, S. (2000/01b). Terapeutiske faktorer i korttidsgrupper. Forskning og klinik [Therapeutic factors in short-term groups. Research and clinic]. *Matrix, 17*(2), 207–237.

Poulsen, S. (2000/01c). Terapeutiske faktorer i korttidsgrupper. Forskning og klinik [Therapeutic factors in short-term groups. Research and clinic]. *Matrix, 17*(4), 419–451.

Pratt, J.H. (1907). The class method of treating consumption in the homes of the poor. *Journal of the American Medical Association, 49*, 755–759.

Rapaport, D. (1951). The autonomy of the ego. *Bulletin of the Menninger Clinic, 15*, 113–123.

Reik, T. (1972). *Listening with the third ear*. New York: Arena Books.

Retterstøl, N. (1979). *Det Psykiatriske Sykehus II* [*The Psychiatric Hospital II*]. Oslo: Universitetsforlaget.

Rickard, H. (1962). Selected group psychotherapy evaluation studies. *Journal of General Psychology, 67*, 35–50.

Roberts, J. (2000). Interventions. In D. Kennard, J. Roberts & D.A. Winther (Eds.), *A workbook of group-analytic interventions* (pp. 12–23). London: Jessica Kingsley Publications.

Robinson, L., Berman, J. & Neimeyer, R. (1990). Psychotherapy for the treatment of depression: A comprehensive review of controlled outcome research. *Psychological Bulletin, 108*, 30–49.

Rosenzweig, S. (1936). Some implicit common factors in various methods of psychotherapy. *American Journal of Orthopsychiatry, 6*, 412–415.

Rothstein, A. (2018). *The narcissistic pursuit of perfection*. New York: Routledge.

Ruud, T. (2015). Routine outcome measures in Norway: Only partially implemented. *International Review of Psychiatry, 27*(4), 338–344.

Safran, J.D., Muran, J.C., Saturday, L.W. & Winston, A. (2005). Evaluating alliance-focused intervention for potential treatment failures: A feasibility study and descriptive analysis. *Psychotherapy: Theory, Research, Practice, Training, 42*(4), 512–531.

Sandahl, C., Lundberg, U., Lindgren, A., Rylander, G., Herlofson, J., Nygren, A. & Åsberg, M. (2011). Two forms of group therapy and individual treatment of work-related depression: A one-year follow-up study. *International Journal of Group Psychotherapy, 61*(4), 539–555.

Sandahl, C., Ahlin, H.N., Asklin-Westerdahl, C., Bjørling, M., Saracino, A.M., Wennlund, Å.U. & Ørhammar, A. (2021). *Why group therapy works and how to do it*. London and New York: Routledge.

Schlapobersky, J.R. (2016). *From the couch to the circle: Group-analytic psychotherapy in practice*. London and New York: Routledge.

Schwarzenbach, F. (1995). A supervisee looks back. In M. Sharpe (Ed.), *The third eye. Supervision of analytic groups* (pp. 107–109). London and New York: Routledge.

Shapiro, A.K. & Morris, L.A. (1978). Placebo effects in medical and psychological therapies. In S.L. Garfield and A.E. Bergin (Eds.), *Handbook of psychotherapy and behavior change: An empirical analysis* (pp. 396–410). New York: Wiley.

Shapiro, D.A. & Shapiro, D. (1982). Comparative therapy outcome research: Methodological implications of meta-analysis. *Journal of Consulting and Clinical Psychology, 51*, 42–53.

Shedler, J. & Westen, D. (2004). Refining personality disorder diagnosis: Integrating science and practice. *American Journal of Psychiatry, 161*, 1350–1365.

Sheehan, D., Javas, J., Baker, R., Harnett-Sheehan, K., Knapp, E. & Sheehan, M. (2002). *Mini international neuropsychiatric interview*. Tampa: University of South Florida Press.

Sifneos, P.E. (1973). The prevalence of 'alexithymic' characteristics in psychosomatic patients. *Psychotherapy and Psychosomatics, 22*(2), 255–262.

Sifneos, P.E. (1979). *Short-term psychotherapy and emotional crisis*. Cambridge, MA: Harvard University Press.

Skre, I., Friborg, O., Elgarøy, S., Evans, C., Myklebust, L.H. Lillevoll, K.,... Hansen, V. (2013). The factor structure and psychometric properties of the Clinical Outcome in Routine Evaluation – Outcome Measure (CORE-OM) in Norwegian clinical and non-clinical samples. *BMC Psychiatry, 13*, 99.

Smith, M.L. & Glass, G.V. (1977). Meta-analysis of psychotherapy outcome studies. *American Psychologist, 32*, 752–760.

Smith, M.L., Glass, G.V. & Miller, T. (1980). *The benefits of psychotherapy*. Baltimore, MD: Johns Hopkins University Press.

Steuer, J., Mintz, J., Hammen, C., Hill, M., Jarvik, L., McCarley, T.,... Rosen, R. (1984). Cognitive-behavioral and psychodynamic group psychotherapy in the treatment of geriatric depression. *Journal of Consulting and Clinical Psychology*, 52, 180–189.

Stokkebæk, A. (2011). *Korttidsterapi i grupper på dynamisk relationelt grundlag [Short-term therapy in groups on dynamic relational basis]*. Copenhagen: Hans Reitzel's Publishing House.

Stone, W.N. (1992). The place of self-psychology in group psychotherapy: A status report. *International Journal of Group Psychotherapy*, 42, 335–350.

Stotsky, B. & Zolik, E. (1965). Group psychotherapy with psychotics. *International Journal of Group Psychotherapy*, 15, 321–344.

Strack, S. (1987). Development and validation of an adjective checklist to assess the millons personality types in a normal population. *Journal of Personality Assessment*, 51, 572–587.

Strupp, H.H. & Hadley, S.W. (1979). Specific versus nonspecific factors in psychotherapy: A controlled study of outcome. *Archives of General Psychiatry*, 36, 1125–1136.

Sullivan, H.S. (1953a). *Conceptions of modern psychiatry* (2nd ed.). New York: Norton.

Sullivan, H.S. (1953b). *The interpersonal theory of psychiatry*. New York: Norton.

Tasca, G.A., Ritchie, K., Conrad, G., Balfour, L., Gayton, J., Lybanon, V. & Bissada, H. (2006). Attachment scales predict outcome in a randomized controlled trial of two group therapies for binge eating disorder: An aptitude by treatment interaction. *Psychotherapy Research*, 16(1), 106–121.

Tasca, G.A., Balfour, L., Presniak, M. & Bissada, H. (2012). Outcomes of specific interpersonal problems for binge eating disorder: Comparing group dynamic interpersonal psychotherapy and group cognitive behavioral therapy. *International Journal of Group Psychotherapy*, 62(2), 197–218.

Thomas, G.W. (1943). Group psychotherapy: A review of the literature. *Psychosomatic Medicine*, 17, 166.

Thomstad, H. & Gydal, M. (1968). Det Terapeutiske samfunn [The therapeutic community]. In R. Alnæs & G. Johnsen (Eds.), *Psykoterapi [Psychotherapy, Volume II: Special part]* (pp. 223–257). Oslo: Fabritius & Sønners Forlag.

Thygesen, B. (2000). *Gruppers individuation- individuation i grupper [The Group's individuation – individuation in groups. Matrix and the collective unconscious. An analytic psychological contribution to group analysis]*. Copenhagen: Dansk Psykologisk Forlag.

Thygesen, B. & Aagaard, S. (2002). Om det sosialt og kollektive ubevisste i gruppeanalytisk perspektiv [About the social and collective unconscious in a group analytic perspective]. *Matrix*, 3, 263–294.

Tillitski, C.J. (1990). A meta-analysis of estimated effect sizes for group versus individual versus control treatments. *International Journal of Group Psychotherapy*, 40, 215–224.

Tracey, T.J. & Kokotevic, A.M. (1989). Factor structure of the working alliance inventory. *Psychological Assessment*, 1(3), 207–210.

Vaglum, P. & Fossheim, J. (1980). Experiences with differential treatment of young drug abusers. A quasi-experimental study of a "therapeutic community" ward in a psychiatric hospital. *Journal of Drug Issues*, 10, 505–515.

Vaglum, P., Karterud, S. & Jørstad, J. (Eds.) (1984). *Institusjonsbehandling i moderne psykiatri [Institutional therapy in modern psychiatry]*. Oslo: Universitetsforlaget.

Vinogradov, S. & Yalom, I. (1993). *A concise guide to group psychotherapy*. Washington, DC: American Psychiatric Press.

Walfish, S., McAlister, B., O'Donnell, P. & Lambert, M.J. (2012). An investigation of self-assessment bias in mental health providers. *Psychological Reports, 110,* 639–644.

Wampold, B.E. & Imel, Z.E. (2015). *The great psychotherapy debate: The evidence for what makes psychotherapy work*. New York and London: Routledge.

Waxer, P.H. (1977). Nonverbal cues for anxiety: An examination of emotional leakage. *Journal of Abnormal Psychology, 86*(3), 306–314.

Weinstock-Savoy, D.E. (1986). *The relationship of therapist and patient interpersonal styles to outcome in brief dynamic psychotherapy* (Doctoral dissertation, unpublished). Boston University, Boston, MA.

Weisz, J.R., Weiss, B., Alicke, M.D. & Klotz, M.L. (1987). Effectiveness of psychotherapy with children and adolescents: A meta-analysis for clinicians. *Journal of Consulting and Clinical Psychology, 55,* 542–549.

Whittingham, M. (2018). Innovations in group assessment: Hov focused group therapy integrates formal measures to enhance treatment preparation, process and outcomes. *Psychotherapy, 55*(2), 186–190.

Widlund, I. (1995). *Den analytiska gruppen [The analytical group. Group analysis in theory and practice]*. Stockholm: Natur & Kultur.

Wiggins, J.S. (1979). A psychological taxonomy of trait-descriptive terms: The interpersonal domain. *Journal of Personality and Social Psychology, 7*(3), 395–412.

Winnicott, D. (1971). *Playing and reality*. London: Tavistock Publications.

Wolf, A. & Schwartz, E.K. (1962). *Psychoanalysis in groups*. New York: Grune & Stratton.

World Health Organization (1992). *The ICD-10 classification of mental and behavioral disorders: Clinical descriptions and diagnostic guidelines*. Geneva: World Health Organization.

World Health Organization (2018). *ICD-11. Clinical descriptions and diagnostic guidelines for mental and behavioral disorders*. Geneva: World Health Organization.

Yalom, I.D. (1975). *The theory and practice of group psychotherapy* (3rd ed.). New York: Basic Books.

Yalom, I.D. (1980). *Existential psychotherapy*. New York: Basic Books.

Yalom, I.D. (1995). *The theory and practice of group psychotherapy* (4th ed.). New York: Basic Books.

Yalom, I.D. & Leszcz, M. (2005). *The theory and practice of group psychotherapy* (5th ed.). New York: Basic Books.

Yalom, I.D. & Leszcz, M. (2020). *The theory and practice of group psychotherapy* (6th ed.). New York: Basic Books.

Zimpfer, D. & Waltman, D. (1982). Correlates of effectiveness in group counseling. *Small Group Behavior, 13,* 275–290.

Index

Note: Page numbers in *italics* indicate figures, and references in **bold** indicate tables in the text

Aagaard, S. 12, 29
action-oriented factor 140
affect control 41
affect tolerance 41
agency 21
aggression 54, 198–199
Ainsworth, M. 39
Alden, L.E. 58
alliance 147–148
altruism 91
analytical culture 162
Anthony, E.J. 6, 10
"atheoretical" clinical-psychiatric examination 46
attachment style 39–40

behavioral tasks 21
beneficiaries of FGAP 33–44; conditions for 33–44; established treatment focus 36; help to explore, as condition of 35; interest in learning, as condition of 34–35; personal resources 36–38; *see also* defense mechanisms; personality traits in FGAP
Bergin, A.E. 135, 139
Bjerke, N.S. 15
blind spots of therapists 126–127, 162
blocktraining course in Norway 14
borderline personality organization (BPO) 44
Bordin, E.S. 88
boundaries and structure focus approach 105–106
Bowlby, J. 39
Burchard, E. 141
Burlingame, G.M. 131, 142

catharsis 92
chain phenomenon 11, 87
Clarkin, J.F. 51, 57
clinical diagnosis 61–64
clinical interview 47–48
clinical quality assurance 125–134; data collection procedures 131–132; outcome measures selection 129–130; process measures choice 131; questionnaires 125, 128–129; structured interviews 125; therapeutic alliance, measures of 131
closed groups 6, 85
cognitive behavioral therapy (CBT) 15, 136, 142, 155
cohesion 147–148
cohesion–outcome relationship 149
cold (reserved) people 60
condenser phenomenon 11, 87
consolidated identity 197
content format 28–29
corrective emotional experiences 100
Corsini, R. 140
co-therapy 139–140
countertransference reactions 164–165
current/immediate level group analysis 12

data collection 131–132
defense mechanisms 40–41, 54; affect control 41; affect tolerance 41; degree of maturity of *41*; mature 54; primitive 54
defenses 198
delayed effect 146
demonstration group 72–84, 168; commonality 82; composition of, discussion 83–84; direct stimulation

82; group composition guidelines 81–83; IIP-C profiles 77; interpersonal problems (IIP-C) 171, 178, 181, 185, 188, 191, 195; introducing 72–84; mental health 174, 180–181, 188, 191; need for 72–78; overall group objectives 79–80; personality 170, 174, 181, 184, 194; personality organization (PO), level of 76, 171–172, 175, 178, 182–183, 189–190, 192–193; precipitating factors (stressors) 169, 173, 176, 179–180, 183, 187, 190, 193; predisposing factors (vulnerability) 169, 173, 176, 180, 183–184, 187, 190–191, 193–194; problem areas 168–170; psychodynamic hypothesis 170–171, 174, 177, 181, 184–185, 188, 191, 194; symptomatic behavior (interpersonal) 169, 172, 176, 179, 183, 190
Diagnostic and Statistical Manual of Mental Disorders 63
diagnostic interview 51
Dies, R.R. 139–140
differentiation phase 28, 94, 96–97, 117–118
district psychiatric centers (DPS) 145, 154–155
dodo bird verdict 142
domineering (assertive) people 60
drive theory 24
dynamic matrix 10, 20, 25, 87

effect size (ES) 141
ego concept 38
ego functions in FGAP 38–44
ego psychology (structural model) 24
ego-training-in-action 11, 87, 93
Elias, N. 9
emotional bonding 88
emotional factor 140
engagement phase 28, 94–96
existential psychology 91
exploitable (focused on the needs of others) people 61

feedback 90–91
Fjeldstad, A. 82, 146–147
Focused Group Analytic Psychotherapy (FGAP) 4, 6, 19–32; brief description 19–20; cohesion in 148; differentiation phase 28; dynamic matrix 20; engagement phase 28; focus and objectives 29–30; focus for therapy 21; foundation matrix 20; framework 22–30; group analysis and, comparison 30–32, **31**; in and by the group treatment 22; individually and for the group 29–30; individual-oriented treatment 20; interpersonal work phase 28; main features of 20–22; matrix concept 20; outcome in 148; phases of 28; preparation of patients 21; process of 86; termination phase 28; theoretical background 23–26; thorough clinical assessment 20; time limitation 22–23; *see also* beneficiaries of FGAP; group analysis (GA); patient suitability evaluation for FGAP; psychoanalytic/psychodynamic theory; supervision in FGAP; therapist in FGAP
formal change theory 137
Foulkes, S.H. 6, 8–10, 12–13, 23, 25–26, 28, 86–87, 89, 116–117, 120
foundation matrix 10, 20, 25, 87
Føyn, P. 154
free-floating attention 110, 160
free-floating group discussion 100
Freud, A. 4, 8–9, 24, 26, 92, 110, 116
Fuhriman, A. 142

Garfield, S.L. 135, 139
Glass, G.V. 141
Global Assessment of Functioning (GAF) 144
Goldstein, K. 8–9
The Great Psychotherapy Debate (Wampold and Imel) 147
group analysis (GA) 8–12; current/immediate level 12; definition of 12; FGAP and, comparison 30–32, **31**; group analytic theory 25–26; group-specific factors 11; matrix 10–11; objectives of 12; primordial level 12; projection level 12; theories and concepts 9–11; transference 9, 12
group climate 131, 148–149
group cognitive behavioral therapy (GCBT) 85
group cohesion 93–94, 131
group cohesiveness 92
group format, dimensions of 26–29; content format 28–29; physical aspects 26; process format 27–28; psychological structure 26; structure format 26–29
group process 85–100; interaction and multidimensional response 90–91;

therapeutic alliance, group cohesion 93–94; therapeutic factors 91–93
group psychotherapy 5, 135–150; change in, factors contributing to *137*; classification 5–6; empirical research on 135–150; Group Questionnaire (OQ-GQ Norwegian) 149–150; in Norway 13–14; outcome research on 141–143; patient characteristics 6; patient flow 6; practice-based clinical research 144–147; psychodynamic short-term groups 143–144; research on 135–136; self-concept, change in 147; thematically oriented 6; theoretical background 6; time-limited psychodynamic group therapy 143; treatment location and duration 6; types of 142; *see also* process research
Group Questionnaire (GQ) 150; Group Climate Questionnaire 148; OQ-GQ Norwegian 149–150
group relationships, cohesion and alliance 147–148
group structure 105–106, 138
group therapy outcomes 140
groups 3–16; closed groups 6; definition 3; early systematic exploration of 3–4; group-specific group factors 87–88; natural groups 3; open groups 6; psychodynamic 7–8; short history of 7; socialization through 11
groups, difficulty of research on 136–141; action-oriented 140; co-therapists use 139–140; emotional 140; formal change theory 137; group structure 138; intellectual (cognitive) 140; patient variables 138; therapeutic factors 140–141; therapist variables 138–139
groups developmental phases (stages) 94–100, **95**; differentiation (2–4 sessions) 94, 96–97; interpersonal work (8–12 sessions) 94, 97–98; opening (engagement, 2–4 sessions) 95–96; termination (2–3 sessions) 94, 98–100
guided facilitation 113, 115–116

Hadley, S.W. 112
Handbook of Psychotherapy and Behavior Change (Bergin and Garfield) 135, 139
Hartmann, H. 55
Henry, W.P. 139
here-and-now, switching to 121–122
Hilsenroth, M.J. 110

homogeneity 81
Hopper, E. 12, 29
Horkheimer, M. 8
Horowitz, L.M. 58

Ianni, F. 40
identity 52, 197; consolidated 197; diffusion 39; mild identity pathology 197; moderate identity pathology 197; severe identity pathology 197
Imel, Z.E. 147
imitative behavior 92
individualized (idiographic) instrument 129
individual-oriented treatment 20
individual therapy 143
inequalities notion 89
intellectual (cognitive) factor 140
intellectualization (dry theoretical discussions) 128
interaction and multidimensional response (feedback) 90–91
internal moral compass 199
International Classification of Diseases (ICD-10) 61
Interpersonal Circumplex (IIP-C) 59, 146–147, 171, 178, 181, 185, 188, 191, 195; in FGAP evaluation 61; norms for 196
interpersonal learning 92–93
interpersonal problems 58–59, 146–147
interpersonal psychoanalysis 91
interpersonal theory 23–24, 40
interpersonal work phase (8–12 sessions) 28, 94, 97–98
interpretation 113, 118–122
The Interpretation of Dreams (Freud) 116
intersubjective phenomenon 117
intervention types in FGAP 114–117; guided facilitation 115–116; interpretations 116–117
interviews for FGAP 46–47; "atheoretical" clinical-psychiatric examination 46; clinical interview 47–48; diagnostic interview 47, 51; psychodynamic interview 48–50; Structured Interview for Personality Organization (STIPO-Revised) 51; traditional interview 46; types of 47–51; *see also* Structured Interview for Personality Organization (STIPO-Revised)
intrasystemic conflict 24
intrusive (uninhibited) people 61

Jensen, J.L. 143
Johnsen, E. 162
Johnson, J. 149

Kanas, N. 141
Kennard, D. 110
Kernberg, O.F. 24, 43, 55, 116, 151
Klein, M. 8

latent connections 22
leadership role in FGAP 101–104
Le Bon, G. 3
level of personality organization (PO) 21
Likert scale 150
Lingiardi, V. 40
long-term group analysis, effectiveness of 144–145
long-term therapy 111, 146, 148–149; group climate development in 148–149; group therapy 136
Lorentzen, S. 15–16
Luborsky, L. 142

MacKenzie, K.R. 94
manifest content 22
Mannheim, K. 8
matrix 10–11, 20
mature defense mechanisms 54
McDougall, W. 4
McNary, S.W. 140
McRoberts, C. 142
mentalization 42
mild identity pathology 197
Milieu therapy 14
Mini International Neuropsychiatric Interview (MINI-PLUS) 63
mirror phenomenon 11, 87
moderate identity pathology 197
moral values (superego-functions) 41–42, 55, 199
Moreno, J. L. 7
motivation 43

narcissism 42, 55; normal narcissism 55–56; pathological narcissism 56
natural groups 3
negative reaction 94
Noah's Ark principle 82, 89
nonassertive (less self-assertive) people 60
normal narcissism 55–56
Northfield experiments 7
Norway, group psychotherapy in 13–16; blocktraining course 14; cognitive behavioral therapy 15; history 13–14; mentalization-based treatment 15; psychodynamic groups 15; psychoeducative groups 15; survey 14–16; training in 14

objective perception 106–108
objective reality 42
object relations 24, 39, 54, 116, 197
open facilitation 113
open groups 6
open systems 10
organizations 3
outcome in FGAP 148
outcome measures selection in psychotherapy 129–130
outcome research on group psychotherapy 141–143
overly nurturant (warm) people 61

pathological narcissism 56
patient characteristics 137
patient self-report (psychometry) 57–61
patient suitability evaluation for FGAP 45–71; clinical diagnosis 61–64; Diagnostic and Statistical Manual of Mental Disorders 63; diagnostic interview 47; International Classification of Diseases (ICD-10) 61; inter-subjective perspective 46; Mini International Neuropsychiatric Interview (MINI-PLUS) 63; psychodynamic case formulation 64–71; questionnaires 46–47; traditional interview 46; see also interviews for FGAP; questionnaires
patient variables 138
pedagogical diagnosis 160
Perry, J.C. 40
personality 36–38
personality disorder (PD) 37, 146, 150
personality organization (PO), level of 33–34, 43–44, 57, 171–172, 175, 178, 182–183, 189–190, 192–193
personality traits in FGAP 38–44; attachment style 39–40; defense mechanisms 40–41; ego functions in FGAP 38–44; identity 39; mentalization 42; motivation 43; narcissism 42; object relations 39; objective reality 42; reality testing 42–43; social conditions 44; subjective reality 43; see also defense mechanisms

personal psychotherapy and supervision, distinguishing 153
personal resources 36–38
phenomenology 63
positive affiliation 94
positive cooperation 94
practice-based clinical research 144–147; long-term group analysis 144–145; personality disorders 146; self-concept, change in 147; short-term group analytic therapy 145; typical patient 145–146
Pratt, J. 7
primary family group 92
primitive defense mechanisms 54
primordial level group analysis 12
principle of interconnectedness 10
process format 27–28
process measures choice 131
process research 147–149; group climate development in 148–149; group relationships, cohesion and alliance 147–148
projection level group analysis 12
psychoanalytic/psychodynamic theory 23–25; interpersonal theory 23–24; intrasystemic conflict 24; object relations theory 24; part-object representation 24; part-self representation 24; two-person relationship 24
psychodynamic case formulation 21
psychodynamic groups 5, 7–8, 12–13, 15
psychodynamic interview 48–50
psychodynamic short-term groups 143–144
psychodynamic time-limited group psychotherapy 154–164; growing interest in 154–164; training in, including supervision 154–155
psychoeducative groups 15

quality assurance 125–134
questionnaires 57–61; cold (reserved) people 60; domineering (assertive) people 60; exploitable (focused on the needs of others) people 61; for FGAP 46–47; interpersonal problems, measuring 58–59; intrusive (uninhibited) people 61; nonassertive (less self-assertive) people 60; overly nurturant (warm) people 61; patient self-report (psychometry) 57–61; in psychodynamic psychotherapy 128–129; socially avoidant (inhibited) people 60; sub-scales 59–61; vindictive (focused on own needs) people 60

reality testing 42–43
retraumatization 100
Rosenberg, B. 140
Rosenzweig, S. 142
Ruud, T. 15

Schwartz, E.K. 8
Schwarzenbach, F. 154
self-concept 147; affiliation 147; autonomy 147; change in 147
self-esteem (sense of self) 52
self-psychology 39
sense of identity 43
severe identity pathology 197
short-term therapy 109–111, 146, 148–149; group climate development in 148–149; group therapy 136
small group processes 137
Smith, M.L. 141
social conditions 44
socialization 87
socializing techniques 92
socially avoidant (inhibited) people 60
standardized (nomothetic) instrument 129
standardized questionnaires 57
"stranger groups" 79
Structural Analysis of Social Behavior (SASB) 147
structural factors 137
Structured Interview of Personality Organization-Revised (STIPO-R) 51–57, 196; aggression 54; clinical assessment level of 52–57; defense mechanisms 54; identity 52; intimacy and sexuality 54; levels 1–3 **53**; moral values (superego-functions) 55; narcissism 55; object relations, quality of 54; representation (sense) of others 54; tolerance and control 54
structure format 26–27
Strupp, H.H. 112
subjective reality 43
sub-scales in questionnaire 59–61
superego-functions 55
supervision in FGAP 151–165; beneficiaries of 155–156; countertransference reactions 164–165; establishing 156; group supervision

model 158, *158*, 159; individual supervision model 157, *157*, 159; intervention of supervisor 160–162; models of 157–159; need for 153–154; other types of learning versus 152–153; purpose/definition 151–152; session activities 159–160; sessions, frequency and duration of 163; supervisor and candidate, contract between 156–157; supervisory problems, examples 163–164; ways 157–159; *see also* psychodynamic time-limited group psychotherapy
systematic exploration of groups 3–4

termination phase 28, 94, 98–100
therapeutic alliance 88, 131
therapeutic elements 140; action-oriented 140; emotional 140; intellectual (cognitive) 140
therapeutic factors 91–93
therapist in FGAP 101–122; action 114; as administrator 5, 102; challenges for 104–106; characteristics 137; focus, staying with 114; greater attention to termination 106; as group member 5, 102; group structure and boundaries 105–106; guided facilitation 113; here-and-now mode work 104–105, 114; higher activity level, challenge 104; interpretation 113; interventions guidelines in FGAP 109–122; as leader and authority 103–104; maintenance of structure 113; modeling 114; no immediate response 114; objective perception or transference, stance of therapist 106–108; open facilitation 113; and patient, contract between 78–79; and patients, relationship 5; responsibilities and tasks 101–104; self-disclosure 114; support and interpretation, balance of (confrontation) 108–109; therapeutic alliance challenge 105; as therapist 102; therapist observation 110; therapist reflection 110–111; time ripe for intervention 111–112; variables 138–139
therapy group 5
therapy outcomes and process, evaluation 125–134; data collection procedures 131–132; outcome measures selection 129–130; outcome of FGAP 129–130; planning and monitoring process methods 129–130; process measures choice 131; questionnaires 125, 128–129, 131; reasons for evaluation 126–128; therapeutic alliance, measures of 131; therapy impact increase 127–128; using measures 128; what to evaluate? 129–130
therapy process; aims of 29; elements forming 88; group analytic views on 86–88; things brought to therapy 88–90
Thomas, G.W. 141
Thygesen, B. 12, 29
time limitation in FGAP 22–23
time-limited groups 35, 81–82, 143
tolerance and control 54
transference 12, 106–108
translation 120
transpersonal perspective of FGAP 25
treatment focus 29, 83
two-person relationship 24

universality 91

verbal method 5
vindictive (focused on own needs) people 60

Wampold, B.E. 147
Whittingham, M. 83
Wolf, A. 8
A Workbook of Group-Analytic Interventions (Kennard, Roberts, & Winther) 109

Yalom, I. D. 91–93